DATE DUE

FAC JUL 23 '99	
Ret'd. AUG 02 '99	

D1445457

Empire and Aftermath

Greek and Latin Studies
Classical Literature and its Influence

Editors

C. D. N. Costa and J. W. Binns
School of Hellenic and Roman Studies
University of Birmingham

Greek and Latin Studies
Classical Literature and its Influence

Empire and Aftermath
Silver Latin II

Edited by
T. A. DOREY

Routledge & Kegan Paul: LONDON AND BOSTON

First published in 1975
by Routledge & Kegan Paul Ltd
Broadway House, 68–74 Carter Lane,
London EC4V 5EL and
9 Park Street,
Boston, Mass. 02108, USA
Set in Monotype Garamond
and printed in Great Britain by
The Camelot Press Ltd, Southampton

ISBN 0 7100 8087 5

Contents

Introduction

T. A. Dorey

The present book deals mainly with writers of a literary period generally known as 'The Silver Age'. This name is not an appropriate one, as it automatically invites comparison with the earlier 'Golden Age' of the late Roman Republic. To make a comparison between the two periods labelled 'Gold' and 'Silver' is to imply a judgment that the writers of the latter period are to be considered inferior to those of the former, to imply, for example, that Suetonius is inferior to Nepos, Tacitus to Sallust, and, in the realm of satire, Juvenal to Horace. It may be argued that there were more mediocre writers in the first century of the Empire than in the last fifty years of the Republic. It would perhaps be more accurate to say that a greater number of mediocre writers from the later period have survived. No doubt the picture would appear different if all Quintus Cicero's tragedies had survived, together with the histories of Lucceius and the epics of Bavius and Maevius.

Velleius Paterculus, whose work is discussed in the opening chapter of this book, is typical of the reign of Tiberius, when the inspiration of the Augustan Age had for the time being spent its force. Yet he was a competent historian according to the standards of his time. Valerius Maximus was one of those compilers of miscellanies whose products are of literary interest rather than of literary merit. The elder Pliny, like so many of the best Romans a combination of soldier, writer and administrator, dedicated his spare time to the production of what was useful, and his works had a strong practical bent. His *Natural History*, however unsophisticated it must appear to the modern reader, contained an assiduously prepared collection of factual information that was greatly prized for many centuries. However, it was with Quintilian that Latin literature began to mount again to a new peak. His work on the education and training of an orator, including a discussion on the principles of education generally, is unique in Latin and outstanding among such works in any language. But what made Quintilian of immediate importance was his insistence on a thorough study of the best literary models for the would-be speaker or writer. The effects of this teaching can be seen in Tacitus and Pliny. A volume in this series has been devoted to Tacitus, whom some have judged to be the greatest Latin prose author – though rather more would allot this position to Cicero. Pliny's *Letters*, which, together with his *Panegyric*, are all that have survived of his literary output, are masterpieces, and should be classed with the work of the other two pre-eminent Latin letter writers, Cicero and Erasmus. Whatever they may lack in spontaneity they make up in sophistication. The final chapter in this book, on Panegyrics, deals with a literary form that came to be of increasing importance in the later years of the Empire and joins chapters in earlier volumes on Ammianus Marcellinus and the *Historia Augusta* as examples of the secular prose literature of the Empire in decline.

This volume marked the end of a stage in the series, as the present editor, having left the *vita academica*, passed on the task to younger colleagues. The series, Studies in Latin Literature and its Influence, now entitled, with a wider range, Greek and Latin Studies: Classical Literature and its Influence, arose out of informal discussions at the Annual General Meeting of the Classical Association held some years ago in Birmingham. Its practical inception was subsequently made possible by an act of faith on the part of the Directors of Routledge. The editors are bold enough to think that this faith was not misplaced and that the series has been of some use to students and to those others who have an interest in Latin literature. If this is so, the credit is largely due to the many scholars, above all those from non-Classical disciplines, who have generously responded to the invitation to contribute a chapter and have often made these volumes the vehicle for the publication of their research.

T. A. D.

Abbreviations

AJP	*American Journal of Philology*
CIL	*Corpus Inscriptionum Latinarum*
CJ	*Classical Journal*
CP	*Classical Philology*
CQ	*Classical Quarterly*
CR	*Classical Review*
CW	*Classical World*
GIF	*Giornale Italiano di Filologia*
HRR²	*Historicum Romanorum Reliquiae*, ed. Peter (vol. I², 1914, vol. II, 1905)
HSCP	*Harvard Studies in Classical Philology*
JRS	*Journal of Roman Studies*
Mnem.	*Mnemosyne*
Mus. Helv.	*Museum Helveticum*
PCPS	*Proceedings of the Cambridge Philological Society*
PBA	*Proceedings of the British Academy*
PW and *RE*	Pauly-Wissowa, *Realencyclopädie der klassischen Altertumswissenschaft*
Rev. Ét. Anc.	*Revue des Études Anciennes*
Rev. Ét. Lat.	*Revue des Études Latines*
RFC	*Rivosta di Filologia Classica*
RM	*Rheinisches Museum*
RQH	*Revue des Questions Historiques*
SIFC	*Studi Italiani di Filologia Classica*
TAPA	*Transactions of the American Philological Association*
WS	*Wiener Studien*

I

Velleius Paterculus

A. J. Woodman

1 Introduction

At the beginning of the first century A.D. Livy was nearing the
end of his massive history of Rome *ab urbe condita*; the final book
was possibly completed in A.D. 12. At the beginning of the second
century A.D. Tacitus was turning his thoughts towards writing a
history of the early empire; he was at work on the *Histories* in
about A.D. 106–7.[1] Between these two focal points almost everything is darkness. The works of those historians who dealt with
res Romanae during this period have not survived – with one exception, Velleius Paterculus, who published a two-volume history
of Rome in A.D. 30. On this account alone Velleius would seem
to occupy an unusually significant place in the tradition of first-
century historiography, yet scholars have curiously insisted on
disregarding him.[2] In an important recent article, however,
G. V. Sumner has at last suggested 'a serious and percipient
reappraisal of Velleius Paterculus as a Roman senator and historian',[3] and the time has now come for a comparable reappraisal
of Velleius as a writer.[4]

We know that Velleius' work was published in A.D. 30 both
because it is not openly hostile to Tiberius' minister Sejanus
(whose downfall in the following year meant an instant and total
damnatio memoriae) and because it is addressed to Marcus Vinicius,
the consul of that year (whose consulship Velleius regularly uses
for dating purposes, as at 1.8.1–4, 1.12.6, 2.7.5, 49.1, 65.2). But
we do not know when Velleius started composing, and all
attempts at finding out have so far been based on a misinterpreta-
tion of what little evidence we have.[5]

The work itself begins with a survey of Greek legend and
history which continues until 1.8.4, when Velleius turns to Roman
history; but no sooner does he reach the rape of the Sabine women
at 1.8.6 than our text breaks off and his account of almost six
hundred years of Roman history (i.e. the greater part of Book 1)

is lost – although a stray fragment on Cimon, which is to be fitted into this lacuna, proves that Velleius was still alluding to people and events of Greek history for at least the fifth century B.C. When our main text resumes (1.9.1) the Macedonian Wars are in progress, and Velleius' narrative carries straight through until the destruction of Carthage in 146 B.C. (1.12–13). At this point Velleius inserts two excursuses, one on Roman colonisation (1.14–15) and one on Greek and Roman literature, with which Book 1 comes to its conclusion (1.16–18). Book 2 resumes the main historical narrative which lasts (after slight digressions on-to second-century B.C. writers at 2.9, and first-century writers and moderns at 36) until chapter 38; here Velleius inserts an excursus on Roman provincialisation (38–9), after which the narrative proceeds more or less straightforwardly right up to the disgrace of Agrippina in A.D. 29, the latest event mentioned in the book (130.4). The work finally concludes with an impressive prayer to the gods of Rome (131).

Even this brief sketch of Velleius' history reveals some highly unusual characteristics, but it is necessary to be selective.

2 *Brevity versus elaboration*

It is clear from the inclusion of Greek history in Book 1 that Velleius saw himself as a 'universal historian' like Cato and Q. Claudius Quadrigarius before him.[6] He was writing Roman history in the grand manner, yet the remarkable fact is that he managed to achieve his goal in the space of a mere two books. 'I hardly know any historical work', pronounced Lord Macaulay, 'of which the scale is so small, and the subject so extensive.'[7] Velleius' achievement must be seen in its true perspective. If we look back over earlier historians who had chosen to trace the history of Rome from its origins down to their own day, we see that they required an ever-increasing number of books for their task: Cato's work, for example, came in seven books, that of Claudius Quadrigarius in twenty-three, and finally that of Livy in one hundred and forty-two.[8] The whole trend of historical writing had been one of narrative-expansion, a trend which was given great impetus by the theorising of Cicero, with his stress on *exornatio* and *exaedificatio*.[9] So far as we know, only the poly-math Varro, Cicero's friend Atticus, and Cornelius Nepos had attempted to write universal histories in summary-form.[10] Velleius may thus be said to have gone against the mainstream of the historiographical tradition.[11]

Why did Velleius adopt this unusual approach? Most scholars, pointing to the number of times Velleius refers to the speed or brevity with which he is writing (1.16.1 'in hac tam praecipiti festinatione', 41.1, 55.1, 108.2, 124.1 'mihi tam festinanti'), have imagined that he was hurrying to meet some sort of deadline and was therefore compelled to be brief.[12] But these scholars have failed to see that 'speed' or 'brevity' (the two are practically interchangeable) were recognised literary virtues of historical writing. Lucian, writing on the art of historiography in the second century A.D. but deriving his instructions from earlier works of a similar nature, said this (*De historia conscribenda*, 56):

> 'Speed' is always useful, especially when there is a lot of available material – which is where you should pursue this virtue, rather than in wording or phraseology. That is, pass over the trivia and less essential topics, but give adequate treatment to important matters. You can actually omit a great deal.

Unfortunately Velleius' preface has not survived to the present day, but it would seem from phrases used later on in his work (55.1 *'promissae* brevitatis fides', 89.6 'memores *professionis* universam imaginem principatus . . . subiecimus') that the preface contained some kind of programmatic announcement of brevity, in reaction to the practice of most earlier historians. The reaction was surely only natural. What point would there have been in compiling a massive history of Rome when Livy had recently done just this in one hundred and forty-two volumes? It was much more practical and original to write a summary, taking *brevitas* and *festinatio* as guiding principles.[13] Besides, Velleius may have been prompted towards this approach by current literary trends outside historiography. At about the same time as he was writing, Valerius Maximus and the fabulist Phaedrus were both referring to *brevitas* in the same self-conscious manner as Velleius, while in the previous reign the architect Vitruvius had done likewise.[14] However that may be, Velleius' insistence on the *brevitas* and *festinatio* of his work should be seen only in terms of a literary convention and nothing more.

It should be made clear at this stage that Velleius was not an epitomator and his work is not an epitome, though often described as such. He is a summary-writer whose work is an original product. Several considerations, including almost every point made in the present essay, show this to be undeniable, but two facts in particular seem decisive. First, it seems clear that for the earlier sections of his work Velleius has used a variety of different sources.[15] Apart from the more conventional references of the type found in most ancient historians (e.g. 1.4.1 'alii . . . ferunt, alii . . .', 1.8.5, 2.4.6, 27.5), he is found referring critically to Cato's work at 1.7.3, and he mentions the *Annals* of Hortensius by name at 2.16.3, while at 25.4 he appeals to an extant inscription to prove his accuracy. Expressions such as those at 1.15.3–5, 23.4 and 53.4 corroborate our impression that Velleius' reading was not restricted to merely one previous work of history. For much of the later part of his work it is generally agreed that he composed directly from his own memory and experiences. Secondly, we should note that much recent scholarship has been devoted to revealing propagandist element in Velleius and to the suggestion that he had a theory of history.[16] Without the help of his preface it is perhaps unwise to define this theory too precisely, but we can say with certainty that at least one of his aims was to provide a singleminded demonstration of Rome's inevitable progress, despite all vicissitudes, towards the ultimate *felicitas* of Tiberius' reign. Other historians had undoubtedly had comparable intentions (for example, Atticus had persuaded Cicero to write history 'ut (patria) . . . per te eundem sit ornata', Cic., *Leg.*, 1.5), but the manner in which Velleius accomplished his purpose (an instance is his attitude towards *otium*) can hardly be derivative.[17] These two considerations should be sufficient evidence to prove the originality of Velleius' work, and if we seek a parallel we should look to Florus in the second century A.D., whose two-volume *imago* of Roman history is also an original product conceived along similar lines.[18]

Velleius' decision to write *summatim* imposed severe limits on his composition, as he frequently remarks.[19] His selection of material would need to be extremely rigorous, and we find that he omits much that we normally take for granted in other more diffuse historians. Take his account of the battle of Pharsalus. Battle scenes were generally a favourite opportunity with Roman

historians for narrative-expansion, and Pharsalus, with its con-
frontation of Caesar and Pompey, was a battle of such significance
that it offered an irresistible chance for vivid, detailed, dramatic
description (Lucan can provide a few hints). Yet here is what
Velleius says of it (52.3):

> aciem Pharsalicam et illum cruentissimum Romano nomini
> diem tantumque utriusque exercitus profusum sanguinis et
> conlisa inter se duo rei publicae capita effossumque alterum
> Romani imperii lumen, tot talesque Pompeianarum partium
> caesos viros non recipit enarranda hic scripturae modus.

(The battle of Pharsalus was a gory day in the history of
Rome; torrents of blood were spilled on both sides when the
rival heads of state clashed together, and one eye, so to speak,
of the Roman empire was gouged out during the massacre
of many great men on the Republican side. Nevertheless
my abbreviated method of writing cannot run to a full
account of the battle.)

Apart from a sparkling metaphor ('effossum . . . lumen') this seems
a very negative method of writing history, hardly likely to
stimulate readers brought up on the theories of Cicero, who had
declared that one of the historian's primary concerns should
be *delectatio lectoris* (*Fam.*, 5.12.4–5). Clearly *brevitas* was not
enough; something more was needed to provide compensatory
interest.

First, Velleius tends to concentrate on the personalities of
history – to such an extent that his work has been described as a
'chronologically arranged portrait gallery of Roman history'.[20]
Character-sketches of the great men of the past are paraded, often
most vividly, before our eyes: Marius (2.11.1), Pompey (29.2–4),
Caesar (41.1–2), Sejanus (127.4); but Velleius is careful not to
forget the lesser lights such as the triple turncoat Dellius who
was consistent in his inconsistency (84.2 'exempli sui tenax'),
or the profligate Julia (100.3 'quidquid liberet pro licito vindi-
cans'), or the German Arminius (118.2 'ultra barbarum promptus
ingenio'). Many of these sketches are sharpened by jingling
word-play, one of Velleius' favourite stylistic devices. Thus
Pompey '*potentia* sua numquam aut raro ad *impotentiam* usus'
(29.3); the German Maroboduus is '*natione* magis quam *ratione*

barbarus' (108.2); and Lentulus could not be secure unless the state was insecure, 'Lentulus vero *salva* re publica *salvus* esse non posset' (49.3). If we compare this last example with instances of a similar idea in other authors (e.g. Cic., *Phil.*, 2.92 'si haec manent quae stante re publica manere non possunt'; Tac., *Hist.*, 3.55.2 'cassa habebantur quae neque dari neque accipi salva re publica poterant'), we can appreciate the skill of Velleius' technique. Yet Velleius' ability at describing character is not restricted to formal sketches. Although Scipio is given a formal sketch at 1.13.3–4 and Pompey a second formal sketch at 33.3–4, both men are contrasted with Mummius and Lucullus respectively, whose characters are not delineated formally but summed up by appropriate anecdotes.[21] Sometimes Velleius allows the characters to emerge from their actions, as in the memorable description of Plancus' nude dance (83.1–2); sometimes they are allowed a few words of direct speech which capture their personality, such as Livius Drusus' comment to his architect (2.14.3 'tu vero, si quid in te artis est, ita compone domum mean ut, quidquid agam, ab omnibus perspici possit').[22]

Second, we should note Velleius' fondness for pointed expressions or antitheses. We have already seen some of these in the previous paragraph, and the 'pointed style' is of course one of the chief characteristics of the so-called 'silver' age of Latin writing, being an especial feature of Seneca and Tacitus.[23] In Velleius, however, such expressions are often not mere *tours de force* for their own sake but a deliberate way of underlining the poignancy of situations which other historians, with more freedom for elaboration, would have felt able to develop, using the full resources of 'tragical' history.[24] Thus Marius spent his exile 'in tugurio ruinarum Carthaginiensium . . . cum Marius aspiciens Carthaginem, illa intuens Marium, alter alteri possent esse solacio' (19.4); during the war with Mithridates the Athenians were forced by siege to keep their bodies within the walls but their hearts without (23.5 'animos extra moenia, corpora necessitati servientes intra muros habebant'); after his death Pompey lived on, if not in body, at least in fame (54.2 'nusquam erat Pompeius corpore, adhuc ubique vivebat nomine'). Again, word-play can be used for additional point: '*spes* de*spera*tione quaesita' (2.5.3, compare Virgil, *Aeneid*, 2.354).

Third, there are occasions when Velleius has expanded his

narrative to deal with episodes which caught his imagination. One example is the battle of the Colline Gate when Sulla defeated Pontius Telesinus. The episode begins with a long sentence (27.1-2, ending climactically with Telesinus' cry 'numquam defuturos raptores Italicae libertatis lupos nisi silva in quam refugere solerent esset excisa'), followed by a shorter sentence describing a lull in the battle much in the manner of Livy,[25] then the death of Telesinus himself described in phraseology reminiscent of Sallust.[26] The episode concludes with a pun on Sulla's agnomen 'Felix' (27.6 'felicitatem diei . . . Sulla perpetua ludorum circensium honoravit memoria'). Another example is the battle of Actium, which is described impressively at 85.1-6;[27] but perhaps the best example is the disaster which overtook Varus and his army in Germany in A.D. 9 and which was presumably of more immediate significance to Velleius and his contemporaries than the battle of Pharsalus. It could hardly have failed to arouse Velleius' own interest, for he himself had served in Germany for several years (104.3); and his treatment of the catastrophe is a valuable indication of his technique (117-20).

The introduction to the disaster is artificial and almost apologetic (117.2 'et causa ⟨et⟩ persona moram exigit'), but this is only to be expected from a writer who has elsewhere expressed his continuous intention of being *brevis* (we shall find other such apologetic formulae at 1.14.1, 1.16.1, 36.2, 38.1, 66.3). Velleius' emphasis on Varus' *persona* is of course typical of his 'biographical' approach to history which has just been discussed. Thus introduced, the episode itself is neatly divided into the *causa* (117.2-118.4) and *ordo* (119.1-120.5) of the disaster, both of which illustrate other and different aspects of Velleius' composition. The former section highlights the *segnitia* of Varus and the *perfidia* of his opponent, the German Arminius, concluding with a long *sententia* on *fortuna*. Although all three elements smack of Velleius the old soldier (the treachery of the enemy and the cruelty of fate), they were also favourite themes in Roman historiography,[28] and just in case we have not noticed them Velleius lists them (in tricolon crescendo) at the beginning of the second section (119.2 'marcore ducis, perfidia hostis, iniquitate fortunae'). Velleius begins this second section by saying that he cannot discuss the *ordo* of the disaster in detail, only its *summa* (119.1). He is as good as his word (the quick-fire phrases at 120.2 read rather like the abbreviated manner of a military communiqué), and his statement shows the principle lying behind his composition: even within a self-acknowledged elaboration of the narrative Velleius cannot forget that he is writing a summary. Nevertheless this four-chapter account of the *clades Variana* is a fairly typical example of Roman historiography in as much as it attempts literary elaboration along traditional lines aimed at stimulating the reader's imagination. Velleius' practice in fact greatly resembles that of Caesar, who in his *commentarii* had managed to combine a disciplined brevity with a highly refined technique of elaboration;[29] yet Caesar had had an incomparably easier task, for not only was the scope of his works much smaller but *brevitas* had always been an indigenous quality of the *commentarius*-genre.[30] This makes Velleius' achievement seem all the more remarkable.

Thus, by vivid characterisation, pointed expressions and selected examples of narrative-expansion, Velleius compensates for his generally abbreviated manner of writing. There are of course other aspects to his resourcefulness, some of which will be studied in the next section.

3 Propaganda and rhetoric

If Velleius' treatment of the disaster to Varus was typical of Roman historiographical technique, the same cannot be said for the excursuses on colonisation in Book 1 and on provincialisation in Book 2, which constitute another unusual feature to be noted in the sketch of Velleius' work given above (pp. 1–2). Whereas Varus was dealt with at the appropriate chronological point in the narrative, these excursuses or surveys have little reference to the main historical narrative but cover the whole range of single large topics which each span several hundred years.[31] Such disruptions of the narrative seem extraordinary, but Velleius himself states that surveys of this type are useful because they allow a whole topic to be treated at a glance (1.14.1 'cum facilius cuiusque rei in unam contracta species quam divisa temporibus oculis animisque inhaereat, . . . non inutili rerum notitia in artum contracta'; 38.1 'ut quae partibus notavimus, facilius simul universa conspici possint': both are apologetic formulae). The practical value of digressions was often mentioned by ancient writers,[32] and Velleius makes it quite clear that no

8

matter how much his excursuses stand apart from the narrative, they are deliberately envisaged in the plan of his work as a whole (38.1 'haud absurdum videtur propositi operis regulae paucis percurrere . . .', cf. 36.2). This is perhaps surprising in a book with the limitations of a summary, but it shows Velleius alive to the practicality of summary-writing in itself, a belief which may have prompted him to write his book in the first place (above, p. 3).

But is practicality Velleius' only motive in writing these excursuses? It has recently been proposed that the excursus on colonisation at 1.14–15 was inserted for propagandist reasons: the gradual diffusion of Roman power is recorded stage by stage in order to show how Italy became effectively united politically.[33] The language used by Velleius (1.14.1 'auctumque Romanum nomen communione iuris') would seem to confirm the hypothesis; but can the same be said for the excursus on provincialisation in chapters 38–9 of Book 2? Here too the language indicates that Velleius' intention is to glorify the military achievements of Rome (and more especially those of Caesar, Augustus and Tiberius), while at the same time reminding his readers of the Augustan Peace.[34] The tone in fact recalls that of the *Res Gestae*, in which Augustus himself had managed to extol the conflicting concepts of war and peace almost simultaneously (12–13, 26–33). The practical benefits of peace were a constant embarrassment to the traditional Roman idealisation of war,[35] so it is hardly surprising that Velleius attempts a reconciliation of the two concepts. He returns to the theme again later, in a brief survey of Spanish history which, though scarcely disrupting the narrative as much as the two excursuses just mentioned, nevertheless deserves to be treated along with them because it covers the whole range of a single large topic and is propagandist in tone (chapter 90). The highly rhetorical survey concentrates for the most part on military perils and reverses, but introduces the Augustan Peace in climactic triumph at the end (90.4):[36]

has igitur provincias tam diffusas, tam frequentes, tam feras ad eam pacem abhinc annos ferme L perduxit Caesar Augustus ut, quae maximis bellis numquam vacaverant, hae sub C. Antistio ac deinde P. Silio legato ceterisque postea etiam latrociniis vacarent.

(These, then, were the provinces which, despite their great
size, extreme wildness and high population, Caesar Augustus
brought to a state of peace about fifty years ago with such
success that during the governorship of C. Antistius, and
subsequently that of P. Silius and his successors, Spain
enjoyed freedom even from terrorists, whereas previously
it had never been free from major wars.)

A propagandist motive can hardly be postulated for the digression on literature with which Book 1 concludes and for which
Velleius apologises in the manner to which we are by now accustomed (1.16.1 'cum haec particula operis velut formam propositi
excesserit, . . . nequeo tamen temperare mihi . . .').[37] Most of the
digression reflects on the phenomenon that the leading writers
of any genre all seem to have lived at more or less the same time
(1.16.2 'cuiusque clari operis capacia ingenia in similitudinem et
temporum et profectuum semet ipsa ab aliis separaverunt'), and
this reflection in turn leads Velleius to consider the problem of
literary decline. Although the background to these chapters is
complex,[38] the problem of literary decline was one which exercised several non-historical writers of the first century A.D.,[39]
and Velleius' quasi-philosophical tone is strongly reminiscent
of discussions to be found in contemporary rhetorical writers.[40]
It may well be that Velleius inserted the whole digression not
because it has anything to do with history (it quite clearly has not),
but because it was based on theories which were currently popular
in the schools of rhetoric. No previous historian had ever included
in his work so extrinsic a discussion, but it shows to what extent
rhetoric was impinging upon historiography and how far a
historian (even a historian operating within the narrow limitations of a summary) could digress from his main theme in order
to provide intellectual stimulation for his readers.

Velleius' obvious familiarity with rhetorical convention derives
from his education. The later stages of a Roman education consisted largely of declamatory exercises in the genres of *suasoria* (in
which one attempted to persuade an imaginary or historical
person to follow or reject a certain course of action) or *controversia*
(in which one attempted to argue one side of a tricky legal
problem).[41] Yet these exercises by no means implied that a young
man dealt mainly with non-historical material. On the contrary,

the subject-matter of a *suasoria* was conventionally historical (for example, 'Cicero deliberates whether to burn his writings if Antonius promises him his freedom on this condition'), while *controversiae* were originally historical in nature and their exponents continued to make great use of historical examples in order to clinch many of their arguments.[42] Evidence of this education is not hard to find in other sections of Velleius' work.[43]

We may take the influence of *controversiae* first. In chapters 127 and 128 respectively Velleius deals with Tiberius' treatment of Sejanus and defends the emperor's favourite against the two main complaints that were levelled at him, that he was Tiberius' *adiutor* and a *novus homo*. In each of these chapters Velleius resorts to techniques of contemporary rhetoric which seem strongly reminiscent of *controversiae*, moving with dexterity from introductory *sententiae* or commonplaces (127.1 'raro eminentes viri non magnis adiutoribus . . . usi sunt', 128.1 'quod optimum sit, esse nobilissimum'), to illustrations or *exempla* from past history (127.1 the two Laelii, Agrippa, Statilius Taurus, 128.1–3 Sp. Carvilius, Cato, Marius, Cicero and others), and finally back to subtle re-statements of his original propositions (127.2 'etenim magna negotia magnis adiutoribus egent', etc., 128.3 'in cuiuscumque animo virtus inesset, ei plurimum esse tribuendum').[44] The arrangement and precision of all this material are singularly impressive,[45] but the language throughout is prosaic and ordinary: instead of the elegant reminiscences of Cicero with which Velleius customarily adorns his work and which are to be seen in profusion in the following chapters, we are given officialese and propaganda (for example, the phrase 'tutelam securitatis' at 128.4).[46] As a result the section reads like an extract from a politically slanted declamation rather than a work of history.

We can now turn to the influence of *suasoriae*. Quintilian tells us (3.8.33) that a popular debating topic for *suasoriae* was the problem 'Where should Pompey flee after the battle of Pharsalus?'. When Velleius reaches the aftermath of the battle in his narrative (53.1), his sentence-structure becomes so schematised and artificial that he would seem to be thinking more of the declamatory topic than the historical situation.[47] A more impressive example occurs later. When Velleius reaches the point in his narrative where Cicero's death is to be recorded (66.2), he breaks out into a direct attack on Antonius for having caused Cicero to be assassinated (66.3–5):

> nihil tamen egisti, M. Antoni (cogit enim excedere propositi formam operis erumpens animo ac pectore indignatio), nihil, inquam, egisti mercedem caelestissimi oris et clarissimi capitis abscisi numerando auctoramentoque funebri ad conservatoris quondam rei publicae tantique consulis inritando necem. rapuisti tu M. Ciceroni lucem sollicitam et aetatem senilem et vitam miseriorem te principe quam sub te triumviro mortem, famam vero gloriamque factorum atque dictorum adeo non abstulisti ut auxeris. vivit vivetque per omnem saeculorum memoriam, dumque hoc vel forte vel providentia vel utcumque constitutum rerum naturae corpus, quod ille paene solus Romanorum animo vidit, ingenio complexus est, eloquentia inluminavit, manebit incolume, comitem aevi sui laudem Ciceronis trahet omnisque posteritas illius in te scripta mirabitur, tuum in eum factum execrabitur, citiusque mundo genus hominum quam ⟨M. Cicero⟩ cedet.

(However, M. Antonius, you achieved nothing – and here I am bursting with such indignation that I feel obliged to go beyond my promised terms of reference – nothing, I repeat, by putting up a price for the excision of that unique voice and the decapitation of such an outstanding individual; you achieved nothing by offering the terms of a hired killer to provoke the death of our erstwhile saviour of the Republic, that great consul. In the event, however, you robbed M. Cicero of no more than the pressures of his everyday life, old age, and an existence which would have been more painful had you become regent, than was his actual death at your hands during the Triumvirate. So far from extinguishing the glorious reputation of his words and actions, you have magnified it: he lives still, and will live on in the memory of the ages; and as long as this world, formed as it is either by chance, providence, or however, – this world which Cicero, almost alone among all Romans, had the powers of observation to penetrate, the strength of intellect to grasp, and the eloquence to irradiate, – as long, I say, as this world remains intact, so long will the glory of Cicero be its

constant companion. All posterity will marvel at the speeches
he wrote against you, and abominate your action against
him. The human race itself will vanish from the earth before
Cicero.)

Velleius' outburst contains the usual apology for his elaboration
of the narrative ('cogit enim excedere propositi formam operis
erumpens animo ac pectore indignatio') and makes effective use
of commonplaces and motifs found regularly in declamation
(e.g. *indignatio* and *fors/providentia*);[48] more particularly, a great
number of these motifs can be paralleled in the sixth and seventh
suasoriae (both on Cicero) of the elder Seneca, Velleius' older
contemporary and a devoted practitioner in the schools of
rhetoric.[49] In fact the whole section would look no more out of
place in these *suasoriae* than, for example, Arellius Fuscus' speech
on Cicero would if it were inserted into Velleius' narrative here
(Fuscus' speech is preserved by Seneca in *Suas.*, 7.8).

4 Types and changes of style

We have already seen some features of Velleius' style in a previous
section (above, pp. 5–8); his treatment of Cicero's death, just
quoted, provides illustration of some different features such as
his fondness for superlatives and for alliteration, '*c*aelestissimi
oris et *c*larissimi *c*apitis'. Superlatives are found perhaps too
commonly (e.g. in the character-sketch of Pompey at 29.3,
'potentiae . . . cupidissimus, dux bello peritissimus, civis . . .
modestissimus, . . . in reconcilianda gratia fidelissimus, in acci-
pienda satisfactione facillimus'); but his employment of alliteration
ranges from the obvious (e.g. 120.1 '*p*erpetuus *p*atronus', 118.2
'*a*rdorem *a*nimi') through many variations to the exceedingly
complex:[50] e.g. 25.4 '*t*abula *t*estatur *ae*rea intra *ae*dem' (aabb), 115.5
'*o*pportuna *v*isa est *v*ictoriae *o*ccasio' (abba), 2.13.2 'ut *m*inoribus
*p*erceptis *m*aiora *p*ermitteret' (abab), 1.9.6 'vel *m*agnitudine regis
Persei vel *s*pecie *s*imulacrorum vel *m*odo *p*ecuniae' (abccab).

Also in the passage on Cicero's death we see Velleius' love of
phraseological pleonasm, 'famam . . . gloriamque'. When Lucian
was issuing his instructions for 'speed' in historical writing
(above, p. 3), he made it clear that the historian should restrict
his selection of material rather than his fullness of phraseology;

and Velleius, despite the severe limitations of writing a summary, constantly aims at fullness of expression.[51] There are instances on every page, with adjectives (e.g. 1.17.1 'aspera ac rudia', 2.11.1 '*h*irtus atque *h*orridus'), participles (2.3.2. 'fugiens decurrensque', 2.16.4 'fluentem procumbentemque'), verbs (122.1 '*e*lucet atque *e*minet', 125.3 '*s*opiit ac *s*ustulit'), or nouns (50.4 'vigore ac fulgore', 57.1 'praesagia atque indicia'). But Velleius' *abundantia* does not stop at individual phrases; whole clauses and sentences are also constructed with this principle in mind, as may be seen by reading his account of Cicero's death, just quoted, or the battle of Actium (85.2–5).[52] Even the long rambling sentences which have been pounced on by the critics (e.g. 41.1–2, 43.3–4) are evidence of Velleius' continual effort at fullness of expression, in the tradition of Cicero and Livy. It is essential that we appreciate this.

When Cicero was expressing his opinions on historical writing in the previous century, he pronounced that a smooth, flowing style was vital; but of the two major historians who followed him only Livy adhered to his advice: Sallust completely disregarded it in favour of an abrupt and contorted style.[53] Both these historians were masters of their respective techniques, and historians of the first century A.D. had a difficult choice left to them. Were they to emulate Sallust or Livy? For many years it has been assumed that they chose to emulate Sallust,[54] yet there is very little evidence to support this contention. Take the case of Velleius. It is certainly true that Velleius' style is much infected with reminiscences of Sallustian phraseology;[55] he had clearly studied Sallust intensively, but no one reading Velleius' work would automatically think of Sallust. On the contrary, we have just seen that he was aiming at a prolixity of style which places him firmly in the tradition of Cicero and Livy.[56] The abruptness of Sallust has been incorporated into the continuous, running style of Velleius. What we must now ask is whether Velleius is typical of other first-century historians.

Of the lost historians who dealt with Tiberius' reign, the two most important are Aufidius Bassus and Servilius Nonianus. A fragment of Bassus on the death of Cicero has been preserved and it provides us with our nearest parallel to Velleius' own style, at least from the point of view of structure.[57] Tacitus links Bassus' name with that of Nonianus (*Dial.*, 23.2) and contrasts them both with the archaic Sisenna and Varro. This implies a stylistic similarity between the two of them, especially since Quintilian also links their names together (10.1.102–3), saying that Nonianus is 'vir . . . sententiis creber sed minus pressus quam historiae auctoritas postulat'. It is thus extremely unlikely that Nonianus, or for that matter Bassus, was a Sallustian;[58] and when Curtius Rufus later wrote his history of Alexander, he too employed an adaptation of the Livian style. There were undoubtedly a few Sallustians, such as L. Arruntius (although, being consul in 22 B.C., he is hardly a first-century writer) and perhaps also Pompeius Trogus, but in general it is much easier to hypothesise Sallustians than confirm them.[59] On the evidence we possess, it would seem that the style beloved of Cicero and Livy retained its popularity with first-century historians, among whom was Velleius, and that when Tacitus looked back to Sallust he 'was to some extent going against the fashion of his age'.[60]

These remarks about Velleius' style should not leave us with the impression that his style is one of monotonous regularity: it has already been seen (above, p. 11) that in chapters 127–8 Velleius changed to a declamatory style more appropriate for argument. That he has this ability to change his style according to his purpose can be gathered from a closer examination of what is perhaps the most important part of Velleius' work, his treatment of Tiberius' reign (126–31).

It is clear from the phraseology at 129.1 ('sed proposita quasi universa principatus Ti. Caesaris ⟨imagine⟩, singula recenseamus') that Velleius has divided his account of the reign into two complementary sections (126–8 the reign as a whole, 129–30 the details of the reign),[61] and that the latter section is intended to illustrate or confirm many of the general statements made in the former. Each of these sections is subdivided in turn: the former into (a) a panegyric of the reign (126) and (b) the discussion of Sejanus (127–8), the latter into (a) the achievements of the reign (129–30.2) and (b) its disappointments (130.3–5). After this comes the concluding prayer (131). Within the space of these six chapters Velleius resorts to four different types of style.

Scholars have often noted the panegyrical tone of the final pages of Velleius' work without, however, appreciating its full extent. If we compare chapter 126 with an actual panegyric, we see that the correspondences in both language and ideas are remarkable: it is almost as if Velleius has written a panegyric proper.[62] Yet we should beware of thinking that Velleius' generalisations, however 'panegyrical', bear no relation to historical fact. Almost every statement can be corroborated in other ancient authorities, an especially instructive parallel being the comparable survey of the years A.D. 14–23 given by Tacitus at *Annals*, 4.6.[63] Velleius has written a manifesto based on the government's record, a type of 'factual panegyric' which assures him of an important place in the development of the panegyrical genre.

No more need be said about the declamatory style of chapters 127–8, discussed above; instead we may pass on to the achievements and disappointments of Tiberius' reign in chapters 129–30. Here almost every sentence is either an exclamation or rhetorical question, and, though factually accurate, the chapters have not failed to provoke severe criticism from scholars who have missed the numerous delicate allusions to Cicero.[64] This section, whatever our judgment on it, ends with a sorry tale of treason in political life and the disgrace of members of the royal family (130.3–5). Such events are gloomy enough in themselves (*dolenda, erubescenda*), but we must also remember that by A.D. 26 Tiberius had abdicated his *cura* of the government in favour of the seclusion of Capri, and that Velleius may well have been unhappy about the subsequent domination of the emperor's minister Sejanus.[65] In striking contrast to the exclamatory enthusiasm of the previous section, the final sentences of Velleius' historical narrative are strangely pessimistic. It is this mood of pessimism, rather than (as is always assumed) unrealistic delight, which prompts Velleius to conclude his work with a prayer to the gods of Rome that they should preserve the good order of things (131):[66]

> Iuppiter Capitoline, et auctor et stator Romani nominis
> Gradive Mars, perpetuorumque custos Vesta ignium, et
> quidquid numinum hanc Romani imperii molem in
> amplissimum terrarum orbis fastigium extulit, vos publica
> voce obtestor atque precor: custodite, servate, protegite hunc
> statum, hanc pacem, ⟨hunc principem⟩, eique functo
> longissima statione mortali destinate successores quam
> serissimos, sed eos quorum cervices tam fortiter sustinendo
> terrarum orbis imperio sufficiant quam huius suffecisse
> sensimus . . .

(Jupiter Capitolinus, and Mars Gradivus, the author and
consolidator of the Roman name, and Vesta, guardian of the
perpetual fires, and all the other gods who have raised this
might of the Roman Empire to the furthest eminence of the
world, I pray and beseech you publicly: guard, preserve,
protect this order, this peace, this prince and when he has
fulfilled the full span of mortal life, ordain successors
who in due time may be able to bear on their shoulders the
burden of the Empire of the world with the steadfastness
that we have seen him bear it. . . .)

The prayer is brilliant in both conception and execution. Not
only has Velleius captured exactly the language and style of
political prayers,[67] but, by evoking the best of Roman tradition
while at the same time looking with concern to the future, he
has managed to strike a tone that equals some of the great
moments in Horace or Livy before him.[68] In almost every aspect
this prayer represents all that is best in Velleius' style.

5 'Habent sua fata libelli'

Velleius, then, has written a universal history of Rome in the
form of a summary, a venture with few precedents in the tradition
of Roman historiography. To compensate for his abbreviated
manner he has resorted to occasional excursuses of either a
propagandist or rhetorical nature, together with a concentration
on the personalities of Roman history; he has found a subtle
blend of brevity and elaboration, of point and fullness of expression. His work is designed to appeal to those who look
for both the *utile* and the *dulce* in their reading; these were, after
all, the traditional aims of historical writing. Unfortunately,
however, his work does not appear to have had the appeal
Velleius intended. It is true that he has an important place in the
development of factual panegyric (above, p. 16); and of the first-
and second-century historians we can say that Tacitus shows
signs of having read him;[69] but the similarities between Velleius
and such writers as Seneca and Curtius Rufus are due more to a
conventional way of looking at situations rather than to any
direct influence of one author upon another.[70] In fact, extensive
emulation of Velleius' style is not to be found until the works of

Sulpicius Severus in the fourth century.[71] Yet if we must admit that 'there is scarcely any ancient book which is so little quoted in ancient or medieval times as the two books of Velleius Paterculus', it is nevertheless equally true to say that he 'succeeded where many Roman historians failed: he somehow found an audience, and survived.'[72]

Despite his survival, however, Velleius has little popularity today: he is 'a historian whom it is now the fashion to dismiss rather than to give oneself the bother of reading'.[73] But it has not always been so. In the seventeenth and eighteenth centuries Velleius was taken seriously. Chapman began the preface to his translation of the *Iliad* by quoting Velleius' estimate of Homer (1.5.1), while Sir William Temple, in his 'Essay upon the ancient and modern Learning', described Velleius as the last strain of the 'height and purity of the Roman stile'; and Dryden, in an 'Essay of Dramatic Poesy', referred approvingly to Velleius' belief in the difficulty of making unbiased historical judgments (92.5).[74] In the eighteenth century Velleius was compulsory third-year reading at Trinity College, Dublin; and Dr Johnson remarked that 'in the study of Latin, it is proper not to read the later authors, till you are well versed in those of the purest ages; as, Terence, Tully, Caesar, Sallust, Nepos, Velleius Paterculus, Virgil, Horace, Phaedrus.'[75] The nineteenth century was more critical. Lord Macaulay said that 'there is an immense quantity of rant, and far too much ejaculation and interrogation for oratory, let alone history'; and Niebuhr observed that 'Velleius is one of those authors who are in ill repute; . . . but we must not lose sight of the fact that he was more talented than his contemporaries; he is in the highest degree intellectual; his observations are exceedingly subtle. He is, moreover, completely master of his theme.'[76] Sainte-Beuve would have agreed, 'un vrai penseur moderne entre les anciens', while Thomas de Quincey has left us some valuable remarks with which it seems fitting to close the present essay:[77]

> How wonderful and pleasing to find such accomplishments of accurate knowledge, comprehensive reading, and study, combined with so searching an intellect, in a man situated as Paterculus, reared amongst camps, amidst the hurry of forced marches, and under the privations of solitary outposts.

Notes

References to Book 1 and to chapters 1–18 of Book 2 of Velleius are always given in full (e.g. 1.12.2, 2.8.3); other references to Book 2 are given in short form since no possible ambiguity can arise (e.g. 66.4). Quotations are generally given according to the 1933 Teubner text (repr. 1968), although I have sometimes made occasional alterations as required. There is in fact no reliable text of V. at present; the most recent, by L. Agnes (Turin, 1969), mainly repeats F. W. Shipley's Loeb text (1924). There has been no commentary on V. in English since the school edition of F. E. Rockwood (Boston, 1893), which is confined only to chapters 41–131. An account of V., the man and his work, is provided by A. Dihle, *RE* 8A1.637–59 (1955), which will soon be supplemented and brought up to date by J. Hellegouarc'h, 'État présent des travaux sur l'Histoire romaine de V.P.', in H. Temporini (ed.), *Aufstieg und Niedergang der röm. Welt* (Berlin, forthcoming), vol. 2.

The study of V. raises a considerable number of complicated problems of which only a few appear in the present essay. The nature of the essay naturally forbids detailed argument even of these few, but I have thought it best to state my belief on various issues and reserve detailed discussion for the commentary which I am preparing and for my paper, 'Questions of date, genre and style in Velleius', *CQ* 25 (1975) – hereafter 'Questions'.

1 On Livy's dates cf. R. Syme, *HSCP* 64 (1959), 27–87; that Tacitus was engaged on the *Histories* in A.D. 106–7 is shown by passages in Pliny's letters.
2 V. is dismissed by F. Klingner, 'Tac. u. die Geschichtsschreiber des 1. Jahrhunderts n. Chr.', *Mus. Helv.* 15 (1958), 194, and ignored by both R. Syme, *Tacitus* (1958), 358 ('the Roman historians subsequent to Livy have perished utterly') and J. Wilkes, 'Julio-Claudian Historians', *CW* 65 (1972), 177–203. Reviewers of Syme's work rightly seized upon this prejudice, e.g. *JRS* 49 (1959), 143; *CR* 9 (1959), 260–1.
3 'The Truth about V.P.: Prolegomena', *HSCP* 74 (1970), 257–97. Sumner's wide-ranging article (to which I shall refer by author's name only) deals with Velleius' family, life, career, and other topics.
4 There is very little recent scholarship on the subject: e.g. in J.-P. Chausserie-Laprée's *L'Expression narrative chez les historiens latins* (1969), a book of 755 pages, there seems to be not one single reference to V.; S. F. Bonner, *Roman Declamation* (1949), 158–60, is useful but brief; A. D. Leeman, *Orationis Ratio* (1963), 248–51, is unsympathetic and R. Rieks, *Homo, Humanus, Humanitas* (1967), 57–67, is superficial.
5 The only sensible comments are those of Cl. Jodry, 'L'utilisation des documents militaires chez V.P.', *Rev. Ét. Lat.* 29 (1951), 271. Sumner's attempt (284–8) is merely a refinement on the traditional, and wrong, view. See now my 'Questions', part I(2).
6 On these historians see above all E. Badian, 'The Early Historians', in T. A. Dorey (ed.), *Latin Historians* (1966).
7 Cf. G. O. Trevelyan, *Life and Letters of Lord Macaulay* (1931), 2.724.
8 On the book-totals of the early historians see Badian (above, n. 6).

9 Cic., *De or.*, 2.53–4, 63. On Cicero's precepts in theory and practice see above all A. H. McDonald, 'The Style of Livy', *JRS* 47 (1957), 155ff.

10 For Varro's *Annalium libri III* cf. Teuffel-Kroll-Skutsch, *Gesch. der röm. Lit.* (1916), 1.333; for Atticus cf. Cic., *Brut.*, 14 'omnem rerum memoriam breviter . . . complexus'; for Nepos cf. Catull., 1.6 'omne aevum [i.e. down to about 54 B.C.] *tribus* explicare *cartis*' (correctly interpreted as an unusually short work by F. Cairns, *Mnem.* 22 (1969), 153–4). Ateius Philologus had provided Sallust with a 'breviarium omnium rerum Romanarum' (Suet., *Gramm.*, 10), but this was probably little more than a note-book.

11 This is not the only matter in which V. has differed from the major historians. From the frequency with which he addresses Marcus Vinicius (more than ten times) we may deduce that V.'s lost preface included a formal dedication to him (so too M. Brożek, *Eos* 52 (1962), 125). Sallust, Livy and Tacitus did not dedicate their works, although some of the lesser historians did (see T. Janson, *Latin Prose Prefaces* (1964), 67 n.10; H. Peter, *Der Brief in der röm. Lit.* (1901, repr. 1965), 242ff.).

12 For example, Schanz-Hosius, *Gesch. der röm. Lit.* (1935), 2.585. Apart from Jodry (above, n. 5) the only scholar to reject this interpretation was F. Milkau (below, n. 50), 10, but he did not argue his case and no one took any notice of him.

13 'Speed' and 'brevity' are common literary virtues (examples in H. Lausberg, *Manual de retórica literaria*, Spanish transl. by J. P. Riesco (1966), 1.268ff.), but also complicated. At *Inv.*, 1.28 Cicero makes it clear that *brevitas* meant one of two things: you could be *brevis* either (*a*) by saying all you wanted to say but attempting to do it in as few words as possible, or (*b*) by cutting down the number of things you wanted to say. I like to call the former 'stylistic *brevitas*' and the latter 'formal *brevitas*': it was the former for which Sallust was famous (Quint., 8.3.82) and which Lucian has already treated at *De hist. conscr.*, 43, but the latter which V. was aiming at. (See further on this ambivalence Plin., *Ep.*, 1.20; C. O. Brink, *Horace on Poetry* (1963), 1.262.) See now my 'Questions', part I(2)–(3).

14 Val. Max, 4.1.12 'sed cum magna *** multa breviter dicenda sint', 6.4 *init.*; Phaedr., 2 *prol.* 11f. 'bonas in partes lector accipias velim,/ita, si rependet . . . brevitas gratiam', 3.10.59f., 4 *epil.* 7 'si non ingenium, certe brevitatem adproba'; Vitr., 5 *praef.* 3 'paucis iudicavi scribendum, uti angusto spatio vacuitatis ea legentes breviter percipere possent.' Valerius and Vitruvius were of course writing handbooks and so were compelled to be brief; but if V. was stimulated by questions of practicality, his 'formal *brevitas*' is a good parallel to theirs.

15 Cf. Dihle, *RE* 8A1.642ff.

16 See I. Lana, *V.P. o della propaganda* (1952), and the judicious article by J. Hellegouarc'h, 'Les buts de l'œuvre historique de V.P.', *Latomus* 23 (1964), 669–84.

17 *otium* is of course only one example, but it rightly caught the attention of J.-M. André, *Rev. Ét. Lat.* 43 (1965), 308–15. I believe, however, that André misinterpreted the evidence and I hope to present a reconsideration, 'Moral and political equilibrium in the Early Empire', in H. Temporini (ed.), *Aufstieg u. Niedergang der röm. Welt* (Berlin, forthcoming), vol. 2.

18 Cf. P. Jal, *Rev. Ét. Lat.* 43 (1965), 358–83, and in his introduction to the Budé Florus (1967). Florus describes his work as an *imago* at 1 *praef.* 3; V. describes his account of Augustus' reign similarly at 89.6 (quoted above, p. 3).

19 He comments on the *forma, modus* or *transcursus* of his work at 1.16.1, 29.2, 52.3, 55.1, 66.3, 86.1, 96.3, 99.4; cf. also 38.1, 89.1, 103.4.

20 H. Sauppe, *Mus. Helv.* 1 (1837), p. 26 of the off-print. This aspect of V.'s work has been noted by many scholars (e.g. Leo, below, n.61), but the monograph devoted to the subject by M. Michels, *De V.P. arte biographica* (1949), is poor. We should of course remember that Roman historians traditionally stressed the part played by individuals in the course of history, cf. Cic., *De Or.*, 2.63; G. Williams, *Tradition and Originality in Roman Poetry* (1968), 619ff.

21 For the technique of contrasting characters (*syncrisis*) cf. F. Focke, *Hermes* 58 (1923), 327ff.; for the use of anecdotes cf. P. G. Walsh, *Livy* (1961), 87f., and his quotation from Plut., *Alex.*, 1.

22 Drusus' remark is perhaps to be traced to the commonplace 'vix quemquam invenies qui possit aperto ostio vivere' (Sen., *Ep.*, 43.4, with W. C. Summers' nn.).

23 For Seneca see W. C. Summers' edition of the *Letters*, xv–xli; for Tacitus cf. B.-R. Voss, *Der pointierte Stil des Tac.* (1963).

24 For 'tragical' history cf. C. O. Brink, *PCPS* 6 (1960), 14ff. (with references).

25 Cf. P. G. Walsh, *RM* 97 (1954), 97–114.

26 27.3 'semianimis repertus est, victoris magis quam morientis vultum praeferens', cf. Sall., *Cat.*, 61.4 'inter hostium cadavera repertus est, paululum etiam spirans ferociamque animi, quam habuerat vivos, in voltu retinens'. On Sallustian influence in general see below, n.55.

27 Cf. A. J. Woodman, *Latomus* 25 (1966), 564–6.

28 For *segnitia ducis* cf. Heubner on Tac., *Hist.*, 2,40; for *perfidia hostis* cf. Otto, *Sprichwörter*, 156, 291 (s. vv. *Graecus, Punicus*: V. has simply brought them up to date); for *fortuna* cf. Otto, ibid., 141ff.

29 See above all P. T. Eden, 'Caesar's style', *Glotta* 40 (1962), 74–117.

30 Cf. Cic., *Brut.*, 262; F. Bömer, *Hermes* 81 (1953), 210ff. We should remember that since V. spent many years as a soldier of considerable responsibility he was doubtless trained in the habit of keeping military memoranda which would necessitate abbreviated writing; the technique may have stayed with him when he came to compose his own work of history.

31 The disruption at 1.14–18 is deliberate since V. wants to separate clearly the end of Book 1 from the beginning of Book 2 ('statui priorem huius voluminis posterioremque partem . . . distinguere', 1.14.1). We should also note that almost all V.'s excursuses are 'woven' into the main narrative to some extent (*subtexturi* is the word he uses, 1.14.1). All the literary excursuses except 1.16–18 are introduced into the narrative chronologically (e.g. 2.9.1 'eodem tractu temporum . . .'); in addition 2.9 is preceded by the theme of *severitas* (2.8) which is resumed at 2.10; after the excursus at 36 V. resumes the narrative at 37.1 with a transitional phrase picking up the end of 35. As for the larger excursuses, 1.14–18

are preceded by the theme of decadence (1.13.5) which is resumed at the very beginning of Book 2; and 38–9 is preceded by a reference to the provincialisation of Syria (37.5, thus introducing the topic of the excursus itself) and concluded (39.3) by the conventional phrase of transition 'sed revertamur ad ordinem' (cf. Fraenkel, *Horace*, 98).

32 Cf. Tac., *Ann.*, 4.5, 12.40.5 'haec, quamquam a duobus pro praetoribus plures per annos gesta, coniunxi, ne divisa haud perinde ad memoriam sui valerent; nunc ad temporum ordinem redeo', 13.9.3. Also Polyb., 38.6.1.

33 Cf. the penetrating article by E. Gabba, 'Italia e Roma nella "Storia" di V.P.', *Critica Storica* 1 (1962), 1ff.

34 The language is martial and bombastic (e.g. 39.1 'fulgentissimum C. Caesaris opus'), but also subtle (38.3): 'immane bellicae civitatis argumentum quod semel sub regibus, iterum hoc T. Manlio consule, tertio Augusto principe certae pacis argumentum Ianus geminus clausus dedit' (cf. esp. Liv., 1.19.1–4, with Ogilvie's nn.). *certa pax* is a slogan, to be compared with *certa possessio* at 89.4 and *certa spes* at 103.5.

35 See Williams (above, n.20), 168–9, 630–1.

36 This sentence recalls Cic., *Leg. Man.*, 31 and *Pan. Lat.*, 8.13.1. For the rhetorical nature of V.'s chapter see, e.g., the highly ornate anaphora of *illae* (thrice), *in illis, illa*; *tot* (twice), *in tantum*; *tam* (thrice).

37 Propaganda has, however, been discerned behind V.'s other literary sections, cf. F. della Corte, *RFC* 15 (1937), 154–9; Lana (above, n.16), 269ff.

38 Cf. F. A. Schöb, *V.P. u.s. literar-historischen Abschnitte* (1908); J. Gustin, *Les péricopes littéraires dans l'ouvrage de V.P.* (1943–4). I have not seen P. Santini, 'Caratteri del linguaggio critico-letterario di V.P.', *Studia . . . A. Ronconi Oblata* (1970), 383–91.

39 Cf. E. Norden, *Die antike Kunstprosa*, 1.245ff., H. Caplan, 'The decay of eloquence at Rome in the first century', *Studies . . . A. M. Drummond* (1944), 319ff.

40 V.'s remarks resemble, in various ways, ideas to be found in Cic., *Tusc.*, 2.5; Sen., *Contr.*, 1 praef. 6–7, *Suas.* 1.3, 7.10; Sen., *Cons. Marc.*, 23.2, *Ep.*, 40.11. Cf. L. Alfonsi, *Aevum* 40 (1966), 564–6, *Euphrosyne* 1 (1967), 183–6.

41 The most recent account is M. L. Clarke, *Higher Education in the Ancient World* (1971), 39–45. See also Bonner (above, n.4).

42 For the historical origins of *controversiae* cf. Suet., *Rhet.*, 1.6.; R. Kohl, *De scholasticarum declamationum argumentis ex historia petitis* (1915). On the use of historical *exempla* cf. Quint., 10.1.34, 12.4.1–2; H. W. Litchfield, *HSCP* 25 (1914), 1ff.

43 I have not seen H. J. W. Verhaak, *V.P. en de rhetoriek van zijn tijd* (1954).

44 Many scholars have noted how chapter 128 especially resembles the common rhetorical theme 'de his qui humili loco nati clari evaserunt' (Val. Max., 3.4), of which examples are found throughout Latin literature. Many of V.'s *exempla* are also standard, cf. Litchfield (above, n.42).

45 See e.g. the ingenious article by R. Syme, *Hermes* 84 (1956), 262–5, on

V.'s choice of Carvilius. It should not be assumed from the above discussion that V. was a sympathiser of Sejanus; there is evidence that he
was not. See too below, n.65.

46 For the notion of *tutela* cf. M. Grant, *Roman Anniversary Issues* (1950),
89–90; J. Béranger, *L'Aspect idéologique du principat* (1953), 204, 257–60,
266ff. For *securitas* cf. H. Instinsky, *Sicherheit als politisches Problem des
röm. Kaisertums* (1952), 15ff.

47 For the sentence-structure cf. de Stefani (below, n.52).

48 For *indignatio* cf. Quint., 6.2.26, Juven., 1.79; for *fors/providentia* cf. Sen.,
Contr., 1 *praef.* 23, Quint. 3.5.6 (there are many other instances).

49 Many of the correspondences between V. and Seneca are noted by
Ruhnken in his comm. on V., by Edward in his comm. on Seneca, and
by C. v. Morawski in a series of articles: *Philol.* 35 (1876), 715–17; 54
(1895), 143–9; *WS* 4 (1882), 166–8.

50 On this cf. F. Milkau, *De V.P. genere dicendi* (1888), 17–25. Milkau's
dissertation is an excellent guide to V.'s style and is far superior to all
others of a similar nature. He also treats word-play and use of words. For
general remarks on V.'s style we may refer to the standard handbooks
such as E. Norden (above, n.39), 302–3, J. W. Duff, *Literary History of
Rome: Silver Age* (repr. 1964), 71ff.

51 Cf. P. Freitag, *Stilistische Beiträge zu V.P.: Pleonasmus und Parenthese* (1942).

52 For detailed discussion of V.'s clauses and sentences cf. E. A. de Stefani,
SIFC 18 (1910), 19–31; the passage on Cicero's death is analysed on pp.
23–4; for the battle of Actium cf. Woodman (above, n.27).

53 For Cicero cf. *Orat.*, 66 'tracta quaedam et fluens . . . oratio', *De Or.*,
2.54 'tractu orationis leni et aequabili', 2.63 'genus orationis fusum
atque tractum et cum lenitate aequabili profluens'; Livy's style was
compared by Quintilian to that of Cicero's ideal historian Herodotus,
in whom 'omnia leniter fluunt' (9.4.18, cf. 10.1.101); for Sallust's style
cf. Quint., 4.2.45 'abruptum sermonis genus', Sen., *Ep.*, 114.17 'ampu-
tatae sententiae et verba ante exspectatum cadentia'.

54 E.g. Leeman (above, n.4), 243, 'There can be no doubt that Sallust's
influence was much stronger than that of Livy.' The main exponent of
this view in recent years has been R. Syme in his *Tacitus* (1958) and
Sallust (1964).

55 Cf. A. J. Woodman, 'Sallustian influence on V.P.', *Hommages . . . M.
Renard* (1968), 1.785–99; also E. Bolaffi, *Sallustio e la sua fortuna nei
secoli* (1949), 192–4.

56 For V.'s emulation of Cicero in other respects also cf. E. G. Sihler,
TAPA 25 (1894), xlv–xlix. For V.'s deviation from Ciceronian clausulae,
however, cf. below, n.64.

57 The fragment is at Sen., *Suas.* 6.23; Peter, *HRR*², 2.96. Apart from the few
linguistic similarities, it is the run of the extract which most resembles V.

58 See now R. Syme, *Hermes* 92 (1964), 408ff., esp. 418.

59 Thus Leeman (above, n.4) devotes pp. 256–7 to proving that Fabius
Rusticus was a Livian, but concludes by stating the opposite (p. 258).
For the Sallustianism of Arruntius cf. Sen., *Ep.*, 114. 17–18; for that of
Trogus cf. M. Rambaud, *Rev. Ét. Lat.* 26 (1948), 171ff.

60 R. M. Ogilvie (ed.), *Tacitus: Agricola* (1967), 24. Only J. Perret before him saw the truth, 'La formation du style de Tacite', *Rev. Ét. Anc.* 56 (1954), 94–7.

61 For a similar division cf. Suet., *Aug.*, 9; cf. F. Leo, *Die griechisch-röm. Biographie* (1901, repr. 1965), 241.

62 An excellent parallel, in view of its similar length, is the epistolary panegyric at *SHA Max. Balb.*, 17. The first scholar to realise the importance of V.'s chapter *qua* panegyric was J. Mesk, *WS* 33 (1911), 85–7, but his remarks left no impression except on M. Durry in his edition of Pliny's *Panegyricus* (1938), 30–1. See my 'Questions', part II(2).

63 On numismatic parallels see Lana (above, n. 16), 185–6.

64 E.g. for the simile of the serpent at 129.3 cf. *Har. resp.*, 55, *Vatin.*, 4; for 'celeritate ac virtute' at 129.3 cf. *Flacc.*, 29, *Phil.*, 10.11; for 'si aut natura patitur aut mediocritas recipit' at 130.3 cf. *Rep.*, 3.18; at 130.5 'levatione periculi aut accessione dignitatis' the word *levatio* is Ciceronian, and for the latter phrase cf. *Fam.*, 2.1.2. Analysis of the clausulae at the end of V.'s sentences in 126–131, however, shows deviation from Ciceronian practice: - - - - ◡ - in Cic. is 7·7 per cent but in V. 25; - ◡ - ◡ - in Cic. is 4·9 but in V. 13·9; - ◡ - - - in Cic. is 16·2 but in V. 11·1; - ◡ - - in Cic. is 25·3 but in V. 11·1. The figures for Cicero are taken from W. H. Shewring, *CQ* 25 (1931), 15ff.; those for V. are my own, although observations on clausulae in V. will also be found in H. Bornecque, *Les Clausules métriques latines* (1907), 571–4. Cf. also L. P. Wilkinson, *Golden Latin Artistry* (1963), 156–62.

65 'The idea that the historian was enthusiastic about Seianus' prospective ascendancy is based on an insufficiently attentive reading of his words.' So Sumner (294), rightly; but unfortunately some of the evidence from which he draws this conclusion is invalid. See my 'Questions', part II(3).

66 I am extremely grateful to Dr R. M. Ogilvie for allowing me to use his translation of the prayer.

67 Compare especially the *vota* of the *fratres arvales* in W. Henzen, *Acta Fratrum Arvalium* (1874), e.g. 110–11. For 'quidquid numinum', an 'escape-clause' similar to that found in many Roman prayers, cf. E. Norden, *Agnostos Theos* (1923), 144ff.; Williams (above, n. 20), 133. For the circumlocutive *sensimus*-clause, typical of sacral language, cf. Henzen (above), and E. Norden, *Aus altröm. Priesterbüchern* (1939), 85–7. The precision and arrangement of the addresses to the divinities are also prayer-features; the metaphor of *cervices . . . sustinendo* is Ciceronian (e.g. *Dom.*, 142, *Sest.*, 138); and for the political tenor of the whole prayer see the themes discussed by Béranger (above, n. 46), *passim*.

68 E.g. Horace's Roman Odes (3.5.10–12, 6.46–7), Livy's preface (5 and 9 as compared with 13), the great speech of Camillus at Liv., 5.52.6–7.

69 For V. and Tacitus cf. G. B. A. Fletcher, *CR* 59 (1945), 47 n.1; *Annotations on Tacitus* (1964); *Latomus* 30 (1971), 146–50. Tacitus' character-sketch of Sejanus (*Ann.*, 4.1.3) also owes a considerable amount to that in V. (127.3–4). It is also possible that V. was read by Lucan (cf. Getty on Luc., 1.135, Francken on 2.88–93) and Martial (cf. N. Scivoletto, *GIF* 8 (1955), 105–15).

70 For such conventionality cf. F. Wilhelm, *Curtius u. der jüngere Seneca* (1928). Scholars have tried to detect verbal similarities between V. and Curtius, e.g. M. Manitius *RM* 47 (1892), 465ff., R. B. Steele, *AJP* 36 (1915), 411.

71 Cf. E. Klebs, 'Entlehnungen aus V.', *Philol.* 49 (1890), 285ff., who also points out similarities with Hegesippus and Solinus.

72 The quotations are respectively from G. A. Simcox, *History of Latin Literature* (1883), 1.439; Sumner, 279. V. is quoted by Prisc., *Gramm.*, 6.63, and schol. Luc., 8.663, 9.178. For the transmission of V.'s text see Sumner, 279 n.129.

73 J. P. V. D. Balsdon, *JRS* 57 (1967), 275.

74 The dates of Chapman's translation are 1598–1611; the remark of Temple (1628–99) will be found in *Collected Works* (1754), 2.174; Dryden's remark (1668) is in E. D. Jones, *English Critical Essays: XVI–XVIII Centuries* (1968 edn), 118.

75 For Trinity cf. M. L. Clarke, *Classical Education in Britain* (1959), 161; for Johnson's comment cf. R. W. Chapman (ed.), *Letters of Samuel Johnson* (1952), 1.7.

76 For Macaulay cf. G. O. Trevelyan (above n.7); for Niebuhr cf. his *Lectures on the History of Rome* (1853), 1.lxxii.

77 C. A. Sainte-Beuve, 'Portraits littéraires: Gabriel Naudé', in M. Leroy (ed.), *Oeuvres* (1949), 2.485; de Quincey, *Collected Works* (1862), 10.231 (also 234n.).

II

Valerius Maximus

C. J. Carter

The great German nineteenth-century historian, Niebuhr, was perhaps exaggerating when he said that the Middle Ages considered Valerius Maximus 'the most important book next to the Bible'[1] but he was certainly well-known and much read by all who counted themselves educated from the time of Charlemagne to the sixteenth century, and when, for example, the foundation statutes of Corpus Christi College, Oxford, were drawn up in 1517, Valerius was one of the four prose authors prescribed for daily lectures to first-year students.[2] Yet a Classics student at University today can normally expect to graduate without ever having read a word of Valerius and unaware that medieval and Renaissance Europe learnt – or thought it learnt – more about the Romans from Valerius than from any other single Latin author. This dramatic change in popularity and importance is only one of the things that makes Valerius so fascinating. He turns up in odd places even today.[3] In many ways Valerius never deserved to survive, and he still obstinately refuses to die. Paradoxes like this surround an author whom modern taste rightly finds one of the most tedious and affected products of the ancient world.

He is known to us by only one work, the *Facta et Dicta Memorabilia* or *Famous Deeds and Sayings,* transmitted in nine books and containing about a thousand stories and anecdotes varying in length from a bare three or four lines to extended and elaborate versions of more than a page.[4] They are broadly classified into ninety-odd groups or chapters, and supplied with chapter headings, not all of which are original.

Book I is devoted to religious topics of the more sensational kind familiar to readers of Herodotus, Livy and ancient historiography in general: the advantages of religious observance, the dire results of its neglect or dissimulation, auspices,[5] omens, prodigies, dreams and finally *miracula*, which also embrace folk-myth wonders such as the Asiatic princess with the double row of teeth, the man who could see across the Mediterranean from Sicily to North Africa and the goats of Cephalonia that drink the wind (I.8.12ff). Book II illustrates traditional Roman customs, institutions and behaviour. In the first half come stories about marriage and divorce, politics and administration, the army, public festivals etc., with a section giving a few comparable foreign practices (II.5); the second half concentrates on those still more emotive sources of Roman self-congratulation – military discipline, the triumph, the censorship, and the perpetual aura of respect traditionally surrounding the distinguished (*maiestas clarorum virorum*) even in the most unlikely or deprived circumstances. In these two books and throughout, the emphasis is on the individual story and the dogged exploitation of its rhetorical, dramatic and moralising aspects. The coverage is not comprehensive, and the examples do not amount to a dispassionate account of each topic. Although his subject-matter is primarily historical Valerius was not writing history,[6] nor was he some ancient sociologist. His work is no more than a product of the declamatory tradition, and this becomes clear as we wade through the relentless stream of stories about Character and Morality in books III–V. The capital letters convey a sense of their pompously didactic tone and Victorian earnestness.

The bulk of book III is made up of sections on bravery (the longest in the work), resolution, self-confidence and constancy, prefaced by a small collection of precocious Roman infants displaying exemplary *Romanitas*. In book IV comes the turn of moderation, abstinence, modesty and friendship; in book V, kindness and mercy, gratitude and ingratitude, and *pietas*, filial, family and national. Between these main sections are a number of shorter and less neatly defined topics – people who rose from humble origins, people who let their noble families down; fathers who loved their children, fathers who were ruthless to their children, fathers who were kind to their children when they were suspected of something, fathers who resolutely faced the deaths of their children; and a title of more immediate appeal these days, *Famous People who indulged in More Outrageous Dress or Behaviour than was Traditionally Acceptable* (III.6). There is no obvious or subtle unity to these books, individually speaking, and their collective content has no aesthetic pattern or logical coherence. Closely related topics or similar stories can be widely separated between books. This again is characteristic of the whole work, and books VI–VIII are even less homogeneous than the previous five, with morals, history, social phenomena and anti-quarianism ranged side by side and a great deal that would be equally or more at home in books I–V. The sixteen stories *On Chastity* at the beginning of book VI echo those on modesty and conjugal love (IV.5 and 6); the next three chapters illustrate freedom of speech and action (cf. IV.8), ruthlessness (cf. V.8) and dignity of speech and action (cf. II.10; VI.2); the fifth chapter, justice in and out of the law-courts (cf. VIII. 1–6); and the remainder, trust in politics, trust between husband and wife, trust between slave and master (cf. III.8; IV.6; V.2) and reversals of character and fortune (cf. III.4 and 5).

Book VII is a similar pot-pourri. The first chapter, *On Good Fortune*, is explicitly linked to the final chapter of the previous book, and the next two – wisdom of speech and action, artfulness of speech and action – also recall chapters in book VI. After a section on military strategy and tactics (cf. II.7; III.7), the rest of book VII skips from six anecdotes about electoral defeats and ten of *Dire Straits befalling Our Nation and Heroes* to three chapters about wills and inheritance – last wills and testaments revoked, last wills and testaments that were not revoked when they should have been, and people who nominated unexpected heirs. These lead straight into the six legal chapters that open book VIII, and again it is a mixed bag. In modern editions the first chapter is a composite one – thirteen instances of the acquit-tal of the guilty, eight very much briefer cases of the condem-nation of the innocent and two adjournments *sine die*, both involving women; this section is followed by some famous civil lawsuits, more trials figuring women, evidence obtained from tortured slaves, famous testimonies and the final *recherché* quirki-ness of *People who committed the Same Offences for which they had Procured the Punishment of Others*. At this point Valerius considered his audience's legal needs had been satisfied, or his own patience or sources were exhausted, and general diversity becomes the order of the day. *Effort and Industry* and *The Uses of Leisure* are succeeded by *The Power of Oratory* and *The Importance of Clear Pronunciation and Apt Gesture* (VIII.7–10), then two meagre sections follow on the Arts – meagre because the foreigners begin to seriously outnumber the Romans, so that the topics are dropped in favour of depressingly familiar matter, *On Longevity, Love of Glory* and *The Rewards of Excellence* (VIII.13–15).

Book IX is more like books III–V and more consistent at first. The main theme is deficiencies of character and Vice, with the first ten sections exemplifying extravagance and lust, cruelty, anger and hatred, avarice, arrogance, treachery, violence including sedition and mutiny, foolhardiness, error, vengeance. But the final five or six chapters return to the world of jumble with *Dreadful Deeds and Wicked Words, Peculiar and Remarkable Deaths, Unmanly Failures to Face Death* (this includes supercilious accounts of elaborate precautions against death taken by foreign tyrants – IX.3.*ext.*2–4), *Confusions of Identity and 'Doubles'* and a last section containing seven pretenders to noble birth and eminence, five Roman, a woman from Milan and an Asiatic tribesman.

Here the *Facta et Dicta* comes to an abrupt halt, without epilogue or final flourish. This is uncharacteristic of Valerius who is chronically effusive and sententious, especially at beginnings and endings, and although the work is the unique survivor of its type, it is unlikely to be complete as we now have it. In the preface to his epitome of Valerius, compiled perhaps in the fourth century, a certain Julius Paris[7] refers to *ten* books of Valerius, but his epitome ends book IX with the same anecdote as the full text; what then follows as book X is a fragment of an entirely different character about Roman proper names, attributed to an earlier epitomator, C. Titius Probus. Figures and numbers are the most unreliable thing about any ancient text, and book-division was also a much more flexible thing in the ancient world: at the one place where the text refers to Valerius, the manuscripts of Aulus Gellius, for example, cite book *nine* for a story that appears in our book *eight*.[8] Since the work has no definable plan, it is impossible to calculate the extent of any loss or know the cause. It could be anything from one or two more stories and a short epilogue, lost with the last leaf of some ancient *codex*, to something very much longer – one or more books, perhaps separated from the extant nine in the days of the papyrus roll and never making that crucial transfer into *codex* form.[9] Further additions might have been halted by Valerius' death. It is useful to clarify the background a little: one cannot be reminded too often, particularly where antiquity is concerned, that the history of the past is 'an enormous jig-saw with a lot of missing parts'.[10]

The stories themselves range from old chestnuts like Marius and the donkey, Coriolanus and his mother, and the air-borne tortoise that reputedly slew Aeschylus (I.5.5; V.4.1; IX.12.2) to the contented suicide of a nonagenarian old lady witnessed by Valerius himself on the island of Cos (II.6.8). The time-span stretches from Romulus to the Emperor Tiberius, though the frequency diminishes rapidly after Caesar's assassination and the battle of Actium. Most stories are about the mighty and exalted, but the lower orders are admitted where their exploits are sufficiently memorable (I.7.4; IV.7.5, etc.). Unless the theme is purely Roman like the military triumph or the censorship, a series of Roman examples is followed by a group of *externa*, chiefly Greek; these are generally fewer and shorter and form about a third of the complete total. When one views the enormous variety of topic and range of material, the appetite is whetted. Unfortunately, the dazzling possibilities of the subject-matter are smothered by Valerius' style, and to tackle the stuff in any quantity becomes an increasingly gloomy and indigestible experience. The approach is uniformly dull, monotonously turgid and oppressively forced, and variations in tone, length of narration and use of direct speech are too sporadic and slight to make any difference. The declamatory conventions of his day have little to do with it. What distinguishes Valerius from Lucan, Seneca, Petronius and Tacitus is supreme mediocrity of talent. He was no spinner of words and whatever the cultural environment a silk purse cannot be made out of a sow's ear.

But before studying his style in greater detail, something must be said about the date of the work, its more precise nature, sources and value to the ancient historian.

Valerius appears to have lived and written during the reign of Tiberius. Augustus is dead (VII.8.6; IX.15.2) and Tiberius is *princeps parensque noster*, a divinity still present to guard and guide in all things (I. *praef.*; II. *praef.*; V.5.3; VIII.13. *init.*). There is no mention of his death or events after it.[11] Pliny the Elder quotes Valerius in book I of the *Natural Histories* as a source for books VII and XXXIII: passages in both these and other books[12] could certainly derive from Valerius though not necessarily from him alone. These are the earliest extant references. The declamatory, pointed style of the work (Seneca the Elder is closest in spirit though superior in quality) is also consistent with an early first-century A.D. date. Attempts have been made to date the *Facta et Dicta* more precisely but scholars disagree whether Velleius Paterculus, who dedicated his *Historiae Romanae* to the consul of A.D. 30, used Valerius or *vice versa* or whether both derived the same or similar material from the same or similar sources; the corruption of Velleius' text adds to the problem. But there has been universal agreement since 1854 that Valerius wrote between A.D. 27 and 31.[13] The evidence is all internal and none of it satisfactory. This is not the place to debate the matter in detail, but the argumentation has a wider relevance, so is worth pursuing a little here. Many a 'dateable' passage in ancient literature is equally suspect.

The whole case rests on a mere three passages. In the first Valerius tells us that his visit to Cos *en route* for Asia Minor was graced by the presence of a certain Sextus Pompeius (II.6.8); it is assumed that this is the Sextus Pompeius who was consul in A.D. 14 and proconsular governor of Asia soon after A.D. 27.[14] The second is the preface to the opening chapter of book VI, Valerius' unctuously gauche invocation to Chastity and 'her persistent guard over the nuptial couch of the Julii' or 'nuptial couch of Julia' if the reading of the manuscripts is accepted.[15] The argument goes that this is an indirect reference to the Empress Livia, who adopted the official name of Julia after the death of Augustus; therefore Valerius wrote the beginning of book VI before Livia's death in A.D. 29. The third passage hysterically denounces the downfall and elimination of an unnamed figure who 'extinguished the light of trust and friendship' and 'endeavoured to wrest the reins of empire from the secure grasp of our beloved Father and Emperor' (IX.11. *ext.* 4 *fin.*). Sejanus is the most obvious candidate and book IX is therefore dated closely after Sejanus' death in October A.D. 31. A neat pattern emerges, pleasing to the bureaucratic tidy mind: Valerius had got to the middle of book II soon after A.D. 27, to the end of book V by 29 and laid down his pen during the winter of 31/32.

There are objections to all these conclusions. In the passage about Sextus Pompeius Valerius does not tell us about any consulship or Asiatic proconsulship. In fact he tells us nothing about his Sextus Pompeius apart from conventional tributes to his superlative character, kindness and eloquence. It is a reasonable inference from the only other place he appears that he was

Valerius' patron (IV.7. *ext.* 2 *fin.*), but here again nothing specific is said or implied about his career or status apart from his 'ruin',[16] the main subject of the passage. Consider on the other hand the eminence of the consul of A.D. 14.[17] He may well have been Ovid's patron and recipient of four of the *Letters from Pontus*.[18] If we can trust Dio, he was a relative of Augustus,[19] though the connection is obscure and may be as vague and remote as indirect kinship with Julius Caesar via his marriage with the daughter of Pompey the Great. As consul of A.D. 14, he also enjoyed a unique distinction. This being the year of Augustus' death, Pompeius and his consular colleague administered the new oath of allegiance to the Senate and people etc.[20] and proclaimed the accession of the monarch Valerius flatters with rhetorical regularity, assisting at the birth of what Valerius calls 'the most felicitous era the Roman people have ever enjoyed' (VIII.13. *init.*). He then secured perhaps the prize proconsular governorship – a Senate appointment, but the holder was unlikely to have been out of favour with the Emperor. Of his subsequent career nothing is known and Tacitus for example has no record that the consul of A.D. 14 was ruined or died in disgrace during Tiberius' reign. It is difficult to believe that Valerius would avoid all reference to his beloved patron's distinguished connections and career if indeed he was the consul of 14, and the straightforward insertion of an 'omitted' *procos.* towards the beginning of the story in book II is no solution to the problem. No, the most economical path is not necessarily the right one, here or anywhere. Let us admit that we do not have a record of all the people in Italy by the name of Sextus Pompeius and that proconsuls were not the only people who visited the provinces during Tiberius' reign. Of the six or so *known* Pompeii,[21] the *eques* who made Tiberius cross on one occasion or the Pompeius who died on a conspiracy charge in the early 30s[22] look much more promising than the consul of A.D. 14.

The invocation to Chastity involves a matter of basic interpretation. It is generally overlooked that Tiberius is a pervasive presence here – Valerius' supreme incarnation of Chastity.[23] The 'persistent guard over a nuptial couch' is a clumsy but simple allusion to the fact that he never remarried. If there is any Julia here it is the obvious one, Tiberius' former wife, the notorious and adulterous daughter of Augustus. It is true, of course, that

Tiberius was her third husband, that they became estranged, that she was sent into exile in 2 B.C. for alleged profligacy, and Tiberius himself may have authorised her starvation to death as one of his first acts after accession. An invocation to Chastity that explicitly embraced such a flagrant example of the very opposite would be tasteless and inept. But Valerius is a tasteless and inept writer and provincial enough not to have known or forgotten a *cause célèbre* fifteen or twenty years past. It is a fallacy to assume that every Roman was omnicompetent and infallibly correct in matters of taste.[24] To inject Livia into the passage, ingeniously exploiting that 'happy' coincidence of name, is a distortion of the natural sense and hopelessly contrived. In any case Livia's fidelity to the dead memory of Augustus was a national legend, and Chastity personified in the form of her son could celebrate, honour and guard her literal or metaphorical marriage-bed irrespective of her existence or present occupancy of the bed. There is no sense in which this invocation had to be written before A.D. 29.

The third passage may well be a diatribe against Sejanus and its melodramatic namelessness and fevered intensity may reflect comparative closeness to the fall itself. If so, a collection of about a thousand separated stories totalling some 80,000 words now depends for its precise dating on this one passage and there are considerations applicable to all dateable references that need scrupulous attention. The first is the question of originality, the second of unity with the surrounding context, both affected by the fluid uncertainties of 'publication' and manuscript circulation in antiquity. The style of the diatribe is not conspicuously different from the rest of the work and displays all the signs of bombastic lubberliness so typical of Valerius. But this is not saying much. In the first century A.D. Italy was full of second- and third-rate declaimers like Valerius and to a large degree their styles will have been indistinguishable. Only writers of genuine talent have distinctive styles that are difficult to emulate. But even if we assume Valerius' authorship, its position is abnormal – a Roman story placed in the *externa*. It could easily have been jotted down and inserted long after the rest was written. A work like the *Facta et Dicta* invites and readily absorbs additions by author and reader alike.[25] The diatribe is not a reliable guide to the date of the rest of book IX, still less the whole work.

The precise date of the work's composition is not a matter of world-shattering importance. Handling familiar material in what was then a universal style as anonymous as modern official-ese, the *Facta et Dicta* was clearly compiled under Tiberius, who is periodically addressed and flattered throughout; exacter dating is a dispensable refinement, but it does no harm to encourage scepticism even in small matters and very minor authors.

About Valerius himself we know nothing. There is no external evidence and the 'Life' found at the beginning of some medieval manuscripts is a medieval distillation of inferences from the work itself. The passage lamenting his patron's downfall seems to indicate a man of little status and small means, but allowances have to be made for rhetorical exaggeration.[26] Numerous references are made to notable Valerii from the past and their exploits, but there are no hints about ancestral connections with the author. Similarly there is nothing to indicate his birth-place or home; he could have been a Roman, an Italian or a provincial.[27] There are frequent stories about generals and armies, but nothing about them suggesting personal experience of military life. The ex-soldier Frontinus, relating the same or similar stories, uses simple technical terms and directer language than Valerius, but it is unsafe to conclude that Valerius never served or fought. He was obviously an educated man with some knowledge of rhetorical theory and his work was primarily of use to students of rhetoric and *declamatores*, but this is not proof positive that he was a practising speaker himself or taught the subject professionally. Which brings us to the question of the nature and function of the work and its background.

The *Facta et Dicta* is a hand-book of *exempla*, i.e. stories or examples of behaviour, attitudes, comments, 'happenings', usually with strong didactic overtones. Such illustrations added colour, variety, interest and persuasiveness to both conversation and formal oratory,[28] just as we enliven discussion today with items from newspapers, general reading or personal experience. History and philosophy provided the chief sources of material, especially the former. Mainly under the influence of Isocrates, Xenophon, Theopompus and other Greek men-of-letters of the fourth century B.C., the boundaries between these and oratory had become less distinct. The Romans inherited this process at an advanced stage: for Cicero, historiography was 'an highly oratorical affair' (*opus oratorium maxime*)[29] and oratory steeped in historical allusions. Cicero also expressed the importance of philosophy to the orator in a passage that touches on the *raison d'être* of *exempla* and demonstrates their use (*Orator*, 4.14–15)

We shall appreciate more fully later on what is here assumed from the outset, that philosophy is indispensable for the production of our orator, not because philosophy is the be-all and end-all but because it helps in the way that physical training helps the actor (I make this comparison because it is often highly appropriate to compare great with small). It is impossible to discourse on a variety of noble topics in a fluent, comprehensive and satisfying manner without a knowledge of philosophy: Socrates, for example, in Plato's *Phaedo* says that Pericles excelled other orators because he had been a pupil of Anaxagoras, the natural philosopher. According to Socrates he learnt much that was sublime and magnificent from Anaxagoras, the source of his fertile eloquence and all-important knowledge of the various emotional reactions stimulated by each type of oratory. Demosthenes may be considered another example: we can appreciate from his letters how frequently he sat at Plato's feet. . . .

Cicero's whole output – speeches, philosophical and rhetorical works, letters – is full of *exempla*, from one-word references to detailed vignettes. A corpus of the more familiar or striking *exempla* naturally accumulated through time in all forms of oratory and in the increasing numbers of histories, biographies and autobiographies that provided their first breeding-ground. Further assisted by the mammoth encyclopaedic labours of scholars and librarians, the standardisation of educational rhetoric and spread of the rhetorical schools,[30] the collection of *exempla* in more readily accessible form as reference books was an inevitable development. Cornelius Nepos, who died in 24 B.C., produced one such collection and Aulus Gellius refers to a story that appeared in its fifth book.[31] Augustus' freedman and Palatine librarian, Hyginus, produced another and Valerius cites the *Collecta* of a certain Pomponius Rufus (IV.4. *init.*). None of these have survived, and there were doubtless many others of which we have no record; some schools of rhetoric are likely to have made their own hand-books or supplemented the editions in general circulation. Similar collections were also available, like Varro's *Human and Divine Antiquities* in 41 books, *Libri Logistoricon* (dialogues with titles like *Marius on Fortune*) in 76, his 15 books of portrait studies of famous Greeks and Romans called *Hebdomades*, Nepos' *De Viris Illustribus* (known to contain at least 16 books and part of which – *Famous Foreign Generals* – has survived), Hyginus' *De Vita Rebusque Illustrium Virorum* or the *Libri Rerum Memoria Dignarum* or *Handbook of Memorabilia* by Verrius Flaccus, who tutored Augustus' grandsons. More specialist works on religion or law will also have been pressed into service. By the early first century A.D. there was an abundance of material to draw on, more extensive than we know, and, apart from the fragment of Nepos, Valerius' *Facta et Dicta* is the sole survivor.

In the preface to book I Valerius describes its composition and purpose in vague, flowery terms:

> The history of Rome and of foreign nations supplies us with many deeds and sayings worthy of remembrance, but they are distributed and spread at large among a host of other writers and cannot be apprehended quickly and concisely, so I have decided to make a compendium of selections from illustrious authorities[32] so that those who want illustrations[33] may be spared the labour of long research. But I have resisted any urge to be comprehensive. . . .[34]

In other words he has compiled the ancient equivalent of a Dictionary of Quotations. The content was universally appealing, especially to students of rhetoric and practising orators, but we cannot tell whether it was the personal manual of a practising rhetorician or the private product of Valerius' leisure or retirement – a sort of commonplace book – which he or others thought worthy of a wider audience and tidied up for publication.

He is normally silent about his sources, unlike Cicero in the first book of *De Divinatione* for example, which at times is a continuous series of *exempla*. Coelius Antipater is cited for C. Gracchus' dream about his brother (I.7.6) and Livy for the vast serpent that terrified Atilius Regulus' army in Africa in 255 B.C. (I.8. *ext.* 19). These are the only two references in book I. There are none at all in book II. 'Reliable authorities including M. Varro' attest the otherwise incredible military exploits of L. Siccius

Dentatus (III.2.24) and in book IV we meet Munatius Rufus' biography of Cato, Pomponius Rufus' *Collecta* and M. Scaurus' autobiography (IV.3.2; 4. *praef.*; 4.11). Thus they trickle on at infrequent intervals. In book VIII the number suddenly rises with Cato's *Origines*, Isocrates' *Panathenaikos* and Cicero's *Pro Gallio* (VIII.1.2; 7. *ext.* 9; 10.3) and an unparalleled outburst at the end of VIII.13 – Cicero's *De Senectute*, Aristoxenus the Musician, Asinius Pollio, Herodotus, Ctesias and Theopompus, Hellanicus and Damastes, Alexander Polyhistor and Xenophon of Lampsachus' *Periplous* tumbling out, sometimes two at a time. This is almost the sum total in the whole work,[35] but only the most gullible of ancient or modern readers will accept the situation at face value. Livy is mentioned the once, Cicero as a source only twice and Pompeius Trogus not at all, but these are almost certainly the ultimate sources for the bulk of the work. A comparison of *De Divinatione I* and book I of the *Facta et Dicta* illustrates the deceptiveness of appearances. Gracchus' dream appears in the Cicero, complete with reference to Coelius Antipater (I.26.56) and flanked by the famous story of the rustic at the plebeian games, Simonides' dream about the corpse on the sea-shore and the two Arcadians at Megara (I.26.55; 27.56 and 57); Valerius includes the same four stories (I.7.4, 6, *ext.* 3 and *ext.* 10) along with twenty others also found in the *De Divinatione*. Valerius could have taken all twenty-four from a copy of the Cicero, but the work is never mentioned.

Source-hunting is a favourite scholarly pursuit and Valerius has received his share of attention.[36] But two factors are commonly ignored or glossed over in many such enquiries – the survival of only a small proportion of what was written in the ancient world, and the misleading assumption that even the best modern texts are identical with their ancient counterparts and reliable bases for detailed comparisons. To take a simple example, Valerius includes the name of the rustic at the plebeian games (I.7.4) and this is not to be found in our texts of the *De Divinatione*. This is not proof of mutual independence: any ancient text of Cicero may have had the name scribbled in the margin or incorporated in the text; it was common knowledge anyway and Valerius could have included it without thinking. We cannot be positive that Valerius originally supplied the name in his version for the same reasons, and his modern editor has to decide between *Latinius* (the reading of the earliest extant manuscripts of the complete text, both of the ninth century) and *T. Latinius* (the reading of the ninth-century manuscript of the late Empire epitome of Julius Paris). A minor example, but the problem it illustrates is a major one. The loss of so much ancient literature also makes the whole business of source-hunting and the tracing of influences a more delicate operation than many of its practitioners seem to realise, and an account of their minute labours often excites a suspicious wonderment that such things should be. It is certainly not to be supposed that Valerius used only the sources he names, nor that he did all the donkey-work himself, or any of it. [37] He had his own epitomators later and there is a strong likelihood that he plundered Hyginus or Verrius Flaccus or some other lost collection. There have been detailed discussions on this point but in default of all other survivors they are academic in the worst sense. The ultimate sources are most likely to have been Cicero and Livy, and it is perhaps true that the very small proportion of Augustan and still fewer Tiberian anecdotes reflects the limits of a single direct source of late Republican or early Augustan date. The lack of contemporary or more original material in the *Facta et Dicta* is not to be construed as modest lack of self-confidence or political caution on Valerius' part. [38] Thus, recent campaigns, victories, heroic exploits and mutinies are ignored in favour of Actium and its predecessors; Marius and Sulla, Hannibal and Scipio appear time and again, but there are no Imperial generals or legates, no Tacfarinas, no Maroboduus, no Arminius, and myriad opportunities to include Livia and Sejanus under a variety of headings are not taken. Even stories of doubtful or unknown date (e.g. VIII.4 on tortured slaves) are much more likely to be Republican than Imperial, and the six different Calpurnii Pisones all belong to the previous century, with no reference to the Younger Germanicus' watch-dog, the notorious governor of Syria.

It can be understood from this that Valerius is of little value to the historian interested in the people and events he mentions. He is at best a second-hand source for everything earlier than Actium and the capture of Alexandria, and this leaves very little. His rhetorical elaboration and clumsy obscurities of style also diminish his reliability and accuracy. Where he conflicts with earlier authors or his testimony is unsupported, he is suspect. The errors and inconsistencies have been diligently hunted down – another favourite scholarly pursuit. Thus in book I Tanaquil is the wife of Ancus Martius, not Tarquinius Priscus, and the Athenians capture Aristomenes of Messana, not the Spartans (I.6.1; 8. *ext.* 15). Glabrio, father and son, are confused (II.5.1) and at III.2.20 Hannibal is found besieging the Romans in Capua whereas, as Kempf succinctly observed, 'the Romans were not in control of Capua at that time, nor did Hannibal ever besiege that city, nor in fact did the events described happen to Hannibal at all: it was Hanno.'[39] Three if not four generations of Scipionic achievements are concentrated in the single person of Scipio Nasica (VII.5.2) and Hannibal is again given the credit for the defeat of the brothers Scipio in Spain (VIII.15.11). In the same book Euclid the geometer is confused with Euclid the Megarian philosopher (VIII.12. *ext.* 1) in a story that Plutarch tells of Eudoxos of Cnidus and Helicon of Cyzicus.[40] This is a brief selection. Kempf devotes seven indignant pages to the topic,[41] waxing particularly wroth over internal contradictions: in book I 'we observe' (*nunc . . . cernimus*) the temple of Juno Moneta on the Aventine (I.8.3) but later on 'we see' (*nunc . . . videmus*) the same well-known building correctly located on the Capitol (VI.3.1). There was a time when passages like this were used to suggest multiple authorship but the indisputable singleness of Cervantes, Thackeray and Tolstoy, all equipped with inconsistencies of this type, has made such arguments less fashionable today.

We have no means of telling which mistakes and confusions in the *Facta et Dicta* are the fault of scribes and misguided annotators of manuscripts, and which are Valerius' or the fault of his sources. Some mistakes can be corrected by a simple change of letter or word, others by the short insertion of a phrase, but economy of means will not distinguish scribal errors from more original ones. All manner of fates might have befallen the text in that gulf between Valerius himself and our earliest manuscripts of the work, and if a Roman cursive manuscript figured somewhere in the lost stages of the transmission the chances of error multiply ten-fold. The other late Empire epitome of Valerius by Januarius Nepotianus mangles things still more and also gives stories that are not in our texts of the *Facta et Dicta*,[42] a powerful reminder of the uncertainties of the ancient scene.

But if Valerius has little value to the historian of events, he has something to contribute to the historian of ideas, providing evidence of a first-century A.D. Roman attitude to the past, the manner and quality of that understanding and the uses to which it was put. But the contribution is slight, adding little to what is already self-evident from the speeches of Cicero, the monographs of Sallust, the extant works of the elder and younger Seneca and the titles of the lost works of Varro. However huge the medieval popularity of the *Facta et Dicta*, the survival of only one more book of Livy or Petronius would be a far greater treasure.

Valerius' style is perhaps the aspect of chief interest today. Disparaging comments have already been made in passing; a closer examination is necessary and proper.

In many respects, and this includes similarity of cultural background, Valerius gives the impression of some ancient Polonius. When Hamlet's mother impatiently requests 'more matter with less art', Polonius protests he uses no art at all and immediately proceeds to play with words and antitheses worse than ever before (*Hamlet*, II.2.97–105):

> That he is mad, 'tis true; 'tis true, 'tis pity;
> And pity 'tis 'tis true: a foolish figure;
> But farewell it, for I will use no art.
> Mad let us grant him then; and now remains
> That we find out the cause of this effect,
> Or rather say the cause of this defect,
> For this effect defective comes by cause;
> Thus it remains and the remainder thus.
> Perpend.

If this obsession with rhetorical figures and verbal relationships is laced with the extravagant crudity of the Players' speeches about rugged Pyrrhus and the mobled queen, the resulting mixture is very like Valerius' Latin. Here is a typical short *exemplum* on the resolution of Cato the Younger (III.2.14):

tui quoque clarissimi excessus, Cato, Utica monumentum est,
in qua ex fortissimis vulneribus tuis plus gloriae quam
sanguinis manavit. siquidem constantissime in gladium
incumbendo magnum hominibus documentum dedisti
quanto potior esse debeat probis dignitas sine vita quam
vita sine dignitate.

(Of your most illustrious demise, Cato, Utica is the memorial: in that city, from those most heroic wounds of yours, more glory than blood flowed. Truly, most resolutely falling on your sword, you provided powerful proof to Man that dignity without life is much more morally desirable to decent men than life without dignity.)

Two things stand out – the concentration of artifice and the general clumsiness, both of which make the 'art' more evident than the 'matter'. The apostrophe of Cato, the personification of Utica, [43] the repetition of superlatives and the other cumbersome sound patterns (especially *monumentum/documentum*), the two pretentious antitheses (the first unnaturally forced, the second a cliché, flourished like a conjuror's rabbit at the climax of the show and having all that animal's wearisome predictability) – it is far, far too much for a story only two sentences long and starting, so to speak, cold. It lacks tact, taste, discrimination and grace: Cato's heroic suicide is lost in the welter, form is elaborated at the expense of content. The contrast with Ciceronian rhetoric is striking. There, effects are prepared for and poised, and, with the greater art that conceals art, the most artificial forms of expression seem to grow from that magnificently versatile and fluid command of vocabulary and sentence-structure with the organic inevitability of a tree. The same formal 'devices' – the word is appropriate in Valerius – mechanically and excessively applied irrespective of subject, soon render the *Facta et Dicta* tedious, and their obtrusiveness is accentuated by the simplistic sentence-structure. It is no defence to say that Valerius' style is 'pointed' or 'Silver', as though a descriptive label explained and justified all. Tacitus and the younger Seneca are 'pointed' and 'Silver' in the same general sense, but even the latter's failings show a degree of linguistic and literary competence unattained by Valerius. In his monumental study of ancient style, Norden opens his very brief discussion of Valerius by describing him as 'the first of a long series of Latin writers whose intolerable artificiality drives one to despair' and refuses to examine what he calls his 'repulsive' style in detail. [44] These are not out-dated or eccentric judgments. The *Facta et Dicta* is an excellent example of the unsuccessful practice of unexceptionable theory.

Comparative analysis is one of the most immediate ways of

appreciating differences of style and their effectiveness. Here are
three passages, one by Valerius, all telling the same story. Since
style demands the detailed study of originals, translations are
relegated to the notes to avoid confusion.

A duo familiares Arcades iter una facientes Megaram
venerunt, quorum alter se ad hospitem contulit, alter in
tabernam meritoriam devertit. is qui in hospitio erat vidit
in somnis comitem suum orantem ut sibi cauponis insidiis
5 circumvento subveniret. quo visu excitatus prosiluit
et iit ad tabernam. cum omnia circa eam quieta vidisset,
lectum ac somnum repetiit. tunc idem saucius obortus
petiit ut saltem mortis suae ultor exsisteret: corpus enim
suum a caupone trucidatum plaustro tum maxime ferri
10 extra portam stercore adopertum. motus his iuvenis
protinus ad portam cucurrit et scelere deprenso
cauponem ad capitale supplicium duxit.[45]

B proximum somnium etsi paulo est longius, propter
nimiam tamen evidentiam ne omittatur impetrat. duo
familiares Arcades iter una facientes Megaram venerunt,
quorum alter se ad hospitem contulit, alter in tabernam
5 meritoriam devertit. is qui in hospitio erat, vidit in
somnis comitem suum orantem ut sibi cauponis insidiis
circumvento subveniret: posse enim celeri eius adcursu
se imminenti periculo subtrahi. quo visu excitatus
prosiluit tabernamque, in qua is deversabatur, petere
10 conatus est. pestifero deinde fato eius humanissimum
propositum tamquam supervacuum damnavit et lectum ac
somnum repetiit. tunc idem ei saucius oblatus obsecravit
ut, quoniam vitae suae auxilium ferre neglexisset, neci
saltem ultionem non negaret. corpus enim suum a
15 caupone trucidatum tum maxime plaustro ferri ad portam
stercore coopertum. tam constantibus familiaris precibus
compulsus protinus ad portam cucurrit et plaustrum,
quod in quiete demonstratum erat, comprehendit
cauponemque ad capitale supplicium perduxit.[46]

C alterum ita traditum clarum admodum somnium: cum
duo quidam Arcades familiares iter una facerent et
Megaram venissent, alterum ad cauponem devertisse, ad

hospitem alterum. qui ut cenati quiescerent, concubia
5 nocte visum esse in somnis ei, qui erat in hospitio, illum
alterum orare, ut subveniret, quod sibi a caupone interi-
tus pararetur; eum primo perterritum somnio surrexisse;
dein cum se collegisset idque visum pro nihilo habendum
esse duxisset, recubuisse; tum ei dormienti eundem
10 illum visum esse rogare ut, quoniam sibi vivo non
subvenisset, mortem suam ne inultam esse pateretur;
se interfectum in plaustrum a caupone esse coniectum
et supra stercus iniectum; petere, ut mane ad portam
adesset prius quam plaustrum ex oppido exiret. hoc
15 vero eum somnio commotum mane bubulco praesto
ad portam fuisse, quaesisse ex eo quid esset in plaustro;
illum perterritum fugisse, mortuum erutum esse,
cauponem re patefacta poenas dedisse. quid hoc somnio
dici potest divinius? 47

The first version is a straight abbreviation of the second, the main
features of the story preserved in the same words but rhetorical
inessentials pared down or omitted. Away go the ponderous
dramatics and stumbling syntax of B's first sentence ('The next
dream, although it is a trifle longer, nevertheless, because of its
extreme distinctness, secures its non-omission') and the obvious
padding in line 7 that expands *subveniret* ('for by his swift advent
he could be extracted from the danger that threatened'). The four
places where simpler, shorter Latin replaces B's studied, self-
indulgent wordiness are best compared side-by-side:

Version A	Version B
6/7 . . . and went to the inn. When he saw all was quiet round the inn, he sought his bed and sleep again.	9/12 . . . and endeavoured to seek the inn in which the other was lodging. To his friend's calamitous misfortune 48 he con- demned a most humanitarian resolution as superfluous and sought his bed and sleep again.
8 . . . sought him to come forth and at least avenge his death.	12/14 . . . begged him, since he had neglected to bring his life aid, not to deny at least murder vengeance.

43

Version A	Version B
10 Moved by this . . .	16/17 Compelled to action by his comrade's highly persistent entreaties . . .
11 . . . and with the discovery of the crime . . .	17/18 . . . and apprehended the cart which had been pointed out in the dream . . .

There is less clutter about A and its preservation of B's pedestrian sentence-structure is in keeping with its modesty of style. In B the same basic sentence-structure conflicts with the outcrops of ambitious phraseology and the mixed vocabulary. Even minor changes of verb contribute to A's lighter tone: 'appeared' or 'arose' (*obortus*), 'covered' (*adopertum*) and 'took' (*duxit*) replacing B's more high-flown 'presented itself' (*oblatus*), 'buried' or 'overwhelmed' (*coopertum*) and 'delivered' (*perduxit*). B's style is restless, unsure, confusing.

The world of version C is accomplished and assured. The almost colloquial simplicity and understatement of the opening clause ('Here is the story of another very clear dream') gives way to the pleasingly varied and unobtrusive symmetries of the rest of the sentence ('These two friends from Arcadia were travelling together and had reached Megara, where the one lodged with an innkeeper, the other at a friend's'). It makes the opening of B seem primitively artificial. C's narrative then unfolds in a beautifully orchestrated series of clauses and sentences that constantly vary in length and type, the complex balancing the simple with sophisticated fluency and ease.[49] The central antithesis (lines 10/11) is clean, quiet and natural, principally because the flow of sound and the rhythm of the words, instinctively sensed by the writer, echo and respond (*sibi vivo . . . subvenisset, mortem suam ne inultam . . .*); there is nothing like this wedding of sound, rhythm and sense in B's antithesis (lines 13/14) and A not surprisingly dispensed with it. The climax in C is masterly (lines 13/19). The foundations are firmly established with the single incisive *petere* and the transparent simplicity of its dependent clauses, a calculated throw-away before the rich excitements that follow. The climax proper shows a fine eye for dramatic detail (the repetition of *mane*, the mention of the peasant-carter, the human touch about asking what was in the cart, the exquisite physical precision of *erutum*).

There is a fine sense of timing in the placing and length of clauses for maximum suspense and impact, particularly in the short sharp succession of clauses at the *dénouement*, where symmetry of construction is varied with great subtlety[50] – a tricolon indeed, but not foisted on the context with frigid disregard for harmony and propriety: here rhetorical precept is vibrant and fully functional. With the ground so fully prepared, even the final rhetorical question can withstand its basic conventionality.

Enough has been said to show the main differences in quality and competence. The worst by far is the middle one – Valerius (I.7. *ext*. 10). The abbreviated version is the work of his epitomator, Julius Paris. The final one is Cicero (*De Divinatione* I.27.57), Valerius' direct or indirect source.

Antitheses and *sententiae*, especially at the beginning and end of anecdotes, personification, apostrophe, rhetorical questions and exclamations, incessant abstraction of the personal or concrete – their interplay has a fascinating awfulness in Valerius.[51] He exhibits the faults typical of poor and affected writing – miscalculated effects; over-explanation; words or phrases repeated several times and then disappearing for long stretches of text; over-elaboration and pretentious diction (*tumor*); ugly rhythms and sound-effects (e.g. *sed sacraria aedificanda sacrificiaque facienda tribuit* VI.5.1c), mixed with a high proportion of slavishly Ciceronian clausulae; clarity inelegantly maintained by the proliferation of *is, ille, suus*, etc., and the simple stacking of clauses in series, joined by *et* or *-que* (*parataxis*) instead of competent subordination and periodicity, or Tacitean marvels of compression or ellipse. Sensitivity to metaphor also separates the sheep from the goats. For much of the time there is instructively little metaphor in Valerius, then comes a harsh and violent concentration. The youth of Manlius Torquatus was 'drenched in the cloud-burst of Fortune's contempt' so that the glory of his old age might 'shine forth all the more radiantly' after the storm (VI.9.1). Parental love is invited to 'unfurl the sails of peaceful and pious affection, voyage with wholesome breeze and import its dowry of sweetness' (V.7. *init*.). There is an arguable dramatic effectiveness to the most famous mixed metaphor in English literature – Hamlet's 'take up arms against a sea of troubles' – but what are we to make of the conglomeration of images in the last paragraph of book VI (VI.9. *ext*. 7)?

Human prosperity is a very fragile and perishable commodity, comparable to babies' rattles.[52] It floods in suddenly, instantly ebbs away. Lacking the support of firm roots, in no place, in no person does it stand steadfast, but hither and thither blown by Fortune's most uncertain blast, those it has raised on high and then forsaken, impoverishing them with unforeseen recoil, these it piteously submerges in the depths of disaster.

In Odes III.29 Horace deliberately adds image to changing image, exploiting the grotesque humour that results and constantly shifting the metaphor's objective focus; Valerius is like the earnest Babu reporting his mother's death: 'Regret to inform you, the hand that rocked the cradle has kicked the bucket.'[53]

There is also some remarkably childish verbal play. Manlius Capitolinus, who precipitated the rout of the Senones (*praecipites agebas Senones*) is flung precipitately headlong (*praecipitatus*) over the Tarpeian rock (VI.3.1a).[54] Cleanthes laboriously draws the waters of wisdom from the well of philosophy (*laboriose haurientem . . . sapientiam*) having sustained the poverty of his youth as a night-time puller of buckets from real wells (*adulescentem quaestu extrahendae aquae nocturno tempore inopiam tuam sustentantem* VIII.7.*ext*.11). The man who claimed to be Octavia's real son was 'conveyed towards the highest ranks of audacity by the bellying sails of presumption until Augustus ordered him to be fixed to the oar of a state warship' (IX.15.2). In the bitterness of his 'fall', Q. Caepio 'outruns' Crassus (*Crassum casus acerbitate Q.Caepio praecucurrit* VI.9.13). As deliberate bad jokes they have some merit: as serious attempts at fine writing and accomplished style, they powerfully suggest the reverse.

Transitions between *exempla* are stereotyped and mechanical. The contrast with Ovid's *Metamorphoses* in this respect is dramatic. Equally wearisome is the regularity of *inquit* after the first or second word of direct speech. What finally could be more sterile than the repetitions, triple tricola, pairs of pairs and noisy climax of his oratorical reflections on the life of Marius (VI.9.14)?

ex illo Mario tam humili Arpini, tam ignobili Romae, tam fastidiendo candidato ille Marius evasit, qui Africam subegit, qui Iugurtham regem ante currum egit, qui Teutonorum Cimbrorumque exercitus delevit, cuius bina tropaea in urbe

spectantur cuius septem in fastis consulatus leguntur, cui
post exilium consulem creari proscriptoque facere
proscriptionem contigit. quid huius condicione inconstantius
aut mutabilius? quem si inter miseros posueris, miserrimus,
si inter felices felicissimus reperietur.[55]

Or the banality of Alcibiades' double fate a page later (VI.9.
ext. 4)?

nam Alcibiaden quasi duae fortunae partitae sunt; altera quae
ei nobilitatem eximiam, abundantes divitias, formam
praestantissimam, favorem civium propensum, summa imperia,
praecipuas potentiae vires, flagrantissimum ingenium
assignaret; altera quae damnationem, exilium, venditionem
bonorum, inopiam, odium patriae, violentam mortem
infligeret. nec aut haec aut illa universa, sed varie perplexa,
freto atque aestui similia.[56]

Valerius then is a declaimer of the worst breed. He has his place
in the history of Latin declamation, but it is easy to understand
why no full-scale analysis of his style and its declamatory characteristics has yet been undertaken. 'Every deed and every saying
sprinkled with sesame and poppy-seed'[57] – an apt description of
his *Facta et Dicta*.

Finally there is the question of influence, difficult in the case
of a reference book: who today acknowledges use of Roget,
Pears' Cyclopaedia or a dictionary? Valerius may have been known
and regularly used by rhetoricians in antiquity but Tacitus and
Quintilian do not mention him and there is no detectable influence
in what survives of their work. The references by Pliny the Elder,
Aulus Gellius, Plutarch and Priscian amount to little:[58] Valerius
is a very minor source in each case and possibly indirect. The
mysterious author of the fourth book of Frontinus' *Strategemata*
was much more heavily in his debt,[59] or was using some lost
source which both he and Valerius were following closely:
nothing is directly acknowledged. In the early fourth century the
Christian apologist and teacher of rhetoric, Lactantius, also seems
to have used Valerius for his *Divinae Institutiones*, again without
acknowledgment. The two epitomes of Valerius by Julius Paris
and Nepotianus have been quoted as evidence of Valerius'
popularity in the late Empire,[60] but the accidents of survival are

no more to be equated with popularity than with merit or significance – the loss of three-quarters of Livy alone shows that, or Catullus' last-minute rescue in the Renaissance. The destruction of only three more Latin manuscripts any time before the ninth century would have consigned all knowledge of the two epitomators to oblivion and made Valerius himself as shadowy a figure as Deculo, Sebosus or Turranius Gracilis.

His influence in later times is a very different matter, much more fully documented.[61] It stems from the slenderest of beginnings, as with all extant Latin literature – in this case from some lost copy or copies made in the eighth or early ninth century in a monastery that was probably north-east France or north-west Germany. In the early ninth century Valerius accordingly came to the notice – among others – of that indefatigable Carolingian humanist and scholar, Lupus of Ferrières. His copy of the *Facta et Dicta* with his own corrections and emendations survives as one of the two oldest manuscripts available today,[62] and unlike its twin it bequeathed a rich inheritance in several ways. From his manuscript Lupus expounded Valerius to his pupils and the extracts taken down by the best of them, Heiric of Auxerre, have also survived in several versions, along with an index to Valerius compiled in turn by Heiric's pupil, Remigius. It was later descendants of Lupus' Valerius which supplied the libraries of the newly established Cistercian houses in the early twelfth century and which brought Valerius to England for the first time, most probably carried across the Channel from Bec or Caen to Canterbury by Lanfranc or Anselm. The preface to William of Malmesbury's *Polyhistor* is the earliest surviving reference to Valerius in England, although 'historians' are specifically excluded from quotation in the text proper. William's *Gesta Regum* and *Gesta Pontificum*, however, may owe something to the *Facta et Dicta* as well as to Suetonius' *Lives of the Caesars*.

Of much greater significance is the interest in Valerius shown by John of Salisbury, Becket's greatest friend, ally and companion-in-exile, 'the most accomplished scholar and stylist of his age, . . . the Erasmus, the Johnson of the twelfth century'.[63] Composed *c.* 1159 and dedicated to Becket (the original, superbly written presentation copy is happily still in England), John of Salisbury's *Policraticus* or *Art of Statesmanship* quotes liberally from Valerius, frequently verbatim for lines at a time. His actual copy of Valerius, fathered way back by Lupus', was left to the library of Chartres cathedral where John died as bishop in 1180. Becket's copy, doubtless procured for him by his friend, went with the rest of Becket's books to the library of that 'medieval All Souls College',[64] Christ Church, Canterbury. This was patronage of the highest, most fertile order and there is evidence strongly suggesting that John of Salisbury, like Lupus before him, corrected and emended his text of Valerius and is responsible for the curiously distinctive 'edition' of the *Facta et Dicta* circulating in England and northern Europe from the late twelfth century.

There are close threads binding Valerius, Lupus of Ferrières and John of Salisbury, but they are only part of a larger tapestry, an example of what was going on *mutatis mutandis* over the whole of Continental Europe. Hardly a monastery will have lacked a Valerius, judging by the regularity of his appearance in extant medieval library catalogues. The spread of the new secular institutions, the Universities, from the twelfth century onwards opened an outlet that was to become a main-stream channel. Valerius was a god-send to a world substantially deprived of Cicero, almost wholly ignorant of Livy and unable to read Greek. The tastes and critical standards indicated by the ornate, highly flavoured but often harsh and fractured Latin of medieval Europe also help to explain the popularity of a Valerius and a Seneca. Lacking competition, offering a *Reader's Digest* short-cut to the history of Rome, with much approved moralising *en route*, the *Facta et Dicta* was a guaranteed success. It was one of Vincent of Beauvais' main sources for the *Speculum Maius*, and at least once it was put into verse, of sorts.[65]

Its heyday came in the fourteenth and fifteenth centuries. The sheer quantity of surviving Renaissance manuscripts – more than of any other ancient prose author, the industrious production of commentaries and epitomes, his direct and indirect influence on works like Petrarch's *De Viris Illustribus*, the early appearance of vernacular translations (by Heinrich Mügeln in German, by Simon de Hesdin and Nicholas de Gonesse in French, by Antoni Canals in Catalan – all in the fourteenth century; there was also an early Castilian version), these are various guides to his pervasive influence. Or we can take the single figure of Petrarch as a microcosmic probe.[66] Valerius heads the list of historians in both accounts of his favourite books and was the model for his

Libri Rerum Memorandarum or *Book of Memorabilia*. References to
the *Facta et Dicta* are frequent in his correspondence and mar-
ginalia. In Paris he studied under Dionigi di San Sepolcro, who
composed the most popular Renaissance commentary on Valerius
between 1327 and his death in 1342. Another of his teachers,
Luca da Penna, also composed a commentary. There is a long
list of Petrarch's friends and acquaintances, led by Boccaccio and
Coluccio Salutati,[67] who are known to have read or quoted or
owned the *Facta et Dicta* and it includes three more authors of
commentaries or epitomes – Giovanni d'Andrea, Benvenuto
Rambaldi da Imola and Giovanni Cavallini. Copies of Valerius
were *de rigueur* in the libraries of the great patrons and all scholars,
and if these and Petrarch represent the pyramid peak of his influence, somewhere amid the pyramid's bulk are those ordinary
readers normally obliterated by history, the record of whose
very existence has hung almost perversely on ownership notes
in manuscripts of Valerius Maximus – people like the French
lawyer, Pierre Gontier, Johannes Vries of Amsterdam, the wife
of Mucilino of Forli, Nicholas of Spoleto, or the Thomas Knyvett
who scribbled his name all over the massive volume that cost
him 8/4d.[68]

Valerius was quick to appear in print after the development
of movable type and the printing press in the second half of the
fifteenth century – another index of significance. The first edition
came from Mentelin's press in Strasbourg most probably in the
summer of 1470, followed by an entirely independent edition the
following year from Peter Schoyffer's press at Mainz, which
became the basis of the first Paris edition in 1475. In the meantime Wendelin of Speier had published the first Italian edition
at Venice in 1471, thereafter modified and reprinted some eighteen
times before the end of the century at the various presses that
quickly sprang up in every major city in northern Italy.

For another hundred years or so Valerius' popularity continued
unabated. Pighius' edition, for example, first published in 1567,
was reprinted nearly twenty times before 1650 and a person of
Montaigne's significance still uses and refers to him.[69] But the
Renaissance rediscovery of the great masters of Classical prose,
the enthusiasm for all things Greek that developed after Boccaccio's reintroduction of the language into Western Europe
and the increasing sophistication of cultural standards began to

make their mark at the expense of the second-rate. The *Facta et Dicta* fell a natural victim. By the seventeenth and eighteenth centuries there was better and more attractive meat in the market – and Livy was frankly easier to read. Even scholars began to shop elsewhere, and the editors of the eighteenth-century *variorum* edition and nineteenth-century Teubner were comparatively little men. Valerius was published in the popular Bipontine and Delphin series in 1783 and 1819, but the standard text today is the Teubner of 1888. There is no Bohn translation, no Oxford Text, no Budé, no Loeb, no version at all in English since 1678.[70] These are eloquent expressions of his contemporary status. Valerius has had a very good run for his money, much better than he deserved. But there is no prospect of a dramatic return to favour. If he still has something of a future on examination papers in Latin Unseens, this, as Valerius himself would have put it, is the last twist of the knife buried in the heart of his present obscurity.

Notes

P-W   Pauly-Wissowa-Kroll, *Realencyclopädie der klassischen Altertumswissenschaft* (1893–).

PIR   Klebs-Dessau, *Prosopographia Imperii Romani* (1897–8).

1 Quoted by Wight Duff, *A Literary History of Rome in the Silver Age* (edn 3, London, 1964), p. 59 and n.2. Augustine surely has the better claim.

2 M. L. Clarke, *Classical Education in Britain 1500–1900* (Cambridge 1959), p. 22.

3 E.g. in the opening chapter of Steinbeck's novel *The Winter of Our Discontent* (1961), where the looseness of reference reflects the character of the speaker.

4 Short: II.6. *ext.* 13; V.3.2d and g; IX.15.3. Long: I.8.2 and 6; II.4.5; III.2.23b.

5 The abbreviated text of one or both epitomes (see n.7) is usually supplied between I.1. *ext.* 4 and I.4. *ext.* 1 missing in all manuscripts.

6 Understandably Valerius was thought of as a historian in the Middle Ages and the myth is still current (cf. *Oxford Classical Dictionary*, edn 2, 1970, p. 1,106).

7 See P-W, 10.686–9. The complete text of the Paris epitome is in the Teubner Valerius (ed. Kempf, 1888) pp. 473–587. The other epitome, by Januarius Nepotianus (see P-W, 9.696), which is possibly later in date, dispenses with book-division and covers only the first two books and part of the third (text in Kempf's Teubner, pp. 592–624).

8 Gellius, XII.7.8.

9 Cf. L. D. Reynolds and N. G. Wilson, *Scribes and Scholars* (Oxford, 1968), pp. 30–1.

10 Cf. E. H. Carr, *What is History?* (Penguin edn, 1964), p. 13.

11 Cf. n.22, the remarks on Seneca, *Tranq.,* XI.10.

12 E.g. Pliny, *N.H.,* VIII. 45 (70) and Val. Max., VIII. 1.8.

13 P-W (series 2), 8.i.90–93. The case was first argued by Kempf in his *editio maior* (Berlin, 1854).

14 Kempf, *ed. mai.,* pp. 3–6.

15 *tu . . . Iuliae ⟨gentis⟩ genialem torum assidua statione celebras.* Pighius (edn 1567) first inserted *gentis,* adopted by most editors since. But see n.24.

16 *iactura.* Valerius' rhetoric is so woolly that it is impossible to decide which of the three chief metaphorical meanings (*bankruptcy, disfavour, death*) is intended.

17 *PIR,* 3 P, 450.

18 *Epp. ex Ponto,* IV.1, 4, 5 and 15.

19 Dio, 56.29.5.

20 Tacitus, *Ann.,* I.7.

21 *PIR* (loc. cit.), 440, 443, 449, 450, 463, 471, 473, 480.

22 Suetonius, *Tib.,* 57; Tacitus, *Ann.,* VI.14. They are not necessarily the same man of course. Seneca, *Tranq.,* XI.10 mentions a Pompeius starved to death by Caligula. It argues a desperate mental economy to pluck the *praenomen* Sextus from thin air, identify Seneca's Pompeius with Valerius' and the consul of A.D. 14 and advance the publication date of book IV of the *Facta et Dicta* to the beginning of Claudius' reign (cf. the garbled account by P. Constant in his edition of Valerius (Paris, 1935), p. ii, where books II and IV are confused). Syme 'suspects' the identification (*AJP,* 1958, p. 21, n.14).

23 Hence the word-order at the beginning of the invocation (*unde te virorum pariter ac feminarum praecipuum firmamentum . . .*) and the imperialistic military imagery (*assidua statione, celebras, praesidio, insignia, munita, numinis respectu*).

24 The emendation *Iuliae gentis* is the unnecessary product of this false assumption. In view of gossip about Tiberius' private life, his invocation as the personification of Chastity is equally tasteless if Valerius was writing in the late 20s or 30s.

25 Cf. the remarks on the Nepotianus epitome (p. 39 above and n.42). The speech by Coriolanus' mother in Livy (II.40.5–8) is interpolated in the text of Valerius' *exemplum* (V.4.1) in certain late manuscripts.

26 IV.7. *ext.* 2 *fin.* Despite P-W (loc. cit.) the phrase *parvulos census nostros* (IV.4.11) is a human generalisation, not a description of Valerius' personal means.

27 References implying familiarity with Rome and its monuments are not proof he was a Roman or knew Rome well. A tomb at Tarentum is treated with equal familiarity (IV.6.3) and if the text is accurate he does not know the geography of the Janiculum (I.1.10).

28 Cf. Quintilian's discussion of *exempla, Inst. Orat.,* V.11.

29 *Leg.,* 1.2.5; cf. *De Oratore,* II. 51–2.

30 See part 3 of H. I. Marrou, *A History of Classical Education in Antiquity* (edn 3, transl., London, 1956; now in Mentor paperback); also S. F. Bonner, *Roman Declamation* (Liverpool, 1949).

31 Gellius, VI.18.11.

32 *ab illustribus electa auctoribus digerere constitui.* The ambiguity is possibly deliberate since *electa* could refer to already existing collections.

33 *documenta*, a somewhat elevated synonym of *exempla* here.

34 The preface to the Julius Paris epitome contains a simpler, clearer statement: 'A supply of *exempla* is of course necessary for orators and declaimers so I have made a one-volume abbreviation of Valerius Maximus' *Facta et Dicta.*'

35 There is a full list in C. Elschner, *Quaestiones Valerianae* (diss., Berlin, 1864), pp. 32–42.

36 Cf. P-W (loc. cit.), 102–14, the best summary.

37 The same applies to Cornelius Nepos who litters his text with 'sources'.

38 Though there may be something in the idea that second-hand contemporary material needed time to mature and become rhetorically acceptable.

39 Kempf, *ed. mai.*, p. 29: cf. Livy XXV. 13–14.

40 Plutarch, *Moralia*, 579 (*De gen. Socr.* 7).

41 Kempf, *ed. mai.* pp. 26–34.

42 See Kempf's Teubner Valerius, pp. 599, 608–10, 616–18, 623 (=Nepotianus 7.3; 9.24 and 34; 15.1 and 17–20; 21.3).

43 For one of the worst examples of personification, cf. II.10.3 *fin.* (the funeral bier of Aemilius Paulus, the conqueror of Macedon, spontaneously borne by Macedonian delegates in Rome at the time): 'Twice, Paulus, Macedonia revealed your illustriousness to our noble city – with its spoils at your safe preservation, with its shoulders at your demise.'

44 E. Norden, *Die antike Kunstprosa* (edn 2, Berlin, 1909) i, p. 303 and for 'das Widerliche seines Stils', p. 304.

45 Two friends from Arcadia travelling together came to Megara; one went to a friend's, the other lodged at an innkeeper's establishment. In a dream the one enjoying his friend's hospitality saw his companion begging him to come to the rescue – the treacherous innkeeper had tricked and trapped him. Roused by this vision he leapt out of bed and went to the inn. When he saw all was quiet round the inn he sought his bed and sleep again. The same figure then appeared all wounded and sought him to come forth and at least avenge his death: butchered by the innkeeper his body was in a cart and hurriedly being taken outside the city-gate, covered with dung. This moved his young friend who forthwith rushed to the gate, discovered the crime and brought the innkeeper to capital justice.

46 Although the next dream is a little longer, it nevertheless secures inclusion because of its extreme distinctness. Two friends from Arcadia travelling together came to Megara; one went to a friend's, the other lodged at an innkeeper's establishment. In a dream the one enjoying his friend's hospitality saw his companion begging him to come to the rescue – the treacherous innkeeper had tricked and trapped him: his swift advent could extract him from the threatening danger. Roused by this vision

he leapt out of bed and endeavoured to seek the inn in which he was lodging. To his friend's calamitous misfortune he condemned a most humanitarian resolution as superfluous and sought his bed and sleep again. Then the same figure presented itself before him all wounded and implored him, since he had neglected to bring his life aid, not to deny at least murder vengeance. Butchered by the innkeeper his body was in a cart and being hurriedly taken to the city-gate, buried in dung. Compelled to action by his comrade's highly persistent entreaties he forthwith rushed to the gate, apprehended the cart which had been pointed out in the dream and delivered the innkeeper to capital justice.

47 Here is the story of another very clear dream. These two friends from Arcadia were travelling together and had reached Megara, where one lodged with an innkeeper, the other at a friend's. They each had supper and retired to bed, but in the quiet of the night the one enjoying his friend's hospitality had a dream in which the other appeared and seemed to beg his assistance because the innkeeper was plotting his death. At first he was terrified, woke from his dream and got up; then he pulled himself together, decided it was nothing after all and lay back down again. When he had fallen asleep, the same figure appeared and seemed to ask him not to let his death go unavenged, since he had not rescued him when alive. His body had been thrust in a cart by the innkeeper and a pile of dung thrown on top. He urged his companion to be at the city-gate early in the morning before the cart left. This dream really roused him. Early in the morning he was there at the gate, ready and waiting for the driver, and asked him what was in the cart. The terrified peasant fled, the corpse was dug out, all revealed and the innkeeper punished. Could there be a dream of diviner inspiration than this?

48 The syntax of *pestifero fato* is ambiguous and has both dative and ablative force, as frequently happens with these identical forms.

49 It is all in indirect speech, the infinitives dependent on *traditum* at the beginning. But these are elegantly varied and the interplay of perfect and present infinitives and pluperfect subjunctives is managed with deceptive ease, the sound-patterns contributing to the effectiveness of the climax. The extent and quality of this subordination are both beyond the writer of B.

50 'Symmetry and consistency . . . are enemies of movement' (Kenneth Clark, *Civilisation* (London, 1970), 12 *init.*). This instinctive variety and slight asymmetry are the crucial life-giving factors.

51 Cf. Nepotianus, *praef.* (Kempf, p. 592): 'Valerius writes what is worth knowing but protracts what should be concise, showing off *sententiae*, piling on the detail and pouring out floods of verbiage. This is the reason why Valerius is perhaps known to comparatively few because involvement and delay offend the eager reader. So I shall prune his over-writing. . . .'

52 *crepundia*, a literary and theatrical image. They were among the conventional instruments of recognition and identification in tragedy and comedy (cf. Plautus, *Cist.* 635–6, 664–5; *Rud.* 1,081*ff.*; Cicero, *Brut.*, 91.313).

53 Cf. Quiller-Couch's essay 'On Jargon' in the Everyman edition of his Cambridge Lectures (London, 1943), p. 92. Valerius is guilty of his two main vices of jargon – 'circumlocution rather than short straight speech' and 'perpetually shuffling around in the fog and cotton-wool of abstract terms' (ibid., pp. 93 and 100).

54 When Livy tells the same story, the play of thought has a mature restraint – *locusque idem in uno homine et eximiae gloriae monumentum et poenae ultimae fuit* (Livy 6.20.12).

55 From the Marius that was so lowly at Arpinum, so socially inferior at Rome, so disdained a candidate for office, emerged the Marius who subdued Africa, who drove King Jugurtha before his victory-chariot, who destroyed the armies of the Teutones and Cimbri, whose double trophies are on display in the city, whose seven consulships make distinctive reading in the *fasti*, who succeeded from exile to consulship and proscribed to proscriber. What is more inconstant or capricious than his career? He will be discovered, depending how you class him, the most wretched of the wretched or most successful of the successful.

56 Two fates, so to speak, partitioned Alcibiades. The one allotted him illustrious nobility, abundant riches, supreme physical beauty, the favouring inclination of his fellow citizens, highest ranks of office, especial reserves of power, the fieriest of intelligences; the other inflicted condemnation, exile, distraint of goods, poverty, national odium, violent death. Neither series was uniform; they were variously interwoven like the ocean deeps a-boiling.

57 *omnia dicta factaque quasi papavere et sesamo sparsa* (Petronius, 1).

58 Pliny, *N.H.*, I (7) and (33); Gellius XII.7.8; Plutarch, *Brutus* 53, *Marcellus* 30; Priscian VI.1.2 (Keil, *Gramm. Lat.*, 2.i, p. 195).

59 Cf. the Loeb edition of Frontinus, pp. xxii–vi, the most accessible summary of the work of Wachsmuth, Wölfflin *et al.*, with the former's list of thirty-two passages common to both (p. xxii, n.3). There are little or no signs of the *Facta et Dicta* in books I–III of the *Strategemata*.

60 Schanz-Hosius, *Geschichte der römischen Literatur* II (edn 4, Munich, 1935), p. 591; Wight Duff (op. cit.), p. 59; *Oxford Classical Dictionary* (loc. cit.). Nepotianus' own comment, quoted above (n.51) is ignored.

61 For the original material in this and following paragraphs and a critical survey of previous scholarly work, cf. my dissertation on the manuscript tradition of Valerius in Cambridge University Library; cf. also the excellent book by Reynolds and Wilson (op. cit., n.9 above) and M. Manitius, *Geschichte der lateinischen Literatur des Mittelalters* (Munich, 1911–31), *passim*.

62 Berne, Stadtbibliothek 366 (=A in Kempf's editions). Its twin (=L), also of the ninth century, is in Florence. I have examined nearly 150 manuscripts and versions of Valerius and have yet to find a descendant of L.

63 David Knowles, *The Evolution of Medieval Thought* (London, 1962), p. 135.

64 Ibid., p. 136.

65 By an eleventh- or twelfth-century Fleury monk, Rodulfus Tortarius. His versification survives in only one manuscript (ed. M. B. Ogle, *Papers and Monographs of the American Academy in Rome*, 8, 1933).

66 Cf. P. de Nolhac, *Pétrarque et l'Humanisme* (edn 2, Paris, 1907); B. L. Ullman, *Studies in the Italian Renaissance* (Rome, 1955); R. Sabbadini, *Le Scoperte dei Codici Latini e Greci ne' Secoli XIV e XV* (Florence, 1905–14), *passim*.

67 Cf. B. L. Ullman, *The Humanism of Coluccio Salutati* (Padua, 1963). Coluccio suggested two emendations to Valerius – *Scipione Asina* for *Scipione Nasica* at VI.9.11 and the insertion of *filius eius* before *qui matrem Idaeam . . . excepit* at VII.5.2; both are occasionally found in late manuscripts.

68 Owners of Vatican, Reg. Lat. 766; British Museum, Burn. 211; Vat. Lat. 1918; British Museum, Add. 11977; Cambridge University Library, Mm.II.18 (2313). The most notable Thomas Knyvett was the Westminster JP who discovered gunpowder in the cellars of Parliament in 1605 but – another case of Sextus Pompeius! – he is unlikely to have been the Knyvett of the Cambridge manuscript.

69 Cf. J. E. Sandys, *A History of Classical Scholarship*, vol. ii (Cambridge, 1908), p. 197, n.5. Constant gives a list of cross-references in his edition (Paris, 1935), ii, pp. 441–2.

70 By Samuel Speed. The Valpy Delphin edition was not followed by a Valpy translation in their popular Family Classics series, but I am working on a Loeb translation and new text; with the generous assistance of the Computing Laboratory at St Andrews I have also computerised the *Facta et Dicta* and made a complete contextual concordance on the lines of D. W. Packard's Livy concordance (Harvard, 1968). To this extent Valerius is entering the twentieth century.

III

Pliny's Natural History *and the Middle Ages*

Marjorie Chibnall

No other encyclopaedia has enjoyed so long and so continuous a vogue as the *Natural History* of the elder Pliny.[1] It was copied in whole or in part throughout the Middle Ages, and has been printed hundreds of times since the first edition of 1469. Even in the mid-twentieth century it may be both read for pleasure and cited in specialized scientific journals as a source of information on the science and technology of the ancient world. Indeed this two-sidedness has characterized its influence since the days of Pliny: compiled by a learned and busy public servant in his spare time for others like him it has never ceased to interest the cultured general reader; but at the same time the information it contains is sufficiently precise to have been of some value to a very wide range of learned specialists. Astronomers, computists, and students of medicine in the early Middle Ages; geographers and early students of botany and zoology from the twelfth and thirteenth centuries; antiquarians, philologists and art-historians from the later Middle Ages, and other encyclopaedists at all times, have dipped into one or more of its thirty-seven books and rarely come away empty-handed. By contrast, other Roman encyclopaedias, such as the compilations of Varro and Verrius Flaccus, failed to survive the early Middle Ages; and some of the most popular medieval encyclopaedias have either never been printed or, like the *Speculum Mundi* of Vincent of Beauvais, not been reprinted since the seventeenth century. Whatever reservations must be made about the influence of Pliny's *Natural History*, its unique qualities and enduring interest cannot be denied.

It was compiled, together with a Roman History and other works now lost, in such spare time as Pliny had during his career in the imperial service; and he completed it in A.D. 75 at the age of fifty-four, two years before his death. In his letter of dedication to Vespasian (the future Emperor Titus) he apologized for the aridity of the work, but justified it as useful, and claimed to have collected 20,000 facts worthy of note from 2,000 books by 100 authors, which in fact is an understatement. Beginning with a short account of the universe and the nature of the world (book II), he passed to a descriptive account of the known world by regions (books III–VI). Book VII deals briefly with man, from his anatomy to his moral qualities; books VIII–XI with animals, birds, fishes and insects; books XII–XIX and XXI with trees, agriculture, vegetables and flowers; books XX, XXII–XXXII with the curative properties of plants and animals, and miscellaneous *materia medica*, books XXXIII and XXXIV with metals, books XXXV and XXXVI with painting and architecture and the materials used for them, and book XXXVII with precious stones. Book I consists of a detailed analysis of the other thirty-six books, and bibliographies of authors consulted. There are many digressions, and the treatment is as unsystematic as might be expected in a Roman encyclopaedia of the first century A.D. Throughout the tone is practical and descriptive: it is intended for the kind of man who might be a military chief or provincial governor, and treats knowledge rather as an adjunct to politics than part of a systematic pursuit of truth. Pliny made use of the Greek philosophers and mathematicians, including Aristotle and Euclid, and cited his sources with precision; but his extracts were usually brief and piecemeal. Whilst serving to familiarize his readers with the work and ideas of many earlier thinkers he did not provide a basis for carrying scientific investigation much further, particularly when the authors he cited became inaccessible. This was, indeed, not his purpose. It meant, however, that though his book helped to transmit a substantial part of the knowledge of the ancient world to the early Middle Ages it did so by preserving, and sometimes even fossilizing, rather than advancing it. Significant advance came only when the more analytical works that Pliny had consulted, and others based on them and written slightly later, like those of Claudius Ptolemy, became available in their entirety.

Important as it was in the work of preservation and transmission of ancient knowledge, Pliny's *Natural History* did not stand alone. Up to the seventh century other scholars still had access to many of the sources he had used. In the third century Solinus put together his *Collectanea Rerum Memorabilium*,[2] an account of the regions of the world with the fables and marvels traditionally attributed to them. Much of the material was taken from Pliny and from works used by Pliny; but the whole character of the collection was different. Solinus accepted everything he related, and went out of his way to recount marvels; there was none of Pliny's occasional scepticism about the legends he heard, no attempt to assign hearsay to its source, and no accumulation of sober and even arid fact to counterbalance the fantasy. His was a world of sciapodes and acephali, dog-faced men, griffins and mantichora and magical stones. Solinus was immensely popular in western Europe and his much shorter work was more freely copied and excerpted than Pliny's; it amounts to a separate source for the superstitions and monsters of the East which were to play an important part in medieval popular culture and art. Another source for a slightly different type of animal legend was the Greek writer known as Physiologus, who wrote a kind of moralized natural history about the second century A.D. It was translated into Latin in the sixth century and became the basis of the popular bestiaries. These belong to a different tradition; although Pliny attributed some moral qualities to animals Physiologus wrote throughout in a vein of pure Christian allegory, and certainly gathered his legends from independent sources. There were some borrowings from Solinus in the later bestiaries, but none from Pliny.[3] The lapidaries, popular treatises on precious stones, had a somewhat different history; but as far as the borrowings from Pliny were concerned the relationship was the same, for little, if anything, came directly from him.[4] Ancient magical books on the properties and healing qualities of precious stones were available in Egypt and Syria; Pliny, Dioscorides and Galen all made some use of the less superstitious parts; less discriminating use was made by Solinus and others after him; and some of the lore passed into Byzantine, Arab and Jewish sources to come back to the West in translation in the twelfth and thirteenth centuries. When Marbod of Rennes composed his *Liber Lapidum* in the twelfth century he used Solinus, Isidore and at least one other compilation from ancient sources: the Plinian material in his treatise was second-hand and submerged in superstition accumulated from divers sources over the centuries.

Among the Latin transmittors of the more academic classical knowledge must be numbered Macrobius, Martianus Capella, Chalcidius and Isidore of Seville. The first two may have known something of the mathematical and astronomical tradition of Claudius Ptolemy though they departed from his views on many matters. Both Macrobius' *Commentary on the Dream of Scipio*[5] and Capella's *De Nuptiis Philologiae et Mercurii*[6] included some cosmography which helped to shape medieval ideas on lines that were sometimes the same as Pliny's, sometimes different. All three, for instance, were convinced of the sphericity of the globe and in general agreement on the zones into which it was divided. That the earth was a sphere had been generally accepted in the ancient world from the time of Plato and the Pythagoreans; and although the basis of their theory was philosophical (that a sphere was the most perfect shape) Aristotle put forward proofs that were augmented by later writers. But the belief that the earth was a flat disc continued to survive among the Jews; and as some passages in the Old Testament (for example Isaiah, 40:22) seemed to lend favour to this view, some of the early Christian Fathers preserved a non-committal attitude. The doctrine of sphericity was, however, kept alive by Macrobius and Capella, until Bede, making some use of arguments he had found in Pliny, finally came down firmly in its favour. As for the zones, there was general agreement that they were five in number: one torrid, two temperate, and two frigid. Macrobius adopted the view of Crates of Mallos,[7] who in the second century B.C. had elaborated a theory of the Pythagoreans. According to Crates the temperate zones were occupied by four great land masses, perpetually separated from each other by two great oceans that encircled the globe, one at the equator, and one extending from north to south at right angles to it through the poles. This view was the basis of the so-called Zone Maps of the Middle Ages. Whilst Pliny believed that the torrid zone was impassable because of its fiery heat and that there might be antipodean races of which we could never gain knowledge, his account was less clear-cut, and he was as much concerned with pointing to the futility of human vainglory when so small a part of the globe's surface could ever be possessed by the human race as with developing any cosmological theory. Macrobius, not Pliny, was the transmittor of the views of Crates. And on some matters where they were in disagreement their divergent views circulated freely side by side in the following centuries. The Greeks from the third century B.C. had understood the relation between the phases of the moon and tidal movements, and Pliny had given a full account of the variations of the tides; but Macrobius brought forward an ingenious 'physical' theory in opposition to this 'astrological' one. He attributed the tidal movements to the collision of the two great ocean currents at the north and south poles; and even the powerful influence of Bede did not eliminate this plausible and unscientific theory, which found favour with William of Conches and earned a mention in most later encyclopaedias.

Indeed only when differences of interpretation exist, or when writers actually cited Pliny by name can we be certain that he was the source of their information. Contrary to a very widely-held opinion, Isidore of Seville made very little direct use of Pliny in his *Etymologies*.[8] He used Solinus freely, and copied passages from Orosius who seems to have used Pliny; but it is doubtful whether he had any first-hand knowledge of more than brief extracts from the *Natural History*. The next clear evidence of significant use of Pliny comes in the time of Bede. Manuscripts were certainly available in several parts of Europe, but the oldest survive in fragments only.[9] A fifth-century palimpsest of Books XI–XV, believed to have been carefully copied from a second century MS., came from Italy to the monastery of Reichenau. Early fragments survive from Nonantula, Lucca and Autun. By the eighth century it is certain that copies of most if not all of the books were in Ireland and Northumbria. How they travelled to Ireland we do not know; some classical works came by way of Spain, but if Pliny took that route it is surprising that Isidore did not use him more directly. They may have reached Northumbria from Ireland or Italy. Irish scholars were using the *Natural History* in Bede's boyhood, and the use made of it by Bede brought it firmly into the centre of medieval studies once again.

Bede's library was rich in the works of the Fathers and in scriptural commentaries; he had few of the Latin classics and knew even Macrobius and Capella only in extracts. He had, however, a number of treatises on the computus, compiled in Ireland, and he had perhaps half the books of Pliny's *Natural History*.[10] To him this was a work of the highest merit – *opus pulcherrimum* as he called it – and he drew freely upon it. He may partly have derived his conception of an ordered universe from Pliny, and his picture of the spherical earth with its five zones, and of the distances between the planets owes much to the *Natural History*. Of greater significance is the precise scientific use he made of it in his computistical works, particularly in *De Temporum Ratione*. Here his immediate preoccupation was with Christian chronology and the calendar, particularly the calculation of the date of Easter; but since the calendar was based on cycles of movements of the moon and the sun, and a lunar month is 29·5306 days and a solar year 365·2422 days the construction of accurate tables demanded a good grasp of astronomy and mathematics. The lunar and solar years could be reconciled only by intercalating a certain number of lunar months every 8, or 11, or 19, or 84 years. Pliny, in dealing with the phenomena of tides, had used an eight-year cycle; Bede preferred a nineteen-year one, but he was able with some difficulty to adapt what he took from Pliny to his own purpose. He shows in fact a mastery of his sources and an ability to interpret them and correct them by observation that is rarely found in either Roman or early medieval writers. Pliny too had a touch of these qualities: they come out clearly in his work on tides, where he went beyond his best authority Posidonius. To earlier calculations of diurnal, monthly and annual tidal periods, and the use of an eight-year cycle, Pliny added the observation that the tides tended to lag behind the period when the lunar control was exerted, and that tides were different in different estuaries. Bede went beyond this; his observation of the varying tides round Lindisfarne taught him that tides can be calculated only for the individual port because of the configuration of the coast, but that it would in fact be possible to calculate tidal tables for each port on the basis of a nineteen-year cycle. This is one of the few occasions where Pliny's work served actually to advance scientific knowledge in a limited field. In a different and much less original way Bede also used material from the *Natural History* for his scriptural commentaries. When writing on the *Song of Songs* he gave detailed accounts of trees and aromatic shrubs taken from Pliny, pointing out that it was impossible for those like him whose whole lives were spent in the northern islands to know anything about the flora of Arabia, Judaea and Egypt except by taking descriptions from writers who knew those regions; and he made some use of Book XXXVII in discussing the various gems mentioned in the Book of Revelation.

It would be quite untrue to claim that Bede ensured the

survival of Pliny, since practically none of the classical texts that survived till the eighth century were subsequently lost, and there were manuscripts of Pliny on the continent. But he helped to popularize his work, and encouraged the copying of extracts from it, so that fragments of Pliny's cosmology became an accepted part of most popular compilations on the subject. An astronomic-computistic collection of the eighth century, which circulated widely on the continent, was probably compiled under the influence of Bede.[11] Possibly, too, Bede's writings stimulated the active use of Pliny in Ireland, where earlier manuscripts already existed, for the *Natural History* was quoted in the next century by John the Scot in his philosophical writings and by the monk Dicuil in a geographical treatise. And on the continent Pliny, with Bede, became the basic textbook of astronomy in the Carolingian schools. Manuscripts multiplied in widely-separated centres from this time; they were to be found not only at Corbie, a famous centre for the dissemination of classical texts,[12] but also at St Denis, Lorches, Reichenau, Bobbio and Monte Cassino in the ninth century. Some of the books became a normal part of the monastic culture of the age.

They were used in particular for astronomical calculations, for medical information, and to furnish illustrations for biblical commentaries and sermons. Medicine had been studied in the earliest Benedictine monasteries; the subject had been encouraged by Cassiodorus, who gave instructions for making an infirmary, urging his monks to learn the nature of herbs and securing translations of the *Herbarium* of Dioscorides, the *De Herbis et Curis* of Hippocrates and other appropriate works for the benefit of those who could not read Greek.[13] Pliny was not in this list, and indeed Dioscorides, who used the same sources, had left much fuller descriptions of curative plants, together with careful drawings; but at some time early in the Middle Ages the *Natural History* gained a reputation for its medical contents that made it familiar at Salerno. Many monasteries cultivated physic gardens. If Walafrid Strabo did not explicitly mention Pliny in his poem, *Hortulus*, on the little garden he planted at Reichenau, we know that there was a copy of part of Pliny in the monastic library at that time, which he could have consulted. A tenth-century list of drugs preserved in the monastery of Jumièges was in the tradition of Pliny and Dioscorides.[14] This interest certainly remained active till the twelfth century, though in 1131 monks were forbidden to practise medicine outside their own communities, and in the next century they were forbidden to practise it at all. There may possibly have been a medical purpose behind an interesting collection of extracts from Pliny that was made at Clairvaux in the twelfth century; for the compiler attempted to rearrange some of the original books so as to bring together the description of a herb and its medicinal uses.[15] Certainly the appearance of a manuscript of Pliny, normal enough in a Benedictine monastery, is surprising in a Cistercian one, for the books in Cistercian libraries showed a strong leaning towards theology and devotional literature, and the pagan classics were rare.[16] But Pliny was often used in Biblical commentaries, as Bede's work shows, and as a background of illustration and allegory in sermons. Even St Bernard could make use of analogies drawn from the physical world in his preaching. 'The sea,' he wrote, 'is the source of fountains and rivers: the Lord Jesus Christ is the source of every kind of virtue and knowledge. . . . If all waters seek incessantly to return to the sea, making their way thither sometimes by hidden and subterranean channels, so that they may go forth from it again in continual and untiring circuit, becoming visible once more to man and available for his service, why are not those spiritual streams rendered back constantly and without reserve to their legitimate source, that they may not cease to water the fields of our hearts?'[17] This picture of the perpetual circulation of the waters of the earth, finding their way by underground channels from the sea to burst forth again at the sources of great rivers, corresponds exactly with the views of Pliny, and may have been derived directly or indirectly from the second book of the *Natural History*. Even in a Cistercian monastery Pliny was not out of place, though it was a place that would have come as a surprise to him.

During the eleventh and twelfth centuries, as schools multiplied in cathedrals and non-monastic communities, there was a revived study of the dormant parts of Classical literature, and Latin translations from the Greek and Arabic made available many Classical texts that had been lost to the west for centuries. As a result Pliny was superseded in the more active and advanced parts of science. Aristotle's scientific works enabled a much more systematic study of the physical universe to be undertaken, and his more advanced logical treatises gave a training in intellectual method that was to lead to genuine scientific experiment as opposed to the cruder *experimentum*, or experience, of Pliny. And the recovery of the *Almagest* of Ptolemy, translated from the Greek by 1160 and from the Arabic by 1175, made possible once again a mathematical approach to astronomy.[18] All Classical and medieval astronomers were handicapped by their belief in a geocentric universe, and also by the theory, widely-held from the time of Plato, that the orbit of the planets was circular. Ptolemy came nearer than any other thinker to reconciling these fundamental errors with observed facts by an ingenious theory of the epicycles; consequently his treatise dominated the mathematical study of astronomy until the time of Copernicus, and the science of the computus based on Bede, Pliny and the Irish collectors was pushed into the background. But before the great age of translations in the second half of the twelfth century Pliny had become firmly established in the cathedral schools. He was read at Chartres, where John of Salisbury knew the *Natural History* and noted with approval his practice of naming his sources, and was a standard text-book at Laon. He was certainly read in the early schools at Oxford, where Robert of Crichlade, from 1141 prior of St Frideswide's, made his abridgment for the use of students – a book that illuminates certain sides of English learning in the early twelfth century.[19]

In the preface to his *Defloratio Historiae Naturalis Plinii Secundi*, which he addressed to students, both monks and scholars, Robert of Crichlade explained that he had compressed the thirty-seven books of Pliny into nine for the convenience of all who wished to read them. There are some hints that he wrote the book in the early part of his life, before he became prior of St Frideswide's and possibly even before he became an Austin canon. If the book belongs to the 1130s it was certainly in use in the schools of Oxford during the obscure period before the emergence of the University. When later Robert published it he dedicated it to King Henry II; but it cannot have been written expressly for him at a date when he was a mere boy with a dubious claim to succeed to the throne. It was not unusual for teachers in the schools to use books for reading with their pupils before they formally published them. The dedication, written some time after Henry's accession in 1154, pointed out that since Henry ruled over so many lands it was fitting that he should know something of the whole world, and referred too to Henry's love of letters; and indeed the book was equally appropriate in the learned court of a cultured king and in the schools. Robert claimed to have preserved Pliny's own words, but to have omitted both information that was no longer of value, such as the names of towns once subject to Rome from which tribute was no longer due, and some of the pagan errors it contained. This in fact is what he did. He condensed the work, producing a scissors-and-paste précis that involved only minor changes in Pliny's wording, and omitting much that might appear redundant in the twelfth century. His treatment of the universe and of man in the second and seventh books shows how he handled the 'pagan errors'. By carefully deleting here a word, here a whole sentence, he eliminated every reference to the world as eternal or divine, so that statements originally embodying Stoic beliefs might be given a Christian interpretation. He allowed the account of the gods of ancient Rome to stand together with Pliny's sceptical comments on the human failings attributed to them in popular belief; and where he did copy a whole chapter that was incompatible with Christian doctrine because it denied the immortality of the soul he added a chapter-heading of his own: *'De errore ipsius Plinii'*. There was no such rubric to the more controversial chapter where Pliny propounded possible limitations on the omnipotence of God, suggesting that he could not make two and two to equal five, or someone who had lived not to have lived. Robert seems, in fact, to have been carefully cutting out the errors that to his mind were too gross to deserve serious consideration, but leaving some controversial, even pagan, statements as debating points for students to sharpen their wits on and improve their comprehension of truth. In the less questionable parts of the *Natural History* Robert's task was more straightforward: simply to eliminate enough details and illustrations to reduce the accounts of regions of the world, animals, plants and gems to manageable proportions. He also added marginal notes of explanation in places; but most of these have been lost.

Robert's *Deflorationes Plinii* is very much of its own day: an interesting example of a type of Christian humanism characteristic of the twelfth century, but a little known one. Only three manuscripts of the twelfth to thirteenth centuries survive, and only brief excerpts have ever been printed. Possibly the copy of Pliny that King John is known to have lent to the abbot of Reading[20] was the abridged Pliny Robert had given to his father. Abridgments of this type belonged essentially to the schools and learned courts of the twelfth century. The growing universities required a more systematic type of learning, and the development of dialectic encouraged the collection of quotations from authorities on every subject as a first step to weighing up their merits. From the twelfth century onwards encyclopaedias were popular sources of instruction. Naturally the great encyclopaedia of Pliny was freely pillaged, and through the encyclopaedias he found a modest place both in the universities of the thirteenth century and in the Dominican and Franciscan schools which developed at the same time in the university centres. The compilers of the early thirteenth century used him far more freely than their predecessors, William of Conches, Alexander Nequam and others had done.[21] Thomas of Cantimpré, a scholar who became a Dominican in 1232, stated in the preface to his *De Natura Rerum* that he was indebted first of all to Aristotle, second to Pliny and third to Solinus. His contemporary, Bartholomew of England, who joined the Franciscans, wrote his *De proprietatibus Rerum* for *'simplices et parvuli'*: beginners and non-specialists. Bartholomew taught in Oxford and had an extensive, first-hand knowledge of Pliny, whom he cited by book and chapter, using possibly the same manuscript as the one that had served Robert of Crichlade for his epitome. His work became a popular elementary textbook, which was rented by medieval booksellers of Paris to students in the Faculty of Arts of the University; but it was also widely read by the less educated, including laymen, and was translated into French, English, Spanish and Dutch before the end of the Middle Ages. An English translation exercised considerable influence on literature in the Elizabethan period. Both these encyclopaedists were used by the Dominican, Vincent of Beauvais, who produced the most comprehensive of medieval encyclopaedias, the monumental *Speculum Mundi*, in four parts about 1244.[22] Vincent's huge compilation was drawn from a multitude of sources in all periods, including his own day. Amongst them Pliny's *Natural History* was important for certain sections of the work, particularly the *Speculum Naturale* and the *Speculum Historiale*.

Vincent's method owed nothing to Pliny. Like other medieval

universal treatises his *Speculum* had a basic plan that was scriptural. The first part, the *Speculum Naturale*, was based on the six days of creation; and within this framework material was minutely subdivided into books and chapters. One relatively new principle was the alphabetical arrangement of some sections. Herbs, trees, animals, reptiles and other creatures were arranged alphabetically, after a brief introductory section on their nature. The alphabetical principle was not unknown: it had occasionally been used in Roman works, but Pliny had not followed it, and it had not been normal in earlier medieval encyclopaedias, though it was coming into use in works of reference in the universities and in monasteries. In large sections of Vincent's work, particularly those concerned with doctrine and morals, Pliny found no place; in many others Aristotle, St Augustine and the earlier Christian encyclopaedists, and the great Arab writers, particularly Avicenna and Averroes, had a very much larger part. Yet even on subjects such as cosmology, where he had been largely superseded by Aristotle and Ptolemy, occasional quotations from Pliny might find a place. Some were familiar tags, such as his clear statement that the globular shape of the earth was self-evident, but could also be proved in various ways, which owed their inclusion probably to their familiarity and the fact that the authorities agreed about them. A succession of encyclopaedias tends to build up a body of accepted clichés, assured of a place in every new compilation as long as they are acceptable and sometimes even after they have been proved wrong, like Pliny's statement that the crocodile could move only its upper jaw. But many of the extracts that Vincent took from Pliny were on topics where doubt still existed, or where Pliny gave information not available elsewhere. As such they are useful pointers to the state of general scientific knowledge in the thirteenth century.

There was virtually no science of meteorology at that date: most normal climatic changes were variously explained in terms of vapours and exhalations. On phenomena such as earthquakes, volcanoes, whirlwinds, thunder and lightning, there was no basis of agreement and a number of ingenious explanations were put forward. Vincent drew in particular on the *De Caelo* and *Meteorology* of Aristotle, the *Quaestiones Naturales* of Seneca, and Pliny's *Natural History* amongst Classical writings, and the encyclopaedias of Isidore and William of Conches amongst later compilations. Often there was little to choose between the ingenious and inaccurate explanations offered; the causes of earthquakes, for example, were variously attributed by Plato to pressure from internal streams, by Aristotle to vapours bursting forth from the centre of the earth, and by Pliny and Seneca to winds driven into the cavities of the earth by great tempests. But Pliny was able to provide a great deal of information about phenomena in widely separated parts of the world. His keen interest in volcanoes, which he believed to be caused by burning seams of bitumen or naphtha wells, had led to his own death during the eruption of Vesuvius. He had collected accounts of the seasons when thunderstorms or hailstorms occurred in various parts of the world; he even had a description of the monsoon in the Indian Ocean. He had heard of islands that had suddenly appeared in the sea after earthquakes, of peninsulas cut off by rivers, and of lands swallowed up by the sea. Vincent assembled this miscellaneous material, to serve as a basis for further observation and hypothesis. He collected also much that Pliny had to tell about Roman economic life, such as the various ways of extracting salt and the best methods of cultivating vines. On agriculture, indeed, Pliny and Palladius were his principal sources of information.

Again, at the time systematic botany was barely in its infancy. Tentative attempts at grouping plants had been made by Dioscorides and a few other writers of herbals, but there was no systematic nomenclature before the seventeenth century.[23] Botany was largely descriptive. Vincent included a few generalizations on the nature of plants from Aristotle, and some divergent opinions; for example, he cited Aristotle's statement that there cannot be differentiation of sex in plants, since if there were they would be more perfect than animals, side by side with Pliny's observations on the two kinds of palm trees. But most of the books dealing with plants were descriptive, with lengthy extracts from Pliny and Dioscorides. Vincent did, however, follow the descriptions of each plant with an account of its curative properties, and for this he drew copiously on the Arab writers Avicenna and Rhazes. It is noteworthy that in spite of the spread of Arab medicine and translations of Galen, Pliny was well-entrenched in *materia medica*, at least at the encyclopaedia level, and was quoted at length by Vincent on the curative properties of minerals and animal products as well as plants.

Zoology, like botany, was still at the stage of observation and collection of data, and was a good deal confused by the intrusion of mythical creatures. Pliny had much to offer Vincent in his descriptions of birds, though his very rough attempts at classification illustrate the lack of scientific method in his approach: he suggested that some birds are diurnal, some nocturnal; some change plumage and song; some are aquatic and others land birds, and that they are distinguished by various types of movement – flying, walking or hopping. Part even of this crude differentiation came from Aristotle, who was also quoted by Vincent. The descriptions, when accurate, had some value. But the sections on birds and, even more, on animals, shaded into legend, and verged on the scientifically useless. Vincent took rather more of his animal lore from Isidore, Solinus and even Physiologus than directly from Pliny. He even included the story of the beaver castrating itself to escape from its hunters, which Pliny had rejected but Physiologus and Isidore had repeated. There was practically nothing from Pliny in the books on the nature of man, and rather more from Solinus and Isidore on the regions of the world. But on a great many topics Pliny's extensive and erudite descriptions were still valued, and anyone going to consult the *Speculum Naturale* on a great variety of subjects ranging from volcanoes to bee-keeping, the types of stone suitable for building, or the medicinal properties of chalk might find the passages he was reading taken straight from Pliny.

What kind of person read these encyclopaedias? They represent only a part of medieval culture; for active scientific experiment and philosophical investigation were being carried on in the university centres by such men as Robert Grosseteste and Albertus Magnus, and were producing an extensive literature of specialist treatises. But they were certainly used in the universities, at least in the lower faculties; and they might also circulate amongst lay people, particularly after translation. They were used by friars to make collections of *exempla* for use in sermons;[24] often it is quite impossible to tell whether a quotation comes direct from Pliny or at second hand through Vincent of Beauvais or Bartholomew of England. Occasionally useful to the specialist, they represented the solid body of general culture in the later Middle Ages. It was a mixed heritage, ranging from Greek mathematics and a nearly accurate calculation of the circumference of the globe to magic and folk-lore. Not surprisingly, the reaction of men of culture and learning to new discoveries and fresh information was by no means logical, and rarely involved simple acceptance. This appears clearly in the widening of geographical horizons; here the views of Pliny on the more remote parts of Asia and Africa proved too tenacious to be uprooted either by the re-introduction of Ptolemy's *Geography* after 1410 or by the actual exploration of the regions described.

Pliny had provided an account of the regions beyond the limits of the Roman Empire drawn in part from contemporary writers of varying reliability, and in part from contemporary second-hand reports. Nero had sent an expedition to explore the upper reaches of the Nile, which enabled Pliny to place the southern-most limit of the *oikoumene*, or inhabited region of the earth, to 4° north, which was 7½° further south than the calculation of Eratosthenes. He had also been able to report that in the southern part of India the shadows fell to the south during part of the year. But many of his sources contained fabulous elements, particularly in the descriptions of marvels and monsters.[25] Pliny made considerable use of Ctesias of Cnidos, who resided at the court of Persia in the early fourth century B.C. and made a great collection of miscellaneous lore. Some of the creatures Ctesias described came from Homer or Hesiod, many others came from myth, or Indian epic, or even from sculptures on the walls of the great palaces of Persepolis. Their widespread origin in popular folk-lore probably accounted for their tenacity: known to the west through Pliny, Solinus, Isidore and Physiologus they repre-sented what travellers expected to find, and often thought that they had found. Foucher of Chartres, who went on the First Crusade and wrote its history, passed rapidly from observation to legend in his account of the various beasts and serpents in the lands of the Saracens.[26] Beginning, 'We saw a strange beast [in Palestine] whose name was totally unknown, larger than a ram, with a face like a he-goat, the mane of a young ass, cloven hooves and a calf's tail', he went on to describe a 'chimaera' seen in Egypt, which appears to have been a giraffe, and then moved into literary sources. From the crocodile (who could move only his upper jaw) and hippopotamus it was only a short step to dragons and the mantichora, described straight from Pliny and

Solinus, with its human head, triple row of teeth, lion's body and scorpion's tail. Foucher's attitude was characteristic of that of the most learned travellers later: a little observation of a few strange new creatures and wholesale acceptance of the rest. John of Plano Carpini, the Dominican friar sent into the steppes of Asia by Pope Innocent IV in 1245 to report on the Mongols, a keen and intelligent observer, was quite prepared to accept the claim of the Tartars that they had seen and killed certain monsters corresponding to the Cyclopedes of Isidore, who travelled by turning cartwheels on their single foot and hand. Almost the only critical note among the travellers was struck by the Franciscan, William of Rubruck, who during his mission to the Mongols made enquiries of the northern tribes 'about the monsters or human monstrosities of whom Isidore and Solinus speak. They told me they had never seen such things, which makes me wonder if there is any truth in the story.'[27] Most other travellers were concerned rather to hear reports of the strange creatures than to question them: the cynocephali, or dog-headed men, were heard of variously in the Andaman Islands, Nicobar, Burma and Russia. In spite of the occasional scepticism of scholars at home, notably Albertus Magnus who found Solinus 'full of lies' but accepted the mantichora, the monsters persisted into the sixteenth century on maps of the world, and in world chronicles from Rudolf of Hohen-Ems in the thirteenth century to Hartman Schedel at the close of the fifteenth, as well as in the natural histories.

Perhaps more surprising is the slow advance of ascertained geographical truths in the face of geographical tradition. Writers continued to describe the uninhabitable torrid zone long after exploration had crossed the equator and Marco Polo and others had brought back information about Madagascar. The slow progress of exploration round the coast of Africa and into the Atlantic was more often described in terms of Classical geography supported by scripture than of the actual discoveries of navigators.[28] The *Cosmographiae Tractatus Duo* of Cardinal Pierre d'Ailly, which was completed about 1414, was based very largely on the newly-discovered *Geography* of Ptolemy, though with some deference to the views of Pliny where they were different. Ptolemy had believed that the Indian Ocean was enclosed by land, whereas Pliny and d'Ailly after him favoured the correct view that it was open, possibly because of the belief recorded as fact by Pliny that Hanno the Carthaginian had sailed from Cadiz to the Red Sea. Again, Ptolemy had calculated (correctly) that the distance from the eastern shores of Asia to Africa was very considerable; the Cardinal, however, maintained that the distance was less than Ptolemy had allowed and could be navigated in a few days if the wind was favourable. In support of this view, which was later to win the approval of Columbus, he cited Pliny. Such an approach may seem natural in d'Ailly, who was a scholar by training; it is more remarkable in the Portuguese navigator, Duarte Pacheco Pereira, who wrote his treatise *Esmeraldo de Situ Orbis* for King Manuel of Portugal *c.* 1505.[29] Pacheco had a considerable knowledge of the West African coast, and he had been to Brazil with Cabral and to India with Albuquerque. His knowledge of the world was extensive; but he chose to quote or even misquote Pliny, Ptolemy, Isidore and the Bible before, and sometimes instead of, referring to his own experience. In his description of the earth he cited Pliny's view that 'the waters are placed in the centre of the Earth' and the statement in the Book of Genesis about the gathering of the waters into one place to prove that the land surrounds and contains the waters of the sea in its centre, and that therefore there is a great land mass beyond the Atlantic Ocean extending from at least 70° north of the equator to 28½° south. The only experience which he cited was that anyone sailing west from Finisterre or any other point in Europe or Africa encountered land. But at this date the coast of the American mainland had not been fully explored, and many of the expeditions had ended in the islands and did not prove the extent of the land mass; knowledge of the size of a few river estuaries might have convinced explorers that a huge continent existed there, but Pacheco said nothing of this. Whatever he may have known from experience, which he termed 'the mother of knowledge', he preferred to express himself in terms of Biblical and Classical tradition. Certainly he had a respect for Pliny, whom he called 'a Roman senator and a most excellent writer'; he may have cited him and other early writers out of an exaggerated respect for authority. But knowledge existed at many levels, and possibly he was translating the new discoveries into terms familiar to his readers, or even to some extent thinking in those terms himself when he turned his mind to literary composition. Many well-worn quotations from Pliny were the commonplaces of all educated men, and it was probably for this reason that so many attempts of scholars and practical men to demonstrate new truths started from this familiar ground.

If Pliny was known to laymen and general readers in hackneyed quotations he was also a scholar's scholar, and as such he was coming into his own again from the fourteenth century onwards. For some scholars the handy snippets of the encyclopaedists were not enough: they were drawn to the Classical writers by a love of all things Roman and a wish to re-create and understand the Roman civilization they admired. Complete or nearly complete manuscripts of the *Natural History* were readily available, though the text was often in a sorry state. All the copyists of Pliny had found him difficult, because of the large number of technical terms and unknown names occurring in the work, and even Bede had misinterpreted him occasionally: the text had deteriorated with repeated copying. In the fourteenth century Petrarch was among the first to take as one of his models all that he could recover of the work of Pliny (*vir curiosissimus* as he calls him) and to attempt to purify the text.[30] He bought an almost complete copy of the *Natural History* in Mantua on 6 July 1350, and was horrified at its corrupt state. 'What', he asked, 'would Cicero or Livy or the other great men of the past, Pliny above all, think if they could return to life and read their own books?' and answered his question with the surmise that they would scarcely recognize these corrupt and barbarous texts as theirs. He immediately began work on the text, emending and annotating it, and the work continued intermittently whenever he had his copy of Pliny by him to the end of his life. But the task was too much even for his enthusiasm and industry: only the first fifteen books and the last four were heavily annotated, and books XX, XXIII and XXIV, all dealing with the medicinal properties of certain herbs and trees, were untouched. Petrarch's special interests were in information about literary figures, anything connected with Roman life including some recipes and cures (though he distrusted doctors and theoretical medicine), and above all the history of art and geography. He marked the names of rivers, lakes and streams with a special symbol, and sketched a chain in outline round the names of the mountains. Whenever he could he verified Pliny's references, whether by urging Boccaccio to come with him in search of the source of the Timavo, or checking

Pliny's geography of Greece against the remarkably accurate mariners' charts of those parts of the Mediterranean. Occasionally he passed beyond correction to pictorial illustration; in Pliny's reference to the river Orga in the province of Narbonne he recognized the Sorgue, and he drew a vivid sketch of the valley of Vaucluse, noting that it was his best-loved retreat north of Italy: '*transalpina solitudo mea iocundissima*'. In contrast to Robert of Crichlade, who had omitted the names of towns subject to Rome from which tribute could no longer be collected, Petrarch eagerly sought further information on ancient cities, visiting them where possible in search of traces of Roman monuments, or perhaps to reinvisage the scenes described by the poets. His humanism was different from the humanism of Robert two centuries earlier; his aim was not to extract from Pliny what seemed relevant to the Christian education of his own time, but to recover the text as Pliny wrote it, to re-create its meaning, and then to bring it up to date through the findings of observation and practical experience since Pliny's day. This attitude arose from an awakening of historical consciousness: an awareness of the difference of the past which had been lacking in most earlier medieval scholars, and which was one of the main incentives to the growth of accurate textual criticism.

By the end of the fifteenth century the popularity of Pliny and the admiration of scholars for the whole of the *Natural History* are plain to see. Lippo Brandolini, for instance, who lived in the second half of the fifteenth century and was famous for his memory, could repeat all the chapter-headings in all its thirty-seven books, and all the notable facts in every chapter.[31] It was one of the earliest classical works to be printed: the first edition appeared in Venice in 1469 from a still imperfect text, and was followed by increased critical activity and a steady stream of new editions. The most eminent early scholars in this field were Hermolaus Barbarus, who produced his *Castigationes Plinii* in 1492–3, claiming to have corrected some 5,000 errors in the text, and Beatus Rhenanus, who corrected the text, from a manuscript that has since been lost, for the edition of Erasmus in 1525. At the close of the Middle Ages, therefore, Pliny was read more widely and more completely than at any time since his own day; and as Latin gave way to vernacular culture his popularity did not decline. There were early translations into Italian and French;

the first and in many ways the most vivid and readable complete
English translation was that of Philemon Holland in 1601. Pliny
continued to be as essential in the library of a cultured English
gentleman of the Jacobean age as he had been in that of an Italian
humanist of the quattrocento[32] and for much the same reason.
Science might advance rapidly and independently, but Pliny's
Natural History – an immense register, as Gibbon called it, of all
'the discoveries, the arts and the errors of mankind' – was still
an essential part of erudition.

Notes

1 The standard edition of the *Historia Naturalis* is by C. Mayhoff (6 vols,
Leipzig, 1892–1909). There is a complete English translation with good
notes by John Bostock and H. T. Riley (6 vols, London, 1855–7). A
French edition and translation now in progress (ed. J. Beaujeu, Paris,
1950–) also contains useful notes.

2 *C. Iulii Solini Collectanea Rerum Memorabilium*, ed. T. Mommsen (Berlin,
1864).

3 See M. R. James, *The Bestiary* (Roxburghe Club, Oxford, 1928).

4 There was nothing allegorical in Marbod's *Liber Lapidum* and the
treatises copied from it: it preserved purely pagan traditions. In the
thirteenth century allegorical lapidaries began to be composed, possibly
in imitation of the bestiaries. See L. Pannier, *Les Lapidaires français du
moyen âge* (Paris, 1882), and V. Rose, 'Damigeron de Lapidibus' in *Hermes*
9 (1875), 471–91.

5 Macrobius, *Commentary on the Dream of Scipio*, ed. W. H. Stahl (New York,
1952).

6 Martianus Capella, *De nuptiis Philologiae et Mercurii*, ed. F. Eyssenhardt
(Leipzig, 1866).

7 See J. K. Wright, *The Geographical Lore of the Time of the Crusades* (New
York, 1925), pp. 18–19.

8 For the sources of Isidore see J. Fontaine, *Isidore de Seville et la culture
classique dans l'Espagne Wisigothique*, 2 vols (Paris, 1959), especially pp.
496–7, 749.

9 For manuscripts of Pliny see the introductions to the editions of Mayhoff
and Beaujeu; also M. Manitius, *Handschriften Antiker Autoren in
Mittelalterlichen Bibliothekskatalogen* (Beiheft zum Zentralblatt für Biblio-
thekswesen, Leipzig, 1935), pp. 120–3; L. D. Reynolds and N. G.
Wilson, *Scribes and Scholars* (Oxford, 1968), *passim*.

10 For Bede see M. L. W. Laistner, *The Intellectual Heritage of the Early
Middle Ages*, chs 8, 9 (Cornell, 1957); and *Bedae Opera de Temporibus*, ed.
C. W. Jones (Cambridge, Mass., 1943).

11 Karl Rück, 'Auszüge aus der Naturgeschichte des C. Plinius Secundus...'
in *Programm des Ludwigsgymnasiums in München* (Munich, 1888), pp. 10ff.

12 See Paul Lehmann, 'The Benedictine Order and the transmission of the literature of Ancient Rome in the Middle Ages', in *Downside Review*, new series, lxxi (1952–3), pp. 407–21.

13 Cassiodorus, *Institutio Divinarum Litterarum*, I, 31, cited A. C. Crombie, *Augustine to Galileo* (London, 1957), p. 10.

14 Charles Cailhol, 'Les drogues médicinales à Jumièges au Xe siècle', in *Jumièges: Congrès scientifique du XIIIe centenaire* (Rouen, 1955), ii, 703–20.

15 D. J. Campbell, 'A medieval excerptor of the Elder Pliny' in *CQ*, xxvi (1932), 116–19.

16 See C. R. Cheney, 'Les bibliothèques cisterciennes en Angleterre au XIIe siècle' in *Mélanges St Bernard* (Dijon, 1953), pp. 375–82.

17 Cited J. K. Wright, op. cit., p. 200; cf. Pliny, II. 66.

18 See C. H. Haskins, *Studies in the History of Medieval Science* (New York, 1960), ch. 5, for the translations; and A. C. Crombie, *Augustine to Galileo* for a lucid general account of the development of medieval science.

19 For Robert of Crichlade see Emden, *Biographical Register of the University of Oxford*, i. 513–14; C. H. Haskins, 'Henry II as a patron of literature', in *Essays in Medieval History presented to T. F. Tout* (Manchester, 1925), p. 75. K. Rück has published extracts from the *Defloratio* in 'Das Exzerpt der Naturalis Historia des Plinius von Robert von Cricklade', in *Sitzungsberichte der K. Bayer. Akademie, Philos-Philol. Classe* (Munich, 1902), pp. 195–285; the bulk of the work is still unpublished.

20 *Rotuli litterarum clausarum*, ed. T. D. Hardy (Record Commission, 1833–4), i.108.

21 For the encyclopaedias see M. de Bouärd in *RQH*, 112 (1930), pp. 258–304; Lynn Thorndike, *A History of Magic and Experimental Science*, 8 vols (London, 1923–58), ii, p. 377 ff.; J. K. Wright, op. cit., pp. 102–6, 404–10. C. V. Langlois, *La Connaissance de la nature et du monde au moyen âge* (Paris, 1911), pp. 128–79 gives a summary of the encyclopaedia of Bartholomew of England.

22 The most recent edition of the *Speculum Mundi* was published at Douai in 1624.

23 See A. C. Crombie, op. cit., p. 115.

24 B. Smalley, *English Friars and Antiquity in the Early Fourteenth Century* (Oxford, 1960), p. 84.

25 See R. Wittkower, 'Marvels of the East', in the *Journal of the Warburg and Courtauld Institutes*, 5 (1942), 159–97.

26 *Fulcheri Carnotensis Historia Hierosolymitana*, ed. H. Hagenmeyer (Heidelberg, 1913), pp. 778–84.

27 For the journeys of the friars see Christopher Dawson, *The Mongol Mission* (London and New York, 1955).

28 See G. H. T. Kimble, *Geography in the Middle Ages* (London, 1938), pp. 208–12.

29 Edited by G. H. T. Kimble for the Hakluyt Society (London, 1937).

30 See P. de Nolhac, *Pétrarque et l'Humanisme*, 2 vols (Paris, 1907), especially ii, 68–82, 269–71. Petrarch's copy of Pliny with his notes is in the Bibliothèque Nationale (MS. Lat. 6802).

31 Lynn Thorndike, *Science and Thought in the Fifteenth Century* (New York and London, 1963), p. 237.
32 The same would be true of an English humanist of the fifteenth century; Pliny's *Natural History* was one of the books given by Humphrey, Duke of Gloucester, to the University of Oxford (N. R. Ker, *Medieval Libraries of Great Britain*, 2nd edn (London, 1964), p. 143).

IV

Quintilian and Rhetoric

M. Winterbottom

Marcus Fabius Quintilianus, public Professor of Rhetoric, tutor of royal children, rich, academic, dry: this hardly sounds the portrait of a revolutionary. And indeed the revolution that he preached in his twenty years of teaching in Rome and in the *Institutio* that was the product of his retirement was rather in the nature of a reaction. The message was that oratory had become corrupt, that it could only be cured by a return to the standards and methods of a century before. We might gauge the strangeness of such a plea by imagining, at the present time, a professor of English Literature who constantly proclaimed that the whole course of poetry since Keats was a mistake and that redemption could only come if poets, with a proper seriousness, returned to addressing nightingales and Grecian urns. But this analogy would miss the richness of implication in Quintilian's standpoint. Oratory – as another chapter in this book explains – was the king-pin of the Roman educational system. Further, oratory was the literary art *par excellence*, and from it poetry and history tended to take their lead. In demanding oratorical reaction, Quintilian was calling for a re-thinking of educational dogma and for a reversal of tendencies that had made the Silver Age of Latin literature.

The return to the past, for Quintilian, was a return to Cicero. An anecdote in the *Letters* of Quintilian's most distinguished pupil, the younger Pliny,[1] illuminates for us what must have been a common attitude to such a return. The orator Regulus on one occasion sought out Pliny because he felt uneasy that he might have given offence by contrasting with Pliny one Satrius Rufus 'who does not pretend to rival Cicero but is content with the eloquence of his own century'. The sarcasm is clear. We know from the *Dialogus* of Tacitus that to the orators of the Silver Age Cicero seemed old-fashioned, crude and long-winded; times had moved on – and brought a new and arguably better style of

79

oratory with them. At the same time, Pliny's reply to Regulus demonstrates the forces to which Quintilian could appeal against this assertion of progress and the inevitability of history. 'Yes, indeed, I do set up as a rival to Cicero,' he said, 'and I am not content with the eloquence of our century. For I regard it as the height of stupidity not to take the best as one's model for imitation.' The concept of imitation, of course, did not rule out the possibility of progress. 'Nothing grows by imitation alone', Quintilian himself remarks (X.2.8). All the same, 'no one can doubt that imitation plays a large part in art' (X.2.1). To have the right models was all-important. The feeling of literary tradition that lies behind such a view was what enabled Quintilian, without patent absurdity, to try to re-direct the course of literary history. The false gods must be replaced by the true; all, then, would be well.

'Let the student who comes to take pleasure in Cicero know that he has made real progress' (X.1.112). This was Quintilian's challenge. Cicero's style, of course, was a thing of the utmost variety: it could be plain or pompous, learned, witty, pathetic. But it had a recognizable unity in humanity and seriousness of intent that could justly be contrasted with the new style. 'When he had matured and learned by experience what the best style of speaking was,' a modern orator says in the *Dialogus* (22.2), 'Cicero attempted passages of greater brilliance and even struck off a few epigrams.' If anything, however, it was the young Cicero who had most vividly presaged the Silver Age – ranting, for instance, on the punishment of a parricide in the *Pro Roscio Amerino* (72) in terms that he himself later admitted to have been altogether too extravagant. And it is significant that the passage is closely imitated in a declamation [2] from the collection attributed (perhaps wrongly) to Quintilian. The mature Cicero controlled himself better; and the prose of the first century A.D. was a reaction against his dignified wordiness, not a natural development of it.

Aper, the modern orator of the *Dialogus*, was pleading a case – and pleading it, in this respect, misleadingly. But Maternus, another speaker, representative, surely, of the view of Tacitus himself, is irrefutable. His thesis is that oratory has changed since the days of Cicero; and changed in a way that leaves no point in mere exhortation to return to Ciceronian techniques. 'What need of long speeches in the senate? Our great men swiftly reach agreement. What need of constant harangues to the people? The deliberations of state are not left to the ignorant many: they are the duty of one man – the wisest. What need of prosecutions? Crime is rare and trivial. What need of unpopular defences? The clemency of the judge meets the defendants half-way' (41.4). To put it less rhetorically, the rule of the emperors – even when they were beneficent – left no real scope for either forensic or deliberative oratory, at least of the kind in which Cicero had made his mark. Words no longer affected important actions or swayed judgments that counted. All that remained was the panegyric; and it is no coincidence that this is the only sort of speech preserved for us other than fragmentarily after the death of Cicero (apart from Apuleius' strange *Apologia*). Nor was there room for the influential orator himself. He was a product of the old turbulent days. 'We are speaking of no inert and passive thing that rejoices in goodness and modesty. Great oratory is the nurseling of licence (which fools call liberty); companion of revolution, inciter of the unruly mob; uncontrolled, unprincipled, insolent, rash, arrogant. It does not arise in well-regulated states' (*Dial.*, 40.2).

This analysis was faultless. An independent political orator was, under the conditions of the principate, unthinkable; at most, a speaker could be a tool of the régime. Quintilian did not see, or chose to disregard, these restrictions. His perfect orator, like Cicero's, was decked out with all talents and all arts; he would defend the innocent and crush crime; but, far more than that, he would shine brightest in greater matters – directing the counsels of the senate and leading the errant people on to the right path (XII.1.26). To this extent, Quintilian was not so much preaching a revolution as crying for the moon. He did see, however, that exhortation was not enough, and that conditions must be changed before states of mind could alter; but the only conditions that he felt at liberty to criticize were educational, and even here he was oddly timid. In the *Dialogus* the character who most nearly represents the views of Quintilian, Messalla, draws a damning contrast between the education of Cicero's day, when orators were trained by example and personal instruction to come up to the merits of the great speakers of the time, and the present system by which youths are automatically sent to a *rhetor*. Here they engage in exercises more concerned with tyrannicide, rape and plague than with sober legal realities. Messalla's diatribe is broken off for us by a defect in the manuscripts mid-way through a sentence that starts: 'But when he comes before real judges . . .' (35.5). And it is certain from parallel sources that what Messalla proceeded to say was that being exposed to reality made young men trained on declamation look merely foolish. It could well be that the lacuna also hides a plea to do away with declamation schools altogether, or at least radically revise their methods. Even this, of course, would have been to treat a symptom of the decline of oratory as though it was the cause; and Maternus' historical exposé would be intended to point this moral. But Quintilian himself was unadventurous even in his recommendations for reforming education. For basically he regarded declamation as a good thing; it was the teachers who had ruined it.

It is to be supposed that Quintilian's lost book on the causes of the corruption of oratory (published a little before the *Institutio*) went into greater detail on this point. It probably drew a parallel between the decline of oratory in Greece after Demetrius of Phaleron, at about whose period declamation was introduced in Athens (II.4.41), and the decline of Roman oratory after the Augustan period when declamation began to flourish in Rome. But, if so, it does not seem to have drawn the conclusion that it was declamation itself that was at fault. At least, in the *Institutio*, Quintilian, while asserting that the licence and ignorance of declaimers was among the primary causes of the corruption of eloquence, put the blame just on the methods of the *rhetores*. The cure was to make the subjects treated by declaimers as near as possible to reality – to the subjects they would have later to treat in court. 'We shall look in vain for wizards and plagues and oracles and melodramatic stepmothers among the legal phraseology of securities and interdicts' (II.10.5). Declamation was instituted as a mirror of reality, and it should not be deflected from reality. But the trouble came when Quintilian considered the practicability of adjusting the exercise in this way. Declamation, when all was said and done, *had* something of display about it, and could not wholly shrug off brilliance and ornament. Moreover, it was good for young declaimers to 'fatten' themselves from time to time on less dry topics. And how difficult it would have been to interfere with the hallowed rules of the game is shown by Quintilian's wistful remark: 'Would that it could be added to normal practice that we should use names, set themes longer and more complex in character, shudder less at ordinary everyday language, and put in jokes' (II.10.9). Why, it may be asked, could not so distinguished a teacher carry out such reforms at least in his own school? The answer seems to have been that the parents, the rich conservatives of Rome, would not have liked it. They may have demanded public declamation on set open-days, when they could come and rejoice in their sons' success: 'They think their children are working only if they declaim as often as possible' (II.7.1) – and that, no doubt, in accordance with the rules to which they had been accustomed in their day. And they, after all, were paying.

Nevertheless, practicably or not, Quintilian made his challenge. It is easy, looking at the massive *Institutio* and observing the scholarly assembling of sources, to regard it as fairly and squarely in a rhetorical tradition. But if it is in a tradition, it is a Greek tradition. As far as Rome went, and forgetting encyclopaedists like Cornelius Celsus, a long book of rhetorical precept was something that went out with Cicero; and even Cicero, once his youthful *De Inuentione* was out of the way, took care to disguise the precept behind a more urbane front than Quintilian assumes. If Quintilian was challenging opinion by harking back to Cicero, he was challenging it by writing a rhetorical handbook at all. Oratory had changed; and audiences had changed accordingly. They liked the short brilliant speeches of today. It was only in the old days that a people still unused to rhetoric would put up with elaborate day-long speeches. 'Then prestige attached to a long preparatory introduction, a narration back to the year dot, a display of elaborate headings, a thousand stages of proof, and all the other things dictated by the dry-as-dust handbooks of Hermagoras and Apollodorus' (*Dial.*, 19.3). And Aper, the modern orator of the *Dialogus*, goes on to say that nowadays all that is out of date; everyone has a smattering of education, and looks for new and exotic tricks in oratory. Now the judges are in a hurry; and they have to be wooed by epigrams and brilliant descriptions. Yet here was Quintilian writing twelve books that constantly allude to Hermagoras and Apollodorus, and inculcate just those technicalities that modern audiences scorned.

Aper's invective goes a long way towards summarizing the content of the *Institutio*. The first two books deal with grammar, various subjects (such as geometry and music) subordinate to rhetoric, and questions about the purpose and definition of rhetoric. Book III discusses the so-called '*status*-lore' – the method, that is, of determining the basis or key issue of a case – and also, rather cursorily, display and deliberative oratory. But Quintilian is most concerned with forensic oratory – both because his tradition always had had this emphasis and because, while epideictic oratory gave little room for extended precept, deliberative oratory was virtually extinct. Accordingly, the rest of the *Institutio* has the law-court in mind – at least when it is not directed to the school-room. Books IV–VI deal with the parts of a speech – proem, narration, division, argument, peroration. Book VII concerns the methods of treating cases of different *status*. Books VIII and IX are about style, particularly the decoration given by tropes and figures and the attainment of rhythmical effects. In Book X Quintilian recommends reading that will nourish the now fully-fledged orator, and discusses imitation and extemporary speaking. Book XI has to do with propriety (that is, with what is fitting in various circumstances), memory-training and gesture. Book XII concerns the moral character of the orator and the various genres of oratory.

This is the barest of summaries. Quintilian goes into great detail, generously illustrates his points from oratory and poetry, and is not afraid to digress. But even from the summary it may be seen where Quintilian's book differs from a normal rhetorical handbook. At the start of Book III we are told that most writers on rhetoric restricted themselves to discussing how materials for speaking should be discovered and dealt with. Quintilian innovated in looking to the child rather than the technique, and in seeing that the whole development was relevant. That is why we are given detailed instruction for the training of boys from birth to their arrival in the school of the *rhetor*; and why the youth emerging from the school is shown the way to a literary culture that transcends technicalities. Further, Quintilian was concerned, for reasons that will be seen later, with the morals of his budding orators. And the preface to Book XII, which pictures the author setting sail on a sea uncharted even by Cicero himself, stresses the importance and originality of this concern. Nevertheless, it remains true that the bulk of the *Institutio* is in the tradition of the 'dry-as-dust handbooks of Hermagoras and Apollodorus'. Let us see how it modifies that tradition.

Rhetoric was a dogma that had been elaborated for centuries – ever since the Sophists of the fifth century B.C. The death of political oratory after the Macedonian conquest if anything stimulated the elaboration; and it was not until the second century B.C. that Greek rhetoricians introduced the *status* theory that is the hall-mark of the mature system, the triumph of academicism. By Quintilian's day the need was not for innovation but for retrenchment and simplification; and this need went happily with Quintilian's own tidy mind. He more than once protests against the tendency of rhetoricians to strive for originality – their 'keenness to pass on something different' (III.6.22). All the same, he took the minutest points seriously. In the same chapter, on *status*, he apologizes solemnly, and with allusions to similar apologies by Hippocrates and Cicero, for changing his mind on the correct way to sub-divide the subject (64). But, significantly, the change of mind was in the direction of simplicity. Typical of his sane attitude is a remark in Book V: 'These are the traditional kinds of proof; it is not enough to pass them on to my reader in mere generalities – for from any one of them an infinite variety of arguments may arise; at the same time, it is humanly impossible to go through all the different sub-headings one by one. Those who have tried to do this have come up against two difficulties at the same time: they said too much, yet they still did not say all there was to be said. And as a result many pupils, falling inextricably into these snares, lost all their natural flair in their addiction to rigid rules; keeping their eye always on their master, they ceased to follow the lead of nature' (V.10.100–1).

This strikes a note very common in the *Institutio*, and it is what Quintilian was answering to those who scorned rules. A traditional triad made the orator the product of three components – natural talent, rhetorical precept and actual practice. No one disputed the value, limited but indispensable, of the last. But the century was much perplexed by the claims of the other two. In Tacitus' description, the orator Aper, though sufficiently well-educated, gave the impression of despising letters 'as though he would win greater fame for his industry if his natural gifts were not thought to depend on the support of acquired skills' (*Dial.*, 2.2). We hear something very like this of Cassius Severus, the first of the 'new' orators: he relied more on talent than on training, and despised even the declamation schools (Seneca, *Controv.*,

III. *praef.* 4 and 12). And, later on, we gain much the same impression of the orator Regulus, whom we saw earlier sneering at Pliny's Ciceronian pretensions. Quintilian names no names, but he is clearly much concerned to counter these subversive views. 'I see,' he says, 'that some people will block my way on the very threshold, contending that eloquence needs no precepts of this kind. They think the ordinary education of the schools sufficient, plus their own talents; and they merely laugh at my painstaking care for detail' (II.11.1).

There follows a vivid description of the excesses to which this sort of attitude could lead. Such people 'boast that they speak on impulse and use strength; they think that, when the theme is fictitious, there is need not for proof or order but merely for splendid epigrams – that is what fills the hall with listeners'. This is the 'naturalist' in the declamation school. But he is let loose in the law-court also; and there his violent abuse and lack of principle has greater dangers. 'They shrink from having to prove their points. They avoid the chill inevitably caused in decadent courts by the details of proof, and look for nothing but what will soothe the ear with pleasures, even corrupt ones. They are concerned only with epigrams, which certainly show up better when their context is so dim and despicable' (II.12.6–7). On the platform, they shout, gesticulate, throw themselves about; and they dub those who have more respect for letters 'witless, bare, cold and weak' (11).

Quintilian's answer to this insult was that an educated orator would be imbued with an instinctive moderation that would avoid such faults. He might be less showy than the untrained, but he would have true force beneath the polished surface. This was what rhetorical training had to offer; and this might be how Quintilian would have answered the criticism that he was too timid in his attack on the educational system of the day: declamation was dangerous if left to the untrained, but in the hands of a responsible teacher, and allied to a thorough training in rhetorical precept and wider literary culture, it could be a worthy method. An orator trained thus would not *want* to titillate the audience with a stream of epigrams; he would know that other things were more important.

At the same time, rules were not enough. They should not become a superstition. In a sensible chapter (II.13) Quintilian firmly puts himself in the opposite camp to those who allowed no exceptions to rules. Rules were originally formulated to help an orator win his case; and if his case so demands he will logically ignore the rules. 'I do not want young men to think themselves sufficiently educated once they have learned off one of the current rhetorical summaries – safe, as it were, behind the dogmas of the experts. Oratory consists in many things: much labour, constant application, varied exercises, frequent practice, deep forethought, the most alert planning' (15). Thus Quintilian's rules may seem complex and rigid; but they are always to be read with this flexibility of principle in mind. And at the start of Book VIII he protests that his rules are not so frightening as they seem: it is just as bad to be deterred from learning by thinking them infinitely complex as to be self-satisfied enough to think them infinitely applicable.

All the same, to modern ears, the *Institutio* does often go beyond acceptable limits of what can be reasonably taught with any hope of success. And it is only right to give, by extended quotation, instances of this failing. Quintilian admits in VI.3.11 that wit and humour are a matter rather of natural gifts and the opportunity of the moment than of precept. But this does not prevent him spending eighteen pages in a minute analysis of types of joke, of which the following gloomy passage (VI.3.61–2) is a fair sample:

> There is an even more ingenious application of similarity when we borrow for one thing what is at home in another; you might call it 'make-believe'. For instance, at a triumph of Caesar ebony models representing cities were carried by in the procession; then, a few days later, the models in Fabius Maximus' triumph were made of wood, and Chrysippus remarked that they were the boxes for Caesar's cities. Again, Pedo said of a gladiator who was chasing another but not striking him: 'He wants to catch him alive.' A resemblance may be joined to an ambiguity. To someone going after a ball with little zest, Gabba said: 'You compete as energetically as Caesar's candidate in the elections' (for the word *petere* is ambiguous, while the resemblance lies in the indifferent attitude). That is enough on this point.

As indeed it is.

The same sort of doubts arise particularly in the chapters on style. It is one thing to know how to classify good qualities in the style of other orators; it is quite another to employ them one-self. For example, Quintilian writes of hyperbole (VIII.6.67–70):

Hyperbole is a fitting exaggeration of the truth; it has equal power in two different directions – in increasing and diminishing. It occurs in a number of ways. We may say more than the actual fact (e.g. 'In vomiting he filled his lap and the whole platform with scraps of food' and 'Twin rocks threaten heaven'), or we may exaggerate things by using a resemblance ('You might believe there floated there the Cyclades uprooted') or a comparison ('Swifter than the wings of a thunderbolt') or certain signs ('She could fly through the surface of unreaped corn without harming the tender ears by her passing') or a metaphor (like the word 'fly' above). Sometimes a hyperbole can be increased by adding another on top, as Cicero says against Antony: 'What Charybdis was so voracious? Do I say Charybdis? If Charybdis existed, she was a single animal: the ocean itself might scarcely seem able so suddenly to have sucked under so many things so widely scattered and dispersed.'

All this is very well, but in practice it could hardly have been of much service. And Quintilian certainly realized that far more important than any such precepts was the reading of good authors and the building up of the *hexis* – the state of mind, the settled habit – of fine expression.

This is how Quintilian came to insert the famous passage in Book X on the Greek and Roman authors that for many is their first and last acquaintance with the *Institutio* (X.1.46–131). Taken out of context, Quintilian's remarks often seem both casual and trivial. It is essential to realize what he was trying to do here. He was not writing a handbook to extant literature, or even attempting, within the limits of space that he set himself, a balanced assessment of the worth of different authors. 'I propose to go through the types of reading that I think particularly suitable for those setting out to become orators' (45). It was normal in ancient literary criticism for judgments to be framed in terms of rhetorical theory; even the excellent 'Longinus' thinks in the rhetorician's rigid categories, and a good deal of his tract *On the*

Sublime is as technical as anything in the *Institutio*. But Quintilian, by design, is even narrower than this: he tells us about each author what may help the budding speaker, and no more. 'Sunt qui Propertium malint' (X.1.93) may seem a brutal dismissal of a fine poet. But the whole genre of Latin elegy is given only four lines: there was nothing for the orator here, unless it was the terseness and elegance that Quintilian felt to reach its height in Tibullus. Indeed there was much positively to be avoided: 'Ouidius utroque lasciuior' – it was not that he was more pornographic than Tibullus and Propertius, but that his style was unrestrained. He could not master his genius – 'too much the admirer of his own talent', as Quintilian had remarked earlier (88) – any more than, in prose, could Seneca, whom 'one could wish had written employing his own talent and someone else's judgment. . . . If he had not loved *everything* that he wrote, . . . he might win the approval of the educated as well as the admiration of schoolboys' (130). Ovid and Seneca are the distinguished relations of the orators attacked by Quintilian for relying too much on their natural gifts and too little on training.

The long passage on Seneca, unchronologically delayed to the end of the chapter, is the key to the rest of Quintilian's discussion of literature. He protests that he was no enemy of his compatriot; his concern was purely educational – all the young men, at the time when Quintilian was a practising teacher, read Seneca and no one else. These youths had to be brought to realize that there were better authors available; and Quintilian's attempt to 'bring back oratory to more austere standards after it had become corrupt and weakened by every sort of fault' (125) inevitably brought him into conflict with admirers of the most extreme exponent of the modern style. The survey of literature from Homer to Vibius Crispus and Julius Secundus is designed to show where these more austere standards were to be sought, who those better authors were. And it is significant that the survey, though it reaches an emotional climax in Cicero ('born by some gift of Providence as one in whom eloquence might try out her full powers' 109), does not stop with Cicero. Cassius Severus, pioneer of the anti-Ciceronian reaction, might be placed among the foremost if his speeches had had more colour and weight (116). Domitius Afer, whom Quintilian had heard as a young man, 'one would not hesitate to include in the company of the great old orators' (118). 'Future writers will have great scope for sincere praise of orators now flourishing: the talents that adorn the forum today are of the first quality' (122). Quintilian, that is, did not wish to forget everything that had happened in the past century. Progress was still possible, but only on conditions. 'I should advise mature students,' Quintilian says in another place, 'to read both the ancients (for if we can take from them their robust virile force and wipe off from it the grime of their period, then this smartness of ours will shine the more brilliantly) and the new authors, for they too have much to be said for them: nature has not condemned us to dullness – it is our fault that we have changed our style of speaking. . . . Older writers surpassed us by their principles rather than by their genius' (II.5.23–4). Quintilian hoped to change the 'principles' – the *propositum* – of his readers. His day had an elegance – *cultus* – that was new and in itself desirable. If it could be harnessed to the seriousness and breadth of Cicero, the perfect oratory might yet be attained.

It is not, then, to be regarded as surprising that Quintilian himself does not write like Cicero. Even in technical matters, there is a gulf between the rather prolix urbanity with which the *De Oratore* dealt with details of rhetoric and the concise business-like methods of the *Institutio*. That is not to say that Quintilian took no trouble to make his book interesting, even, in a mild way, artistic. In III.1.4 he quotes Lucretius' famous dictum on the need to smear the rim of a bitter cup with honey. Elsewhere, he says, he has added a certain amount of 'brightness' (*aliquid nitoris*; compare a similar remark in II.10.12 on the style of de-clamation compared with real oratory); and it worries him that in the third book the subject may cause there to be more worm-wood than honey to the reader's taste. Yet even here he contrives to be more interesting than his rivals; and in general he tries to vary the tone of his treatise, and not allow precept to go on too long without relief. It may be observed how the prefaces to individual books, while marking off the firm structure of the work, bring variation by striking a more personal note; at the same time, they are cunningly related to the subject of the succeeding chapters. Thus the preface to Book IV aims to capture the good-will and attention of the reader in the same way as the exordia that he proceeds to discuss; and the famous preface to Book VI on the death of Quintilian's wife and children precedes discussion of epilogues and the appeal to emotion.

It remains, however, that Quintilian rarely writes a sentence that could be mistaken for one of Cicero's. The Silver Age shows even in a passage like the following where it is only a question of words that have fallen out of currency (I.6.42):

> Neque enim *tuburchinabundum* et *lurchinabundum* iam in
> nobis quisquam ferat, licet Catō sĭt aūctōr, nec *hos lodices*,
> quamquam id Pōllĭōnī plăcēt, nec *gladiola*, atqui Messala dixit,
> nec *parricidatum*, quod in Caelio uix tolerābĭlĕ uĭdētūr,
> nec *collos* mihi Caluus persuaserit: quae nec ipsi iam dicerent.

> (No one in our day would tolerate *tuburchinabundus* and
> *lurchinabundus*, even though they have the authority of Cato,
> or *lodices* in the masculine, although Pollio likes that, or
> *gladiola* – yet Messala said this – or *parricidatus*, which is
> scarcely to be borne in Caelius; nor will Calvus persuade
> me to say *colli*. They themselves would not use these words –
> nowadays.)

The variety of ways in which Quintilian gives the authorities for the words he cites, the flashes of cretic rhythm and the final epigram all show him using the rhetorical techniques of his age to expound something not in itself very amenable to rhetoric.

Moreover, when he does pull out all the stops, Quintilian is clearly not *trying* to write like Cicero. The lament for wife and children is moving enough; but its rhythms and mood are those of the first century A.D. (VI. *praef.* 12).

> Tuosne ego, o meae spēs ĭnānēs, labentis oculos, tuum
> fugientem spĭrĭtūm ūidī? Tuum corpus frigidum exsānguĕ
> cōmplēxūs, animam recipere auramque communem haurire
> āmplĭūs pŏtŭĭ, dignus his cruciātĭbūs quōs fĕrō, dignus his
> cogitationibus.

> (Child of my empty hopes, did I see your fading eyes, your
> departing breath? Did I endure, once I had embraced your
> body, cold, bloodless, and received your spirit, to breathe
> any longer the common air? Worthy am I of these agonies
> that I bear, worthy of these thoughts.)

This is grave, and, in its way, effective; but it is not Cicero. And when Quintilian says that his dead wife was so young that her loss could be regarded as 'inter uulnera orbitatis' (the phrase is hardly translatable, but the meaning is that her death was like the death of one of Quintilian's children), the declamation school is very close (VI. *praef.* 5). Similarly when a diatribe is launched against the modern method of bringing up children to precocious debauchery (I.2.6–7):

> When a child is not yet bringing out his first words, he
> already knows the meaning of 'purple', already insists on
> the choicest dye. We train their palates before their tongues.
> They do their growing in litters; if they touch the ground,
> they hang on hands that support them on each side. We
> are gratified if they say something particularly daring; words
> that we should scarcely tolerate from Alexandrian slaves
> we greet from our children with a kiss and a laugh.

All this scarcely differs in language and sentiment from Seneca. We know that Quintilian meant what he said; but this was a century in which even sincerity was expressed artificially.

A fortiori, in matters of language, we do wrong to impose on Quintilian a desire to be Ciceronian. '*renuntiare officiis* occurs thrice in Seneca, in Pliny the younger and even in Ciceronian Quintilian.' So, at one point, Summers, one of the best commentators on Silver Age Latin. Quintilian did not proscribe – and could not have proscribed if he had so wished – words that originated after Cicero. He is an author of the Silver Age; and he was in revolt not against anything that had happened to the Latin language, or even against the new smartness in itself: only against the slickness and superficiality that all too easily went with that smartness. The answer was breadth of interest; and Cicero was the key to this, not because he had lived a century before, but because he had been broad in the way that mattered.

Professor Clarke elsewhere in this volume shows how meagre was the influence of Quintilian on the educational methods of the Middle Ages. The question of his influence in rhetoric is hardly separable from that other problem. But it may be remarked here that, striking as is the lack of interest in the *Institutio* during the Middle Ages, his neglect in the later centuries of antiquity is

even more extraordinary. The name of Quintilian attached itself
to two collections of declamations, known as the Minor and the
Major. The Minor, which may perfectly well have some direct
connection with the teaching of the master, are preserved only
by the most tenuous thread of manuscripts. The Major were more
popular; and they at least can claim to have been quoted by res-
pectable authors of late antiquity. The *Institutio*,[3] however,
scarcely causes a ripple in the same period. The use made by
St Jerome of a single chapter of the first book is quite exceptional.
Scholars have hardly been able to dredge a convincing reminis-
cence out of Augustine; rather later, Boethius seems to have had
a phrase from Quintilian's criticism of Seneca at the back of his
mind while he was writing his *Consolatio Philosophiae*.[4] It may not
be coincidental that the Seneca passage comes in a part of the
Institutio that we find excerpted for a brief 'Quintilian on authors'
during the Middle Ages. The *Institutio*, in fact, was too long a
book, and too technical, to win many readers. Only another
Spaniard, Isidore, seems to have paid much attention to it;
and, ironically enough, though he employs it on grammar and
even on music, he looks elsewhere for information on rhetoric.
One or two shadowy rhetoricians, especially Julius Victor, made
use of Quintilian; extracts from the *Institutio* attached themselves
to certain manuscripts of the great Cassiodorus (who indeed
himself seems in his commentary on the Psalms to have gone to
Quintilian for a few definitions), and there are more in a wonder-
ful eighth-century manuscript (Paris Lat. 7530) from Monte
Cassino. That is virtually all.

Manuscripts of the *Institutio* emerge for us first in the ninth
century, one group from central France, the other probably from
Italy. There are not many now, and there probably never were
very many more. One (indeed the most important) of the French
group (the Berne MS. 351) was, it would seem, the property of
the proto-humanist Servatus Lupus, abbot of Ferrières on the
Loire. The details of Lupus' dealings with Quintilian are revealing. Twice he wrote in search of manuscripts of the author, once
to York when he had no text at all, and once to Rome when he had
merely a mutilated text (as indeed the Berne manuscript is). But
he profited little from such of Quintilian as he managed to come
by. Perhaps he did not read all that he had. Lupus' method with
his books was to read them carefully, making corrections where

necessary and noting interesting words in the margin. This process in Quintilian proceeds little beyond Book II; and I have seen no sign in Lupus' letters of any use made of the *Institutio*. A monk of St Gall two hundred years later was rather more energetic. He had access to a complete text of Quintilian (now in Zürich), and he corrected it for about three-quarters of the way; then, shortly after writing in the margin a despairing couplet about the difficulty of emendation where one has no exemplar to help one, he too turned to other matters.

A still more persistent monk, this time at Bec, produced an elegant and intelligent abbreviation of the *Institutio* in the middle of the twelfth century (Paris MS. Lat. 14146). He, like Lupus, had only a mutilated version to work from; but he spread his interests widely, and did not fight shy of the technical details, though he tended to omit the examples. All the same, it was these details that presumably put people off in the Middle Ages. Quintilian was a great name, a revered 'author'. But when it came to reading him, it became clear how little there was in common between ancient rhetoric – elaborate dogma for the speaker in Roman court or senate – and the medieval *ars dictandi* that concerned itself with less august situations. Only a John of Salisbury could get much out of the *Institutio*; and he, after all, read everybody. The ordinary man was more at home with the brief extracts on morality and etiquette that went the rounds of medieval France as part of the *Florilegium Gallicum*.

In the fourteenth century Petrarch, like Lupus before him, searched for Quintilian; found him; then gloomily deplored his mutilated state. Even the part of the book available to him, however, was more than enough for Petrarch. His tiny notes and shrewd emendations in the margins of the Paris MS. Lat. 7720 stray little outside the first and twelfth books. And indeed it was only in the fifteenth century that Quintilian really met with any wide appreciation. Gasparino Barzizza was even prepared to provide a completion of the still mutilated *Institutio*. But this kindly thought was made unnecessary by the discovery of a complete text – made by Poggio in a squalid tower at St Gall, where the very manuscript laboured on so lovingly over three hundred years before at last came to light. This in 1416; and perhaps a hundred manuscripts dated between then and the end of the century testify to the popularity of the book in Renaissance

Italy, France and Germany. The great Lorenzo Valla covered the margins of his manuscript (Paris Lat. 7723) with commentary; and his emendations win for Valla the right to be called the first editor of Quintilian.

The story after that is of a slow fading, marked by a steady decline in the number of editions produced as the centuries passed. Nowadays the average classics undergraduate never opens the *Institutio*. If this were a sign that rhetoric is dead, there would perhaps be no need for grief. And indeed, for the moment and in this country, it *is* dead. But persuasion lives on, and always will live. It is here that Quintilian remains relevant. For it is the great virtue of the *Institutio* that it faces up to the dangers of persuasion. It makes some show, at least, of replying to the criticisms that Plato had voiced long before. 'Most people,' writes Quintilian (II.15.24), 'content to read a few clumsy excerpts from Plato's *Georgias* . . . have fallen into the serious error of believing that Plato held that rhetoric was no art but a mere knack of giving pleasure.' Despite the arguments that follow, Quintilian himself over-estimates Plato's enthusiasm for rhetoric and confidence in the possibility of a just orator. But Plato's criticisms are always in the back of his mind. This is one of the factors that led him to reject definitions of rhetoric that made it only a means of persuasion (II.15.2 *ff.*). If it were that and that only, it would have to be judged simply on its results, on its success in winning cases. But an orator can be good even if he loses his case; and others – prostitutes, flatterers, seducers – are persuaders without being orators. The solution for Quintilian was to import a value judgment into his definition. Rhetoric is the 'knowledge of how to speak *well*' (II.15.38); and the orator – as Cato had said – is the *good* man who is skilled at speaking (XII.1.1).

Quintilian devotes a whole chapter to a quasi-philosophical 'proof' of the virtues of this definition. 'Well, let us grant, what is in fact impossible, that we have found some bad man who at the same time is supremely eloquent. Nevertheless, I shall deny that he is an orator. . . . He who is called in as counsel for the defence needs to have trustworthiness that avarice cannot corrupt, influence deflect or fear break down. Or are we to give the sacred name of orator to a traitor, a turncoat, a conniver?' (XII.1.23–4). In this passage, Quintilian's procedure is particularly transparent. An orator must be a good man by definition. Anyone who is not good is ruled out automatically – ruled out, that is, by force of logic; not, however, ruled out of worldly influence. And this was where the rub came. You can refuse to give the name of orator to the corrupt barrister (or the unscrupulous advertising agent); but if he is doing well out of his corruptness, he will not be unduly offended.

It was the custom of the ancient literary critic to avoid mention of living writers. This meant that Quintilian was relieved of the necessity of mentioning one of the most notable and notorious speakers of his day, one who looms large in the letters of Pliny – the Regulus, in fact, who thought he might have offended by commenting on Pliny's Ciceronianism. This man was one of the class of *delatores*, the informers, who, as was natural, flourished under the principate. They were encouraged by a law that gave successful prosecutors a share in the estates of their victims, and further encouraged by emperors who found them useful agents of their régimes. A number of the most distinguished orators of the century – Domitius Afer and Vibius Crispus among those mentioned by Quintilian – were tarred with this brush. By the end of the century the *delatores* were important people. Regulus, who had ruined noble families under Nero, came into his own under the Flavians; his crimes under Domitian, remarked the benign Pliny (*Epp.*, I.5.1), were no less heinous than those under Nero – merely better concealed. These crimes brought him the consulship, at a date unknown; their instrument was an abusive and violent style of oratory. He called Rusticus 'that Stoic ape'; and we can measure his quality from another remark to Pliny – '*You* think one has to go through all the details in a case; I see the throat at once – and grip that' (*Epp.*, I.20.14). Here was the spirit that felt the prolixity of Cicero to be out of date. But Regulus' own talents were, at least in Pliny's view, unimpressive: 'Weak lungs, indistinct speech, hesitant tongue, snail-like imagination, no memory, nothing but an insane genius. Yet, thanks to this very shamelessness and madness he has come to be regarded as an orator' (*Epp.*, IV.7.4). Not, we imagine, by Quintilian. This Regulus – and there were other speakers like him – was on two counts opposed to every Quintilianic ideal. He was lacking in the technical make-up of the orator; and he was a bad man. Quintilian's book might have been written as a protest that such a man could go so far. Regulus, someone said of him, was a bad man unskilled in speaking (ibid., 5). Cato's definition, and Quintilian's, was overturned.

On the practical level there was nothing that Quintilian could do about Regulus or his like; though there was a revulsion against informers at the beginning of the reign of Trajan not long after the publication of the *Institutio*, there is no reason to suppose that it was caused by the *Institutio*. For one thing, writing under Domitian, Quintilian could not be too specific in his plea for moral standards to be applied to oratory. But the plea remains impressive; it is one that is rarely made, but that should never be silenced:

> I have tried, as far as a man could, to contribute something to the technique of speaking; and I should deserve ill of humanity if I were making ready this weapon for the use of the highwayman, not the soldier. And, quite apart from myself, Nature, in the very gift to man by which she shows herself to have been particularly generous to him and particularly to have separated him from other animals, Nature herself will prove to have been no parent but a stepmother if she designed the power of speech to be the companion of crime, the opponent of innocence and the enemy of truth. (XII.1.1–2)[5]

Notes

1 I.5.11. I have discussed this and other matters arising in this chapter in an article in *JRS* 54 (1964), 90–7.
2 299 (p. 181, Ritter).
3 See F. H. Colson's edition of Book I (Cambridge, 1924), xliiiff.
4 See my note in the *Bulletin of the Institute of Classical Studies* 14 (1967), 83.
5 I have left this chapter largely as it was written in 1967. In the meantime G. A. Kennedy has provided an excellent general survey in *Quintilian* (New York, 1969).

V

Quintilian on Education

M. L. Clarke

When Quintilian wrote his *Institutio Oratoria* he had had twenty years' experience of teaching, which he had combined with practice as an advocate. He had been the first occupant of the chair of Latin rhetoric at Rome endowed by Vespasian from public funds, and he had now retired. He was not a young man with new ideas, not a radical thinker, not a theorist starting from first principles. He was a successful teacher giving to the world the fruits of his experience. He fully accepted the educational system in which he had been brought up and within which he had taught, and to understand his work we must understand what this system was.

It was what would today be called a three-tier system. The first stage was that of the primary school, the *ludus litterarius*, which taught reading and writing and probably some elementary arithmetic. This was followed by the school of the *grammaticus*, who taught language and literature, after which the boy went on to the third stage, that of the rhetoric school, where he learned to express himself orally and in writing. This course was pursued simultaneously in two languages, Greek and Latin; indeed in the earlier stages Greek had priority over Latin. The reasons for this were historical. The first teachers of grammar and rhetoric in Rome were Greeks, who taught in Greek and assumed that their Roman pupils would know their language and want to acquire their culture. The Romans developed their own Latin schools, but the Greek schools continued to function and the Romans continued to attend them. Thus in Quintilian's day the Greek grammar school was as much a feature of a Roman's education as the Latin, and he would know his Homer as well as he knew his Virgil. There were some who continued the double course, Greek and Latin, to the final stage and studied rhetoric in both languages simultaneously; the younger Pliny studied under the Greek rhetorician Nicetes as well as under Quintilian. [1] Quintilian himself, however, does not require a training in Greek rhetoric, and there were probably not a few who dropped their Greek studies after the grammar school stage. When the first Latin school of rhetoric was opened in the early first century B.C. Cicero was advised against attending it, and as a young man he declaimed in Greek more often than in Latin because the best teachers were Greek. [2] Since his day, however, Latin rhetoric had grown in prestige and Greek had suffered a relative decline.

Grammar and rhetoric were only two of a number of subjects which according to ancient theory an educated man ought to know. In Quintilian's scheme of education boys at the grammar school stage would also study geometry and music, and at the same time would have some physical training and lessons in voice production. A Roman boy who followed this curriculum would be in a position not unlike that of a modern English schoolboy working for Ordinary Level in two languages and two other subjects, with classes in physical education and elocution. But unlike his modern counterpart he would not, it seems, study them all in the same school. A school meant a teacher, perhaps with an assistant, and there were as many schools as there were subjects. The Greek *grammaticus* taught Greek 'grammar', the Latin *grammaticus* Latin, and the other subjects had their separate schools. How concurrent study under separate teachers was arranged is not clear from Quintilian, who at this point confines himself to rhetorical questions designed to convince the reader of a boy's capacity to take in a number of subjects at once. One thing, however, is clear. It was expected that this general education should be completed before the boy proceeded to the rhetoric school. Learning to speak and write was in Quintilian's opinion too exacting to allow of any other simultaneous study. [3] It is clear too that there were relatively few who studied these other subjects: the main stream of education was that which led through grammar to rhetoric, and Quintilian has to argue against those who thought it unnecessary to learn anything else. [4]

At what age did a young Roman enter on the study of rhetoric? On this point Quintilian is content to say only that he should move up from the grammar school when fit to do so, [5] but there are passages in his work and elsewhere which indicate what was the normal age of entry. 'Boys', he writes, 'are transferred to these teachers when they have nearly reached maturity and stay with them when they have become young men.'[6] Elsewhere he refers to students of rhetoric as *pueri* and *iuuenes* or *adulescentes*, and he advises sparing the voice in the transition period between boyhood and adolescence.[7] Boyhood (*pueritia*) officially ended with the assumption of the *toga uirilis*, which took place at about the the age of sixteen, and it is clear that the younger pupils at the rhetoric school would be below this age. Evidence from later antiquity suggests that we can take fifteen as the normal age for entry.[8]

Quintilian again declines to lay down any general rule for the leaving age,[9] but we know that the younger Pliny started on his career at the bar in his nineteenth year, and this was the age at which, at a later date, St Augustine began to teach.[10] There would be some who left earlier and went over to other studies, such as law or philosophy,[11] and others who stayed on later (some teachers, according to Quintilian, kept their pupils unduly long),[12] while adults, even senators, sometimes visited the schools, or even attended them regularly.[13] We should, however, probably be justified in taking eighteen as the normal leaving age. Quintilian's school then corresponded, as regards the age group involved, more or less with a Scottish university in the early nineteenth century or with the fifth and sixth forms of a modern English grammar school.

Such was the educational system of Quintilian's day; what did Quintilian make of it? His own teaching experience was confined to the school of rhetoric, but he recognized that the final stage of an orator's education depended on what had gone before, and he had his own views on even the earliest stages. He dissents from those who think education should not begin before the age of seven; he criticizes the common practice of teaching the names and order of the letters before their shape, approves another common practice, that of giving children ivory letters to play with, and recommends the use of model letters cut into a board which the child can follow with his pen.[14]

The work of the grammar school had two sides to it, language and literature, or, as Quintilian puts it, *recte loquendi scientia* and *poetarum enarratio*.[15] It will be observed that the literature course was confined to poetry; oratory belonged to the rhetoricians, philosophical writing to the philosophers and teachers of history were non-existent. Expounding the poets meant teaching correct reading aloud, explaining the metre and diction and elucidating the mythological references. With regard to the last task Quintilian deprecates a pedantic display of learning; otherwise his discussion of the grammar school curriculum is chiefly remarkable for his anxiety to avoid anything that could be regarded as morally objectionable. 'There are passages in Horace', he writes, 'which I should not like to have to explain.'[16] He is referring to the Odes, which even in Victorian England were read unexpurgated.

The division of functions between grammarian and rhetorician had the curious result, or would have had if each school had stuck to its traditional tasks, that in the grammar school the boy did no composition and in the rhetoric school he did no reading. In practice, however, the division was not strictly maintained. The course in rhetoric began with a series of graded exercises in composition known as *progymnasmata*, and the more elementary of these Quintilian, presumably following current practice, assigns to the grammar school. Some grammarians went further than this: they handled all the progymnastic exercises and even started their pupils on declamation.[17] This development Quintilian deplores. His view is that each profession should stick to its own sphere.[18] Apart from the fact that this principle might have been invoked against the compromise which he adopts, he seems somewhat short-sighted here. A system under which composition is combined with the reading of literature would appear to be better than one under which the two are taught by different masters at different stages of a boy's school career.

The strict demarcation between the two professions made it difficult to include any reading of authors in the school of rhetoric. In the Greek schools historians and orators were read, but not in the Latin. Quintilian tried to introduce such reading in his school, but the experiment was a failure. Tradition was too strong, and his pupils preferred to take his speeches as a model rather than Cicero's. Moreover, the exposition of texts was regarded as below the dignity of the rhetorician. Quintilian had to acknowledge failure and content himself with recommending this method to posterity.[19] Presumably, however, he encouraged out-of-school reading. The younger Pliny, doubtless a model pupil, describes how he went on with his studies (he was reading Livy) during the eruption of Vesuvius; he was then aged seventeen, and, as it was August, would be on holiday from school.[20]

The function of the rhetorician was to teach the theory and practice of speaking. Instruction consisted in part of lectures on rhetorical theory, in part of declamation. Though rhetorical theory occupies the major part of the *Institutio*, it probably did not bulk very large in Quintilian's teaching. Certainly he had a greater interest in the subject than some of his contemporaries, who were scandalously ignorant of theory and thought that declamation comprised the whole of rhetorical teaching,[21] but though he believed a knowledge of the Art of Rhetoric to be essential, it is unlikely that he devoted more than an occasional course of lectures to it. He tells us of two such courses, one of two days' duration for the younger pupils, which would be a simple outline of accepted doctrine without refutation of rejected opinions, and a longer course for the older ones.[22] Some of the latter was incorporated in the *Institutio*; but in writing this work he made a number of alterations and additions, and his treatment of the subject as eventually published was more detailed than anything he had given in his school teaching.[23]

The main activity of Quintilian's school, as of other schools of rhetoric, would be declamation, that is the making of practice speeches on set themes, whether of a deliberative character (*suasoriae*) or a forensic (*controuersiae*). The usual routine was for the master to choose a theme, discuss and analyse it and then give a model declamation.[24] The pupils would prepare their own speeches on the set themes and on certain days would deliver them in class.[25] The 'Lesser Declamations' ascribed to Quintilian give us a good idea of what went on in the classroom. In this collection, which originally comprised as many as three hundred and eighty-eight declamations, we have what are apparently the notes taken down by a pupil perhaps of Quintilian himself. The material is divided into *Sermo*, the teacher's preliminary discussion of the theme, and the declamation itself. It is clear that the same teacher is speaking throughout, and the whole collection can perhaps be taken as reproducing a complete course in declamation. To the modern reader it seems a curriculum of wearisome monotony.

Declamation was in origin and intention a preparation for real life, for the oratory of the law courts and of politics. But under the Empire it had lost touch with reality and become an end in itself. The themes set tended to be fantastic and melodramatic and the treatment was equally unrealistic. Serious argument was avoided; all was sacrificed to immediate effect. Superficial sparkle and clever but shallow epigrams were what won applause, and those who emerged from the schools found it hard to adjust themselves to the realities of the courts. Quintilian made it his business to counteract the harmful influence of declamation as it was then practised. He was not one of the *scholastici*, the rhetoricians who spent their whole lives in the schools and accepted their values without question. He started teaching only after some years of practice in the courts, and he continued such practice while he was teaching. He was well aware of the factors that made for success in the advocate's profession and of the poor preparation afforded by the contemporary schools. But though a severe critic of declamation, which he considered to be the chief cause of the corruption of oratory, he had no desire to get rid of it; he regarded it as a valuable exercise which had been badly misused. [26] He insists that it should be looked on as a preparation for the oratory of the courts; the subjects, therefore, should be as realistic as possible and the speeches should be modelled on real pleading. [27] But in practice he had to compromise: he is prepared to admit that declamation involves an element of display and to allow students occasionally to handle incredible and poetic themes. [28] His purpose is, he says, to train an orator, but to avoid criticism from students he also includes what has relevance only to scholastic practice. [29] Throughout his work there are numerous references to *controuersiae* which show that he had the schools in mind as much as the courts; his section on deliberative oratory is almost entirely concerned with *suasoriae*, and leaves the reader with the strong impression that such exercises were quite useless as training for speaking in the senate or advising the emperor. [30] Though he aims at educating an orator Quintilian seems at times to be educating a declaimer.

Quintilian is sometimes praised for the breadth of his outlook, for his belief that the orator should be well read and equipped with wide and varied knowledge. He was certainly a man of wide knowledge and interests, but at the same time he was very much the professional rhetorician, inclined to magnify his subject unduly and unwilling to allow encroachments on it. Though he dilates on the capacity of the human mind to take in a number of subjects at the same time, he confines the study of such subjects to the grammar school stage, while the elaborate programme of reading which he draws up in his tenth book is designed for the adult who has completed his schooling.[31] Moreover, he regards everything else, mathematics and music, literature, law and philosophy, as subordinate to rhetoric and as contributing to oratorical ability. Even if we accept his view that eloquence is the highest gift of heaven to mankind and that all else should be sacrificed to its attainment, we may still wonder whether better results might not have been attained with a less exclusive concentration on the art of speech. There is evidence from Quintilian himself that his pupils were sometimes afflicted by a morbid self-criticism which reduced them to silence.[32] Perhaps they would have found more to say if they had had some relief from the endless routine of learning how to speak. Where the school of rhetoric was concerned Quintilian forgot what he had written of the grammar school stage: 'Variety of itself refreshes and restores the mind. . . . Who can fail to be deadened if he has to listen the whole day to one teacher, whatever his subject may be?'[33]

The teachers of the ancient world were originally specialists who claimed only to give instruction in their own subject. But when an educational system became established under which the years of boyhood and adolescence were spent in the charge of two of these specialists, the *grammaticus* and the rhetorician, people came to expect something more from school than mere instruction in literature and in the art of speaking. They paid some attention to the sort of qualities a modern parent values, good moral tone, good discipline, perhaps even a 'happy atmosphere'. As modern parents do who have any choice in the matter, they discussed schools. It was not then as it is in modern England, a matter of choosing between day and boarding school or between independent and state school: the choice was between different schools of the same type or (as it was in England in the time of Locke) between school and education at home under a private tutor. Quintilian's discussion of the latter question shows that men were influenced not only by purely academic considerations. In favour of the private tutor two arguments were advanced: that schools corrupted morals and that a boy got on better if he could command the full attention of his teacher. Quintilian answers the first by saying that morals could be corrupted just as much at home, and the second by pointing out that the best teachers did not become private tutors and that a good school-master would give individual attention to a promising boy. There were also in his view positive arguments in favour of school. It provided a better preparation for life than the privacy of home; boys acquired the ability to get on with people (for that is roughly what the Latin *communis sensus* means), and learnt from their fellows by competition and emulation; finally the friendships made at school lasted for life.[34] Quintilian, then, was aware that a school (even one without the numerous extra-curricular activities of modern English schools) could contribute something more to the lives of the young than training in a particular branch of knowledge.

We have mentioned good moral tone as one of the qualities men looked for in a school and this was certainly something which Quintilian regarded as of great importance. The orator for him should be first and foremost a good man: virtuous living was more important even than high oratorical ability.[35] We should remember that there was then no church to train the young in the principles of right conduct; and the philosophers, the profes-sional teachers of morality, influenced only a relatively small num-ber, and apart from this were in bad odour when Quintilian wrote, had in fact been expelled from Rome by Domitian. It was left to the rhetoricians to do their best by precept and example to make their pupils not only good speakers but also good men.

When Quintilian writes of the morality of schools it is clear that he is thinking partly, perhaps mainly, of sexual morality. One might think that homosexuality would not have been a serious problem in the Roman schools as the boys lived at home and the younger ones were carefully guarded by their *paedagogi* or slave tutors. But Roman parents and teachers were certainly concerned about it. For this reason Quintilian was not in favour of allowing the older and the younger boys to sit together,[36] and no doubt he separated them in his own school. The younger Pliny, giving advice on the education of a good-looking boy who had hitherto been taught at home, emphasizes that his rhetoric school must be strict and above all morally pure.[37] The fact is that not all teachers could be trusted in this respect,[38] and some of the boys were corrupted by their home background. A striking passage in Quintilian throws a lurid light on the home life of some of the wealthier Romans. 'Would that we did not ourselves ruin the characters of our children. We spoil them in infancy by indulgence. The soft upbringing which we call being kind weakens all the sinews of mind and body. . . . We are delighted if they say anything over-free; words which would not be permitted even in favourite slaves from Alexandria are greeted with laughter and a kiss. There is nothing surprising about this. We have taught them, they have heard us use the words. They see our mistresses and male concubines, every party is loud with indecent songs, and things shameful to speak of are witnessed. Hence comes habit, and habit becomes second nature. The poor creatures learn all this before they know that it is wrong; this makes them enervated and effeminate. They do not get these vices from school; they bring them to school.'[39] Even those who spoilt their boys and allowed them to be corrupted at home perhaps hoped that they would acquire better habits at school. For them no less than for strict parents like those of Pliny's circle Quintilian's care for his pupils' morals would help to recommend his school.

Quintilian's morality, though not uninfluenced by the prevailing philosophy of Stoicism, was a matter of instinct and tradition as much as of reason and theory. He was not the sort of man to argue and question as his contemporary Epictetus did; but one can imagine that his rebukes and his commendation would be listened to and remembered. He has been described as 'the sort of person we should regard today as a first-rate headmaster of a public school of healthy moral tone, high standards of intellectual performance, and slightly conservative tradition.'[40] Such men may not have the profoundest insights into human conduct, but parents willingly entrust their children to them.

Along with sound moral principles went a sympathy with and interest in the young. Quintilian clearly enjoyed teaching; even in retirement he still writes of *'adulescentes mei'*.[41] He believes that the young should enjoy their studies, or if they cannot do that should at least not dislike them.[42] He warns against discouraging by undue severity.[43] He knows the value of play and recreation.[44] He would have the schoolmaster observe the different characters and abilities of his pupils and apply different methods accordingly.[45] He disapproves of the then prevalent practice of beating, and for good reasons. First, it is a degrading punishment suited only to slaves; second, those who do not respond to verbal correction will not respond to beating, but will merely become hardened to blows; finally beating would be unnecessary if the *paedagogi* (who not only accompanied boys to school but also saw that they did their work) performed their task properly. After giving further reasons he sums up: 'No one should be allowed too much power over those who are helpless and easily victimized.'[46]

His attitude to education is summed up in his admirable sketch of the ideal schoolmaster:[47]

Let him above all adopt the attitude of a parent towards
his pupils and think of himself as taking the place of those
who have committed their children to his charge. He should
neither be vicious himself nor tolerate vice in others. He
should be strict without being gloomy, genial without being
slack; otherwise the first quality will make him disliked, the
second will bring him into contempt. He should have much
to say on what is good and honourable; for the more he
advises the less he will punish. He must not be prone to
anger, though at the same time he should not ignore faults
that need correction; he should be straightforward in his
teaching, ready to take trouble, assiduous but not excessively
so. He should willingly reply to questions, and should
himself question those who do not ask. In praising the
compositions of his pupils he should be neither grudging nor
effusive; the former causes a distaste for work, the latter
complacency. In correcting faults he should not be harsh,
and certainly not insulting; there are some teachers whose
rebukes give the impression of dislike, and this has the effect
of discouraging many from study. . . . Pupils rightly
instructed regard their teacher with affection and respect.
And it is scarcely possible to say how much more willingly
we imitate those whom we like.

It may be asked whether there was anything original about Quintilian's work or whether he did no more than express the best educational thought of his day. He was certainly not a radical reformer: the cast of his mind was on the whole conservative, and much of what he advocated was probably familiar at the time of writing. To give one instance, his belief that a good teacher should take account of the different natural abilities of his pupils, which according to a modern writer 'strikes a new note in education', [48] was, as Quintilian himself says, the accepted view. [49] On the other hand, he clearly formed his own views, and his work bears the mark of a definite personality. It was he and not someone else who wrote the *Institutio*, and the *Institutio* was different from any other ancient treatise on rhetoric.

What Quintilian himself regarded as important in his work can be seen from the preface to the first book. The main points he makes here are two, that the whole of education from infancy upwards is relevant to the training of an orator and that the orator should be a good man. His belief in the importance of the early stages of education involves him in general pedagogic questions which in all probability had hitherto interested only the philosophers. Not to mention Plato and Aristotle, the Stoic Chrysippus had written a work on education to which Quintilian more than once refers. [50] The treatise on education ascribed to Plutarch, which is more or less contemporary with Quintilian's *Institutio*, is evidently the work of a philosopher, or one influenced by philosophy, and not of a rhetorician. Quintilian was perhaps the first to use the educational ideas of the philosophers in connection with the established system of literary and rhetorical education. His second point, that the orator should be a good man, was hardly new (Cato had long ago defined the orator as *uir bonus dicendi peritus*), but it had some new implications for teaching. Quintilian's hope was that rhetoric would be able to absorb what was valuable in the moral education given by the philosophers. As things are, he admits, we cannot do without the teachings of philosophy, but he hopes the time will come when the perfect orator will claim them as his own and restore philosophy to its position as a part of eloquence. [51] In the meantime Quintilian's strong emphasis on morality might well suggest that in practice philosophical schooling was unnecessary for one trained in rhetoric on his principles.

A book about education by a successful schoolmaster will convey to posterity something of the author's character and qualities as a teacher, but if we want to know what he was really like we should if possible turn to his pupils to see what they thought of him. In the case of Quintilian one of his pupils, the younger Pliny, provides us with a little evidence. It is not to be found in his actual references to Quintilian, which tell us little,

but in his devotion to oratory and literature, his interest in
education, and particularly in the way he speaks of his schooldays.
Asked to help in choosing a school for a friend's nephews he
went round the schools to see what they were like; he enjoyed
renewing his youth and reviving memories of 'the happiest days
of one's life'.[52] It is not everyone who can say this with sincerity
of his schooldays, and it can be taken as a tribute to the kindly
personality of Quintilian and his ability to arouse an interest in
study. Pliny also bears out Quintilian's claim that friendships
made at school last for life: his close friend Voconius Romanus
had been at school with him, and as Voconius was a connoisseur
of oratory and came from Quintilian's province of Hispania
Citerior, we can be confident that the school was that of
Quintilian.[53]

Conjecture, and it is no more than conjecture, has numbered
two other distinguished writers among Quintilian's pupils,
Juvenal and Tacitus. If Juvenal was taught by Quintilian, he
was not exactly an admiring disciple. His references to him have
been interpreted as providing evidence of hostility,[54] and even if
there was no active hostility, it was certainly no great compli-
ment to attribute his success, as Juvenal does, merely to luck.[55]
On the other hand, there are passages in the *Satires* which
suggest that Juvenal may have got some of his ideas from Quintilian, as where he writes of the bad influence of parents on their
children,[56] or where he invokes a blessing on those *qui praeceptorem
sancti uoluere parentis esse loco*,[57] though in the latter case we begin
to have doubts about Quintilian's influence when we read on and
find that Juvenal seems to think the chief function of a parent is
to wield the rod.

Tacitus too is, if anything, critical of Quintilian.[58] If we accept
the view now favoured by scholarly opinion that the *Dialogus*
was written after the death of Domitian, we might well suppose
that it was the publication of the *Institutio*, following on Quintilian's now lost work on the causes of the decline of oratory,
which led Tacitus to think and to write on the subject.[59] Evidently
he did not share Quintilian's optimism about the future of
oratory;[60] he recognized, as Quintilian had not done, that circumstances had changed since the days of Cicero and great oratory
could not flourish under the imperial system.

Quintilian's work was in fact out of date even when he wrote.

There was little scope for his ideal orator-statesman in the reign of Domitian. Quintilian looks back to the past rather than forward to the future, and for this reason he had, so far as we can judge, little influence in the Roman world after his death. He was remembered, it is true, as a great rhetorician. The attribution to him of the 'Greater Declamations' is evidence of this. But it is also evidence that his work was ill understood, for these compositions have little of those virtues of style and treatment which he tried to inculcate. The Latin rhetorician of the second century of whose methods as a teacher we know most is Fronto, and he seems quite uninfluenced by Quintilian. His excessive interest in stylistic elegance and his addiction to rare and archaic words would hardly have met with Quintilian's approval. Nor was Quintilian's hope that rhetoric could absorb and supersede philosophy fulfilled. The teaching of Fronto, *uir bonus* as he doubtless was, could not satisfy Marcus Aurelius.

If Quintilian's work was out of date at the time of writing, even more did it become so with the spread of Christianity. Not that the Christians were uninterested in education: from the beginning the Church was essentially a teaching institution, and such works as Augustine's *De Catechizandis Rudibus*, Gregory of Nyssa's *Catechetical Oration* and John Chrysostom's *De Inani Gloria* show that churchmen were aware of the importance of education and of educational method. But their purpose was quite different from that of Quintilian. They did not aim at worldly distinction; they were uninterested in success in the forum and the senate. They taught Christian doctrine and practice: their textbooks were not rhetorical handbooks or speeches of Cicero but the Scriptures. The means they used were different too. They did not attempt to reform the secular schools: they taught rather through the home and the church. Christian parents were expected to teach the faith to their children; converts had to undergo a course of instruction before admission to baptism, while teaching continued through life in the regular services of the church. Moreover, Christian education was designed for everybody, and not only for children of well-to-do parents, such as would attend Quintilian's school.

Schools of rhetoric continued, but the subject was not one which churchmen regarded with much favour. It smacked of deceit and vanity and worldly ambition; an applicant for baptism who had followed the regular course in grammar and rhetoric would, St Augustine notes, have to unlearn something of his pride in his accomplishments.[61] If this was the attitude of the church, it was not to be expected that much attention would be paid by churchmen to Quintilian's work. Yet there was much in his first book which could be adapted to any form of education, and St Jerome drew heavily on that book in the letter he wrote to Laeta prescribing a course of Christian education for her daughter.[62] The method is Quintilian's, but the purpose of Jerome's instructions, and perhaps the sex of the person for whom they were designed, might well have 'made Quintilian stare and gasp'.

Quintilian was not forgotten in the Middle Ages,[63] but his work was unlikely to have much influence on education so long as social life and intellectual ideals remained so far removed from those of Quintilian's day. At the end of the tenth century, it is true, Gerbert was teaching rhetoric at Rheims, and treating it not merely as one of the traditional 'arts' but as the crown of education; but there seems to be no evidence that he knew Quintilian's work.[64] It is perhaps only in the school of Chartres in the twelfth century that we can find Quintilian exercising a real influence in medieval education. The well-known description by John of Salisbury of the methods of teaching followed there[65] is based on Quintilian's directions on *praelectio* in the grammar school, and it is reasonable to assume his teachers, William of Conches and Richard l'Évêque, and before them Bernard of Chartres, based themselves on Quintilian, or at any rate, since the school of Chartres was essentially one of grammar, on his first book. In two respects, however, the method of Chartres differed from that of Quintilian. First, Bernard used corporal punishment as a means of inculcating his lessons; and second, he taught verse composition. There appears to be no evidence that boys in the Roman grammar schools were made to write verses; this is rather one of the legacies of the Middle Ages.

The humanist interests represented by the school of Chartres were soon eclipsed by the growing prestige of Aristotelian logic. In the medieval universities, when philosophy was added to the traditional Arts curriculum, and the Arts faculty was regarded as subordinate to the higher faculties of theology, law and medicine, there was little room for the studies with which Quintilian was concerned. It was in Italy of the fifteenth century, with the growth of a more secular outlook, of an interest in literature and eloquence and a desire to recover something of the way of life of ancient Rome, that an interest in Quintilian revived.[66] Various names could be mentioned as significant in this connection. There is Petrarch, who in 1350 addressed a letter to Quintilian and who, comparing the *Institutio* with the Declamations, then believed to be Quintilian's work, recognized that he was a better teacher of oratory than orator.[67] There is Poggio, who discovered the complete text of the *Institutio* at St Gall in 1416; Vittorino da Feltre, the famous humanist teacher, who, according to his biographer, 'gave the highest praise to Quintilian as the best authority as regards both life and learning';[68] and Valla, who had a great admiration for Quintilian and claimed to know him almost by heart.[69] Educational writers of the fifteenth and sixteenth centuries regularly draw on Quintilian. As the best Roman authority on education his reputation stood high. 'I observe,' says Erasmus in one of his educational treatises, 'that Quintilian has given thorough instructions on these matters, so much so that it seems the height of impudence to write on the same subject after him.'[70] We find him followed even where he advocates beginning Greek before Latin, a procedure which was quite impracticable in the modern world so long as Greek grammar books were written in Latin. 'First of all the Greek, as Quintilian will have it; secondly the Latin,' says Rabelais's Gargantua in his instructions to Pantagruel.[71] Erasmus also reproduces Quintilian's precept, and Sir Thomas Elyot in his *Governour* follows him.[72] Battista Guarino, however, though otherwise much indebted to Quintilian, recognizes that he cannot be followed in this respect.[73]

The humanist educators, great as was their respect for authority, did not attempt to reproduce Quintilian's educational programme unaltered. They laid more stress than he did on the influence of the home (in this respect the Plutarchian treatise on education, which was available in a Latin version from 1411, was more congenial to them) and on physical education, and they were concerned, as Quintilian of course was not, to combine an education in literature and rhetoric with Christian piety. On one or two points doubt might arise as to the compatibility of ancient ideals with Christianity. The doctrine of original sin makes

Erasmus hesitate to go all the way with the ancients in their belief in the value of education,[74] and Quintilian's disapproval of beating might seem to conflict with the scriptural precept 'He that spareth the rod hateth his son'. Roger Ascham pointed out that this applied to parents rather than to schoolmasters and observed with some justice that in the ancient world the master confined himself to teaching and left others, the father and the *paedagogus*, to correct manners, so that the schoolmaster could do without the rod.[75] Erasmus is bolder in rejecting scriptural authority. The precepts of Solomon, he says, may have been suited to the Jews of old; *nunc oportet Hebraeorum dicta civilius interpretari*.[76] In general the humane side of Quintilian, his ideal of the master as the kindly sympathetic teacher who makes himself loved as well as respected, was readily accepted. Accepted, that is to say, by educational theorists; how far their ideas percolated to the schoolrooms is another matter.

It was Quintilian's first book, with its general educational precepts and directions on grammar school teaching, that was most influential. The Renaissance teachers were more grammarians (in the ancient sense of the word) than rhetoricians. Useful as Latin eloquence still was, it could hardly claim the same importance as it had had in Quintilian's day, nor was it exercised, as it had been in the ancient world, primarily in the law courts.[77] The course in rhetoric provided in the Renaissance schools was therefore a good deal shorter than that given in those of ancient Rome. A common scheme was one in which a course in grammar and literature was followed by a year of rhetoric; this was the system in the Jesuit colleges, in those of the Oratorians and in the University of Paris.[78] In the English grammar schools there was no class specifically devoted to rhetoric and little formal teaching of the subject; composition was practised concurrently with the reading of texts. Even where there was a rhetoric class, its curriculum was less specialized than that of Quintilian's day. In the Jesuit schools 'rhetoric' included verse composition, in Greek as well as Latin.[79] Moreover, the reading of authors, which Quintilian had tried in vain to introduce into the Roman schools, became a recognized part of rhetoric. The ancient disciplines of grammar and rhetoric were in fact combined; the schools of modern Europe did not, like those of Rome, separate the study of literature from the teaching of composition.

Quintilian's work was at one time used in the teaching of rhetoric, but it did not maintain its position. Muretus, who lived from 1526 to 1585, remarks that when he was a boy the *Institutio* was carefully expounded in the schools, and no one was considered a good teacher of eloquence who did not use it in exercising his pupils; at the time of writing, however, things had changed for the worse, and the young now used inferior handbooks and compendia.[80] It is easy to see why this should have been so. The *Institutio* was too detailed and too much concerned with forensic speaking to be of much use as a text book. At the end of the seventeenth century, according to Rollin, Quintilian was unknown to the schools and little read outside. While teaching at the University of Paris Rollin had often wanted to use him, but was aware that his students would find him too long and too technical; he therefore produced (1715) an abbreviated edition for class use.[81] By then formal rhetoric had lost ground, and in teaching the art of speaking, or writing, the tendency was to lay less stress on rules than on the value of models. Locke in his *Thoughts on Education* (1693) explains that he has said little about rhetoric and logic 'because of the little advantage young people receive by them',[82] and elsewhere he remarks that 'we are more apt to learn by example than by direction'.[83] Quintilian would not have agreed with this depreciation of the subject he professed, but he too, as his tenth book shows, was well aware of the importance of reading for the formation of style and of the value, as well as the limitations, of imitation.

Locke's attitude to rhetoric is in keeping with the spirit of independence found throughout his work on education. Mankind had now moved away from the old respect for authority and admiration of the ancients, and the influence of Quintilian on educational thought and practice had markedly declined. Locke does not mention him in his *Thoughts on Education* and appears to be quite uninfluenced by him. It is significant that he can discuss the relative merits of school and education under a private tutor without any indication that Quintilian had discussed the same problem and had reached the opposite conclusion to his.

In the last two centuries or so Quintilian has probably exercised little direct influence on education, and to the modern educationalist his method may seem primitive, his psychology unscientific and his whole aim irrelevant to the requirements of the present day. Yet he deserves to be remembered with respect. In the first place for his belief in education. It is a mistake, he says, to suppose that intellectual ability is confined to a few: learning is as natural to mankind as flying to birds and galloping to horses. The fact that boys often show promise which comes to nothing is a sign that it is not nature which is at fault, but the way they are handled; some may gain more than others from study, but no one will gain nothing.[84] Quintilian may not have been a believer in universal education, but his principles, if carried to their logical conclusion, would lead to what is now the accepted ideal. Secondly, we should remember him for his humanity, his belief that education can be a pleasure both for the teacher and for the learner. All those who have laboured to make the path of learning easier for the young should remember him as a pioneer. Finally, it is to him surely that the teaching profession owes something of its present prestige. The fact that a distinguished ancient writer, a respected figure in the society of Rome, was himself a schoolmaster, and did not think it below his dignity to write on the details of his scholastic work, must have had some influence in raising the status of schools and teachers in the world of the Renaissance and consequently of modern Europe.

The content of his educational programme is not likely to have much appeal in an age which has turned its back on the rhetorical ideal. But at least Quintilian provides a workable compromise between the various aims of education. It is not at all clear, says Aristotle, whether education should be concerned with those studies 'which are useful in life, or those which make for goodness, or those which advance the bounds of knowledge'.[85] It is still not at all clear. Today the practical side of education, training for a career, remains inevitably of prime importance. We make much, in universities at any rate, of 'studies which advance the bounds of knowledge', research as we call it. We think less of goodness than the ancients did, and less than our ancestors did in the nineteenth century when Tom Brown's father sent him to Rugby to be made a Christian and a gentleman; at the same time we still look to schools to provide some sort of training in morality, the more so now that the influence of the church and of the home is weaker than it once was. Quintilian was not much concerned with advancing the bounds of knowledge, but at least he applied high standards of scholarship to his own subject. Aristotle's other aims, practical and moral education, he did his best to combine. His school provided what was in effect a professional training, even though he would have regarded the career of an advocate as more than merely one of the professions. At the same time he regarded goodness as even more important than professional competence. He expressed his ideal in the formula *uir bonus dicendi peritus*. The modern teacher would substitute for *dicendi* the various techniques that are useful in the modern world. He might substitute for *uir bonus* 'an integrated personality', or whatever is the fashionable phrase, but essentially his aim would be much the same as Quintilian's.

Notes

(References, unless otherwise stated, are to Quintilian)

1 Pliny, *Epp.*, VI.6.3.
2 Suetonius, *Rhet.*, 2; Cicero, *Brut.*, 310.
3 I.12.12.
4 I.10.2f.; Apuleius, *Flor.*, 20.
5 II.1.7.
6 II.2.3.
7 II.2.9, 14; II.4.8, 10, 14; II.5.2, 21; II.7.2; V.10.96; V.12.22; VII.3.30; X.5.17; XI.1.55; XI.3.28–9; Seneca, *Contr.*, 3, *praef.* 15; Tacitus, *Dial.*, 35.3.
8 This was the age at which St Augustine left the grammar school at Madaura (*Conf.*, II.3.5–6). At this age too Eunapius enrolled among the pupils of Prohaeresius (Eunapius 493) and Paulinus of Pella finished with grammar and was ready to proceed to rhetoric (*Eucharisticus* 113–26).
9 XII.6.1.
10 Pliny, *Epp.*, V.8.8; Augustine, *Conf.*, IV.1.1–2.
11 XII.3.11–12.
12 XII.11.14–15.
13 Pliny, *Epp.*, II, 18; VI.6.3.
14 I.1.18, 24–5, 27.
15 I.4.2.
16 I.8.6.
17 I.9.6; II.1.1–6.
18 II.1.4–6.
19 II.5.2–3.
20 Pliny, *Epp.*, VI. 20.5.
21 II.1.2; II.10.2; II.11.1–2.
22 I. *praef.* 7; cf. VIII. *praef.* 1.

23 I. *praef*. 8.
24 For evidence, though this is hardly required, that Quintilian himself declaimed. see XI.2.39.
25 I.2.23–4; II.7.1; X.5.21; Juvenal, VII.160–1.
26 II.10.3. Cf. (e.g.) V.12.17–23.
27 II.10.4, 8.
28 II.10.6, 12.
29 II.10.15. For cases where school practice was different from that of the courts or where specific advice is given to declaimers see, e.g., IV.1.46; IV.2.28, 97; V.10.96; V.13.36, 45, 50; VII.1.38; VII.2.55–6; VII.3.20; XI.1.55.
30 III.8.
31 X.1.4.
32 VIII. *praef*. 31; X.3.10–15.
33 I.12.4–5.
34 I.2. But Quintilian assumes that the first stage of education will be conducted at home. Children of the wealthier parents would escape the *ludus litterarius*.
35 I. *praef*.9; I.2.3.
36 II.2.14.
37 Pliny, *Epp.*, III.3.
38 I.2.4; II.2.15.
39 I.2.6–8.
40 E. B. Castle, *Ancient Education and Today* (1961), p. 136.
41 VII.3.30.
42 I.1.20.
43 II.4.10.
44 I.3.8–10.
45 I.3.1–7; II.8.1.
46 I.3.13–17.
47 II.2.5–8; cf. II.9.
48 W. Boyd, *History of Western Education* (8th edn, 1966), p. 72.
49 II.8.1.
50 I.1.4, 16; I.3.13; I.10.32; I.11.17.
51 XII.2.9.
52 Pliny, *Epp.*, II.18. Cf. II.3.6.
53 Pliny, *Epp.*, II.13.4–5; III.13; VI.33.7–11; X.4.1.
54 W. C. Hembold and E. N. O'Neil in *CP* 54 (1959), pp. 100–8; W. S. Anderson in *Yale Classical Studies* 17 (1961), pp. 3–93.
55 Juvenal, VII. 188–98.
56 Juvenal, XIV.1f.
57 Juvenal, VII.207–10.
58 See R. Syme, *Tacitus* (1958), pp. 114–15.
59 The parallels between the *Dialogus* and the *Institutio Oratoria* point to the priority of the latter. See H. Bardon in *Rev. Ét. Lat.* 19 (1941), pp. 113–31; R. Gungerich in *CP* 46 (1951), pp. 159–64.
60 X.1.122.
61 Augustine, *Cat. Rud.*, 9.13.

62 Jerome, *Epp.*, 107.4.

63 See Colson's edition of Quintilian I (Cambridge, 1924), pp. xlix–lx; P. Lehmann in *Philol.* 89 (1934), pp. 349–83; Priscilla Boskoff in *Speculum* 27 (1952), pp. 71–8; R. Johnson in *For Services to Classical Studies*, ed. M. Kelly (Melbourne, 1966), pp. 79–102.

64 *Patrologia Latina* 138, p. 103; J. Havet, *Lettres de Gerbert* (Paris, 1889), no. 44; Colson, Quintilian I, p. xlix.

65 John of Salisbury, *Metalogicus*, I.24.

66 See Colson, Quintilian I, pp. lxiv–lxxxix; W. H. Woodward, *Studies in Education during the Age of the Renaissance* (Cambridge, 1906), *Vittorino da Feltre and other Humanist Educators* (Cambridge, 1897).

67 Petrarch, *Epp. Fam.*, 24.7. See P. de Nolhac, *Pétrarque et l'humanisme* (Paris, 1907) II, pp. 84–5, for the identification of Petrarch's 'liber quem de causis edidisti' with the Declamations.

68 *Commentarius Platinae de Vita Victorini Feltrensis* in T. A. Vaiani, *Cremonensium Monumenta* (Rome, 1778), p. 23.

69 Valla, *Opera* (Basle, 1540), p. 477.

70 Erasmus, *Opera* (Leyden, 1703), I, 522–3.

71 Rabelais, *Gargantua and Pantagruel*, Bk II, ch. 8.

72 Erasmus, *Opera*, I, 521; Elyot, *Governour*, Bk I, ch. 10.

73 W. H. Woodward, *Vittorino da Feltre*, p. 167.

74 Erasmus, *Opera*, I, 502.

75 Ascham, *Scholemaster*, ed. 1927, p. 48.

76 Erasmus, *Opera*, I, 507.

77 See P. O. Kristeller, *Renaissance Thought* II (1965), pp. 9–10.

78 H. C. Barnard, *The French Tradition in Education* (Cambridge, 1922), pp. 9, 161; *Ratio . . . Studiorum Societatis Jesu* (Rome, 1606), p. 78.

79 *Ibid.*, pp. 94, 112.

80 Muretus, *Variae Lectiones*, XVIII, xv.

81 *M. Fabii Quintiliani Institutionum Oratoriarum libri XII ad usum scholarum accommodati* (Paris, 1760), pp. xli–xliv; cf. Rollin, *De la manière d'enseigner et d'étudier les belles lettres* (Paris, 1728), I, p. 3.

82 Locke, *Some Thoughts on Education*, 188.

83 Locke, *Works* (1824), II, p. 407.

84 I.1.1–3.

85 Aristotle, *Politics*, 8.1.4. Ernest Barker's translation 'which advance the bounds of knowledge' for τὰ περιττὰ may be open to criticism, but it serves my purpose.

VI

The Letters *of Pliny*

Betty Radice

The younger Pliny (generally so called to distinguish him from
his uncle) was a fairly typical senator of the late half of the first
century A.D. He was a landowner with properties in his native
region of Como, in Tuscany and on the coast of Latium, near
Ostia, and had a town house on the Esquiline. He was an active
member of the Roman bar, particularly in the Chancery (Centumviral) Court, and in the Senate when trials involved problems
of finance. He moved through the regular *cursus honorum* to the
consulate, held two treasury posts and two priesthoods, was
president of the Tiber Conservancy Board, and, as the climax
to his career, he was the emperor Trajan's special representative
sent out to deal with irregularities in the previously senatorial
province of Bithynia-Pontus. He was thrice married, but childless,
and he had a large circle of friends, ranging from obscure people
in Comum he had known as a boy to personalities as distinguished
as Licinius Sura and Tacitus. He wrote light verse, rather badly,
and gave readings to his friends of his poetic efforts as well as of
his speeches; his official *gratiarum actio* to the emperor for his
consulship he expanded and published, and this has survived as
the first in the collection known as the *XII Panegyrici Latini*. He
also wrote letters to his friends over a period of about twelve
years, and later selected personally those he thought most suitable
for publication (247, arranged in nine books), while his official
correspondence with Trajan (121 letters, all but fourteen covering
the two-year period of his service in Bithynia and Pontus) was
posthumously published as a tenth book, presumably unrevised.

It is primarily as a letter-writer that Pliny is remembered, and a
few of his letters always spring to the mind – his eye-witness
account of the eruption of Vesuvius which destroyed Pompeii
and Herculaneum; his exchange of letters with Trajan on the
subject of the Christian communities in Bithynia; his detailed
description of his country houses; perhaps too some ghost

stories or the boy-and-dolphin friendship at Hippo Diarrhytus.[1] But there are many reasons why his letters should be read as a whole. The personal letters provide us with the fullest self-portrait of any Roman we know, with the possible exception of Horace, and they are genuine social history of the greatest importance for a badly-documented period, the reigns of Domitian, Nerva and Trajan. The official letters of Book X give a vivid picture of the problems confronting an official on tour in a disturbed province and are also first-hand evidence for the workings of the imperial bureaucracy. Moreover, the letters are highly readable, both for their content and their style. No one would think of Pliny as possessing a creative imagination or sustained literary genius, but he is an intelligent man, sensible, honest and pleasant even when he may seem over-conscientious or a little priggish, and what we learn from him about the circles he moved in offers a salutary contrast to the highly-coloured picture of Roman society given by his contemporaries, Juvenal, Martial and Tacitus. He has what makes a good letter-writer, a keenly observant eye and a gift for description, and the versatility of his Latin prose is a perpetual pleasure. At his best he can certainly stand second to Tacitus, as he always hoped to do.

All the facts of his career and daily life come from a few inscriptions and his letters. He was the son of Lucius Caecilius Cilo of Comum, and both the Caecilii and his mother's family, the Plinii, owned property in the district to which several letters refer.[2] As he tells us that he was seventeen at the time of the eruption of Vesuvius in August 79,[3] he must have been born in late 61 or early 62. His father died early, and he then had Verginius Rufus as his guardian – the famous Rufus who had put down the rising of Vindex in Nero's reign, and whose state funeral in 97 is described in an early letter.[4] As he tells us that there was no school at Comum, we presume that he was educated at home under a *grammaticus*, and then came to Rome where he attended the lectures of Nicetes Sacerdos, a well-known rhetorician from Smyrna, as well as those of Quintilian;[5] in Rome he would see more of his mother's brother, the elder Pliny, and he and his mother were both at Misenum where his uncle commanded the fleet at the time of the eruption. Fortunately for us, Pliny stayed at Misenum when his uncle crossed the bay and was suffocated in the fumes.

He inherited the full estate, and his change of name indicates that he was adopted as a son in his uncle's will: henceforth his official name was Gaius Plinius Luci filius Caecilius Secundus.[6] He was still only eighteen when he began his legal career with a success at the Centumviral Court,[7] and at about the same time he married his first wife, of whom nothing is known. He began his senatorial career with a minor magistracy as one of the decemviri *stlitibus iudicandis* presiding over the four panels of the Centumviral Court, and was then military tribune, probably for no more than the minimum six months, serving with the Third Gallic legion in Syria as auditor of the auxiliary forces' accounts.[8] There he met the philosophers Artemidorus and Euphrates, banished from Rome by Domitian. After another minor office (*sevir equitum Romanorum*) he was *quaestor Caesaris*, attached to the emperor's staff as bearer of his messages to the Senate, and then *tribunus plebis*,[9] a position he took very seriously, to the extent of suspending his practice in the law courts. Domitian allowed him to move on to the praetorship without waiting for the statutory year's interval; the exact date is uncertain, but most probably Pliny held office in 93.[10] In the same year he acted for the prosecution in the first of the big public trials which were to occupy so much of his time, when Baebius Massa was convicted in the case brought against him by the province of Baetica.[11] Massa retaliated by charging Herennius Senecio, Pliny's colleague in the case, with *maiestas*. Senecio was one of the leaders of the so-called 'Stoic opposition' to the Flavian emperors, and his conviction and execution mark the start of the reign of terror associated with Domitian which is described in Tacitus's *Agricola*. The leaders of the opposition were put to death and many of their supporters were exiled; later on Pliny was to recall that he was in danger of his life as the thunderbolts fell all round him,[12] but in fact he emerged unhurt, and his career was advanced by a three-year appointment at the military treasury (*curator aeraii militaris*).[13]

Soon after Domitian's assassination in 96 Pliny came forward to vindicate the name of Helvidius Priscus, one of the Stoics executed in 93, by denouncing his prosecutor, Publicius Certus. The letter describing this episode gives a clear picture of the feeling of uncertainty in the Senate at the start of Nerva's reign.[14] No one was anxious to rake up the misdeeds of the recent past, and all that resulted was that Certus was passed over in the consular elections, though as an official at the Treasury of Saturn he would expect to proceed to a consulship. Soon after, he died, and Pliny succeeded him as *curator aerarii Saturni*, another three-year office, which he held with his friend and colleague Cornutus Tertullus from 98 until they were suffect consuls together in September and October 100.[15] This was the occasion when Pliny delivered his speech of thanks to the emperor Trajan which he later revised and amplified for publication in the form in which we have it, as the *Panegyricus*.[16]

Pliny continued to be active in the courts during his official engagements. He wrote to Trajan early in 98 to ask permission to conduct the prosecution against the governor of Africa, Marius Priscus, while still in his treasury post, and soon after Priscus was convicted in January 100,[17] Pliny agreed to act for the province of Baetica in their case against the governor Caecilius Classicus;[18] Classicus was convicted in 101. After his consulship he was often busier than he liked, either in the Senate or in the Centumviral Court, and he looked forward to honourable retirement.[19] He was also frequently called on to act as assessor in the City prefect's court or to Trajan himself,[20] and there were still two more big public cases to occupy him: he defended two ex-governors of Bithynia, Julius Bassus during the winter of 102–3 and Varenus Rufus in that of 106–7.[21] His reward of merit for distinguished public service came in 103 when he was elected augur to fill the vacancy left by the death of Julius Frontinus – he had asked Trajan for a priesthood on an earlier occasion, and why it was not granted is unknown.[22] (A brief inscription found near Como describes him as *flamen* of the deified emperor Titus, presumably an honour bestowed by his native town.) He also accepted another three-year office in 104, with responsibility for keeping the banks of the Tiber in repair to prevent flooding and for maintaining the sewers of Rome (*curator alvei Tiberis et riparum et cloacarum urbis*).[23] Finally came the appointment to go out to the province of Bithynia-Pontus as Trajan's representative with special powers (*legatus propraetore consulari potestate*), and he was doubtless chosen as a recognized expert on finance and on Bithynian affairs after his defence of the two senatorial governors, Bassus and Rufus. He arrived in Bithynia in time for Trajan's birthday celebrations on 18 September,[24] but the year could be 109, 110, or 111; as the letters break

off before mention of celebrations at the beginning of his third
year of office, it is presumed that he had died, possibly while on
tour in Pontus.

No more is known about his second wife except that she died
just before the trial of Publicius Certus in 97,[25] but Pliny continued to correspond with his mother-in-law, Pompeia Celerina,
and to handle her affairs for her. His young third wife, Calpurnia,
appears several times in the *Letters*. She was the orphaned
granddaughter of Calpurnius Fabatus, a wealthy landowner of
Comum, who appears from the tone in which Pliny sometimes
addresses him to have been a rather irritable old gentleman;
he evidently undertook the management of Pliny's estates in the
district.[26] There are several touching letters of affection and pride
concerning this young wife, and Pliny's grief over her miscarriage
and subsequent sterility is very real.[27] One feels that Trajan's
conferment of the privileges of parents of three children (*ius
trium liberorum*) would bring little consolation. Calpurnia went
out with him to Bithynia, and the official correspondence ends
with Pliny explaining to Trajan that he had broken his rule not
to use the imperial posting service for personal journeys when she
wished to hurry back to Comum to be with the aunt who had
brought her up, on hearing of her grandfather's death. Trajan's
reply, though formally phrased, is appreciative of the integrity
of his loyal servant, and it is also perhaps befitting that the last
word we have on Pliny shows him to be an essentially domestically
minded man (Letter X.121; Trajan to Pliny):

> You were quite right, my dear Pliny, to feel confident of my
> response. You need not have had any doubts, even if you had
> waited to ask me if you could expedite your wife's journey by
> making use of the permits which I issued to you for official
> purposes; it is her duty to make her visit doubly welcome to
> her aunt by her prompt arrival.

It was entirely suitable for him to seek a wife in his native
region, to which he remained sentimentally attached – though his
visits north could never be frequent, as his public duties in Rome
left him with little time for long journeys. 'I wonder how our
darling Comum is looking,' he writes to Caninius Rufus ('quid
agit Comum, tuae meaeque deliciae?'), and elsewhere remarks
that however troublesome it is to be an absentee landlord, he

will never part with his mother's estates. [28] He was a substantial benefactor to the town, building and endowing a library, offering to pay one-third of a resident teacher's salary if a school is set up, making provision for destitute children from a rent-charge on his property, and leaving the town more than two million sesterces in his will. [29] The older men who had influenced his youth were northerners: Verginius Rufus was a native of Milan and owned property in the Como district, and Vestricius Spurinna's wife, Cottia, has a Celtic name from the neighbourhood of Turin. As well as the landowner Caninius Rufus, the lawyer Annius Severus and the *decurio* Calvisius Rufus receive several letters with commissions for the benefit of Comum, while old school friends like Atilius Crescens and Romatius Firmus are given financial help and good advice. Humbler folk, too, had reason to be grateful: Metilius Crispus for a capital sum and equipment to raise him to centurion's rank, an old nurse for the income from a small farm. There is a Maximus from Verona, and Minicius Acilianus comes from Brescia with a mother from Padua. This group of correspondents is important for historians, as it provides evidence for the part played in the affairs of the capital by the natives of the Cisalpine Gaul region, and also exhibits the qualities of character, industry, responsibility and loyalty which Pliny possessed himself and which are not easy to find in the persons described by his contemporaries.

This provincial background was shared with the leaders of the 'Stoic opposition' – its leader, Thrasea Paetus, was a native of Padua. His long opposition to Nero and execution in 66 are best known from Tacitus (*Annals*, XVI); his father-in-law, Caecina Paetus, had joined in the conspiracy of Scribonianus against Claudius and had been obliged to commit suicide. [30] Pliny quotes Thrasea with admiration more than once, and pays tribute both to his wife and Caecina's (the younger and the elder Arria). Thrasea's daughter, Fannia, married Helvidius Priscus, and he too was executed for sedition by Vespasian; he left a son by his first wife, another Helvidius, who in his turn was put to death by Domitian in the purge of 93 along with several of his supporters, while others (including Fannia) were exiled and did not return until after Domitian's death. [31] It was then that Pliny delivered in the Senate what was considered one of his best speeches, to vindicate Helvidius, and later on, when Helvidius's daughters both died in childbirth, he says again that 'my love of their father has remained constant since his death, as my defence of him and my published speeches bear witness' ('nam patrem illarum defunctum quoque perseverantissime diligo, ut actione mea librisque testatum est . . .').[32] This record of devotion to a cause spanning four generations clearly made a great impression on Pliny, perhaps the more so as he was not himself cut out to play the martyr. It may well have been an embarrassment to him when the exiles of 93 returned to find that he had not suffered in any way, and had even accepted from Domitian his post at the military treasury. It is surely significant that he never mentions this in the *Letters* – it is known only from the relevant inscriptions – which suggests that he wished his readers to forget that he owed anything to the emperor whom he never fails to represent as a monster of tyranny. I do not think we should judge him as a collaborator, in the modern sense of the word: he was not really politically minded, and his professional interests were almost entirely legal and financial. It would be fairer to see in him an example of what prompted Tacitus to write about Agricola that 'even under bad emperors there can be great men' ('posse etiam sub malis principibus magnos viros esse'); for honesty and competence can survive, despite a corrupt regime.

More than a hundred people receive letters from Pliny, and many more are mentioned in the correspondence. Some of these (Mustius, Venator, Sardus, and the several individuals under the name of Maximus) have not yet been identified. A few, like Caninius Rufus of Comum, are fairly well defined in the *Letters* but are unknown outside them. Some are well known from other literary sources, such as Verginius Rufus, or the jurist Titius Aristo, often quoted in the *Digest*, while others (Calpurnius Macer or Sosius Senecio, for example) have their careers documented in inscriptions. There is naturally no indication in the *Letters* that the two young men whose early success at the bar gave Pliny such pleasure[33] were later to reach the consulate and marry into the imperial family: Fuscus Salinator's wife was the daughter of the sister of the future emperor Hadrian, and Ummidius Quadratus was to marry the sister of Marcus Aurelius. Erucius Clarus, standing for the tribunate about 101, was consul in 117, one of Trajan's legates in the Parthian War and, according to Dio, the captor of Seleucia. The more one looks into the list of correspondents in the light of independent sources, the more the historical importance of the *Letters* is revealed, both for what they include and what they omit. In the literary field, Tacitus and Suetonius receive letters; Silius Italicus is mentioned but receives nothing; Martial's death is reported and the fact that he wrote verse to Pliny and received his travelling expenses home to Spain. But there is no mention of Juvenal, nor of Statius, though he and Pliny had a mutual friend in Vibius Maximus. There are interesting omissions too amongst the political figures of the period. It has been pointed out that no one from the Republican or Augustan aristocracy receives a letter, though Pliny is always glad to hear of promising young men in 'noble families'. Neratius Priscus, the jurist, receives letters, but his brother, Neratius Marcellus, does not, though Pliny refers to the military tribunate he offered Suetonius. Juventius Celsus, Julius Frontinus and Javolenus Priscus are also mentioned, but if Pliny had copies of letters he wrote to them, he does not include them in the published selection. This confirms what we know of him elsewhere, that he is not a social climber, and suggests that the people who receive his letters are genuinely amongst his friends.

It seems probable that Pliny's basis for selecting his letters was literary. The opening dedicatory letter (to Septicius Clarus, to whom Suetonius also dedicated his *Lives of the Caesars*) starts: 'You have often urged me to collect and publish any letters of mine which were composed with some care. I have now made a collection, not keeping to the original order as I was not writing history, but taking them as they came to my hand. . . .' ('frequenter hortatus es ut epistulas, si quas paulo curatius scripsissem, colligerem publicaremque. Collegi non servato temporis ordine (neque enim historiam componebam), sed ut quaeque in manus venerat. . . .') In fact the order of the letters in each book is artfully designed to give a lively variety of tone, the longer serious letters relieved by short notes, and every book having a selection of legal and political themes, descriptions of scenery or natural phenomena, letters of advice and recommendation, literary criticism, eulogies of great men or women, neatly phrased jokes or courtesy notes, and occasional moralizing. There has been some skilful editing within several letters: requests for 'four marble columns, any kind you think suitable, and marble for building the floor and walls' of a new temple on Pliny's property must surely have had some measurements given in the original, and Annius Severus of Comum could hardly have had a pedestal made for a bronze statue if he was not given its size.[34] Many letters, too, start with a sentence which supplies the context: 'You want me to read through some of your poems while I am away on holiday. . . .' 'Thank you for asking me to send you a description of my uncle's death so that you can leave an accurate account of it for posterity. . . .' 'You urge me to give a reading of my speech to a group of friends . . .'[35] In general Pliny keeps to the principle that each letter should deal with a single theme, though sometimes he follows the scholastic 'rule of three'. At the same time, he never fails to give the impression that these are genuine letters, however carefully composed and presented, and he draws the distinction himself between what he writes and 'a sort of pupil's exercise for a letter' ('scholasticas atque, ut ita dicam, umbraticas litteras')[36] which would be more like Seneca's *Epistulae Morales*.

The order of the books is roughly chronological, though not, as he says, the letters in each book, and very few can be firmly dated. Positive dates range from the death of Verginius Rufus in 97 (his funeral is described in II.1) to the consulship of Valerius Paulinus referred to in IX.37 and known to have been held in September-October 107. There is no evidence on how and when the books were published, and no real agreement amongst scholars, though it is generally thought that they came out in groups, possibly in threes, none before the death of Pliny's *bête noire*, Regulus, in 104, and certainly none after his own departure for Bithynia. The time after his last big public case (that of Varenus, ending in 107) would seem to be the most likely for Pliny to have time for revising and editing his letters – earlier on he always writes about being busy with his speeches – and it is noticeable that Book IX contains more letters than any other book, but mostly short ones, literary or reflective; the only long one on a professional subject (IX.13) describes his speech in vindication of Helvidius Priscus over ten years ago. There is a hint in one letter that Pliny was beginning to feel that retirement from active life would leave him with less to write about,[37] but there is no formal ending to the personal correspondence. Probably its publication was cut short by the Bithynian appointment; he had long looked forward to increased leisure for his country pursuits and literary interests, but he was never to know it again.

It is wholly characteristic of the man that the practical problems which faced him and the stimulus of a completely new type of public responsibility brought out the best in him; and yet the prospect of some years' absence from Rome and Italy could not have been altogether welcome. Apart from his service in Syria as a young man he had not travelled further than Como or Campania, as far as we know, and his pleasure was always in the lovely natural sights of Italy rather than in conventional sight-seeing. His profession, too, had kept him occupied in Rome with Chancery work and with public trials in the Senate, two of which (those of Julius Bassus and Varenus Rufus, whom Pliny had defended in 103 and 106–7) were for maladministration by senatorial governors. It seems likely (as was said above) that Trajan chose Pliny for the post both for the inside knowledge of Bithynian affairs he had gained in these trials and because he was a recognized expert on financial problems.

Bithynia had been left to Rome by the will of its last king in 74 B.C., and had been extended eastwards to cover the western part of Pontus by Pompey, who reorganized the whole area as a Roman province and laid down its constitution by the *Lex Pompeia* to which Pliny often refers. This must have covered taxation and rules for military service generally, though the Greek cities appear to have had considerable local autonomy. Nicomedia and Amastris were the capitals of the two halves of the province, but only Chalcedon and Amisus enjoyed freedom from Roman intervention as *civitates liberae ac foederatae*, and in Trajan's time there were only two *coloniae*, Apamea and Sinope. Byzantium, on the European side of the Bosporos, was administered with Bithynia. Since the reorganization of the empire by Augustus, Bithynia-Pontus had been a senatorial province governed by a proconsul. Some of these are mentioned by Pliny – Lappius Maximus under Domitian, for example, and Servilius Calvus under Nerva. It is clear from the correspondence that the proconsuls had considerable latitude in jurisdiction, and some of their rulings were quoted as precedents. There were also edicts and rescripts of the emperors on specific points which were open to interpretation in similar but not identical cases. The mere fact that the province had brought actions against two recent proconsuls showed that there was need for a proper investigation, by someone who had overruling authority acting in the emperor's name. Pliny was accordingly sent as *legatus propraetore consulari potestate* to tour the province, send back reports, and settle all he could on the spot. There were three main types of problem: the existence in several of the Greek cities of hostile factions which could be politically dangerous; the near-bankruptcy of several cities owing to unwise and unregulated public spending; and irregularities in administration both general and local due to dishonesty, ignorance or inefficiency.

The problems raised by the Christian communities[38] come under the first head, for though Pliny's investigations made him conclude that there was nothing to be found but 'a degenerate sort of cult carried to extravagant lengths' ('nihil aliud inveni quam superstitionem pravam et immodicam'), he had to see that their meetings were discontinued 'after my edict, issued on your instructions, which banned all political societies' ('post edictum meum, quo secundum mandata tua hetaerias esse vetueram'), and he felt there was a risk of their fanaticism spreading to rural districts. Trajan somewhat reluctantly permits the free city of Amisus to continue having a benefit society 'if the contributions are not used for riotous and unlawful assemblies, but to relieve cases of hardship amongst the poor' ('si tali collatione non ad turbas et ad inlicitos coetus, sed ad sustinendam tenuiorum inopiam utuntur').[39] But he flatly refuses Pliny's request for permission to form a company of firemen for Nicomedia, even though the numbers were to be limited and the persons hand-picked (X.34; Trajan to Pliny):

> I have received your suggestion that it should be possible to form a company of firemen at Nicomedia on the model of those existing elsewhere, but we must remember that it is societies like these which have been responsible for the political disturbances in your province, particularly in its towns. If people assemble for a common purpose, whatever name we give them and for whatever reason, they soon turn into a political club. It is a better policy, then, to provide the equipment necessary for dealing with fires, and to instruct property owners to make use of it, calling on the help of the crowds which collect if they find it necessary.

There is plenty of evidence for the mismanagement of civic finance, a lot of it due to extravagant public building due to inter-city rivalry. This is confirmed by the speeches of Cocceianus Dio (Dio Chrysostom) who also features in the *Letters* in connection with building schemes at Prusa and an acrimonious lawsuit arising out of them. [40] Prusa also has bad debts and still needs new public baths; Nicomedia has thrown away large sums of money on two abortive attempts at making an aqueduct; Nicaea has spent more than ten million sesterces on a theatre which is half-built and already cracking and subsiding as the site was never surveyed; Nicaea is also rebuilding its *gymnasium* without proper plans or adequate foundations; and Claudiopolis is trying to build an enormous public bath on a totally unsuitable site. Sinope has no proper water-supply, and Amastris should have its open sewer covered in the interests of public health. [41] Trajan refuses requests for architects and land-surveyors to be sent from Rome, for they are needed there for his own building schemes; Pliny is to find local men or use his own judgment. Only for a complicated plan (obviously dear to Pliny's heart) for improving communications at Nicomedia by connecting its local lake with the sea by means of a canal does Trajan tell him to send to the army commander of Lower Moesia for a military engineer. [42]

The other irregularities reported cover a wide range, and though some may seem trivial in themselves, Pliny's concern is always to obtain a general ruling where the *Lex Pompeia* seems inadequate and subsequent decisions of the proconsuls lack proper precedent. In some cities people previously sentenced to the mines or the arena are found to be working as public slaves and receiving salaries, in another men sentenced to banishment by one governor are still at large and plead that their sentences were subsequently reversed; at Prusa a 'philosopher', Flavius Archippus, produces letters from Domitian to prove that his sentence for forgery has been rescinded. Sometimes Pliny asks for guidance on a religious matter (the moving of a temple, for instance) or for rulings on the proper age of entry to a local senate or the legality of senators paying entrance fees. The legal status of foundlings or of people born free and later reduced to slavery also has to be defined. Trajan's replies are brief and to the point; some may have been left to the official secretariat while others have a more personal ring, but the principles for Pliny's guidance are explicit: traditions must be respected, administration must be in the interests of the province, and retrospective action for offences dating a long way back serves no useful purpose. On this point, this letter is typical (X.111; Trajan to Pliny):

> It is true that I have issued instructions forbidding public grants of money, but grants made a long time previously ought not to be revoked nor rendered invalid, lest we undermine the position of a great many people. Let us then leave out of consideration any features of this case which date back twenty years, for in every city the interests of individuals are as much my concern as the state of public funds.

So much has been said in the past about Pliny as a pusillanimous bureaucrat, unable to decide the most trivial matter without refering to Trajan, that it still has to be emphasized that in a period of rather less than two years Pliny addressed only sixty-one letters to Trajan; if the testimonials and formal letters of congratulation on official anniversaries are excepted, Pliny wrote not more than forty times asking for guidance on specific points or reporting progress on a question previously raised. Most of these letters fall into the first year of his appointment, and presumably as he gained in experience, he was able to act increasingly on his own initiative, as Trajan intended he should. We simply do not know how many decisions he took without reporting them. But though his legal training is evident in his wish for properly defined terms of reference, the general impression he gives in the letters of Book X is one of practical activity and good sense. On matters of water-supply, sewage and drainage he writes with knowledge gained on the spot and reinforced by his general interest in problems of hydraulics and civil engineering: he had, as we know, sat on the Tiber Conservancy Board, and he knew Julius Frontinus, whom he succeeded as augur;[43] Frontinus had been *curator aquarum* in 97, and Pliny may well have known his expert treatise *De aquis urbis Romae*. Consequently, when Nicomedia's water-supply demands an aqueduct Pliny writes: 'I have been myself to look at the spring which could supply pure water, to be brought along an aqueduct as originally intended, if the supply is not to be confined to the lower-lying parts of the town. . . .' He looks personally at Sinope: 'I think there is plenty of good water which could be brought from a source sixteen miles away, though there is a doubtful area of marshy ground stretching for more than a mile from the spring.'[44] Though he requests (and receives) an engineer for the projected canal at Nicomedia, he makes more than one personal tour of inspection and offers a choice of solutions for the problem of not losing all the water from the lake through the canal. Trajan's reply has a hint of affectionate amusement for Pliny's enthusiasm ('manifestum, mi Secunde carissime, nec prudentiam nec diligentiam tibi defuisse circa istum lacum. . . .') (X.62; Trajan to Pliny):

> I can see, my dear Pliny, that you are applying all your energy
> and intelligence to your lake; you have worked out so many
> ways of avoiding the danger of its water draining away, and so
> increasing its usefulness to us in future. You choose, then, the
> way which best suits the situation. I am sure Calpurnius
> Macer will not fail to send you an engineer, and there is no lack
> of such experts in the provinces where you are.

These interests are in keeping with the Pliny we know in the personal letters. He mentions his two villas on the shores of Lake Como 'which give me a lot of pleasure but a lot of hard work' as he is busy building additions to improve their existing amenities: they are nicknamed Tragedy and Comedy, as one is high on the rocks as if raised on *cothurni*, while the other is low down by the water, wearing *socculi*, the comic actor's slippers.[45] The *suburbanum* at Laurentum[46] is described in loving detail, carefully planned as it is to fit in with its site by the sea, to enjoy wide views and receive the maximum of sunshine to warm it in winter, while there are rooms which are shaded and well ventilated for summer use. Linked with the main building by a covered arcade (*cryptoporticus*) is a suite of rooms which Pliny specially loves, as he had them built himself ('diaeta est amores mei, re vera amores: ipse posui'). Only one thing is lacking, running water, and the house has to make do with the wells and springs which are near the surface all along the shore. ('haec utilitas haec amoenitas deficitur aqua salienti, sed puteos ac potius fontes habet; sunt enim in summo.') On his property near Tifernum on Tiber he had more scope. The house is built on the foothills of the Apennines in the sort of scenery familiar to anyone who knows Tuscany – the mountains and woods above, the vineyards

below, and then the ploughland and the meadows which are
'bright with flowers, covered with trefoil and other delicate
plants which always seem soft and fresh, for everything is fed
by streams which never run dry. . . .' The formal garden is
terraced and planted with shrubs and clipped box hedges, but
a good deal of the letter is devoted to what Pliny calls the *hippo-
dromus*, evidently a landscape garden shaped like a Roman *circus*,
with plane trees and laurels for shade, paths and lawns and beds
of roses and acanthus. With mountain water piped at pressure
he can really enjoy himself (V.6.36–40):

At the upper end of the course is a curved dining-seat of white
marble, shaded by a vine trained over four slender pillars
of Carystian marble. Water gushes out through pipes from
under the seat as if pressed out by the weight of people sitting
there, is caught in a stone cistern and then held in a finely-
worked marble basin which is regulated by a hidden device so
as to remain full without overflowing. The preliminaries and
main dishes for dinner are placed on the edge of the basin, while
the lighter ones float about in vessels shaped like birds or
little boats. A fountain opposite plays and catches its water,
throwing it high in the air so that it falls back into the basin,
where it is played again at once through a jet connected with
the inlet. Facing the seat is a building which contributes as
much beauty to the scene as it gains from its position. It is
built of shining white marble, extended by folding doors which
open straight out into greenery; its upper and lower windows
all look out into more greenery above and below. A small alcove
which is part of the room but separated from it contains a bed,
and although it has windows in all its walls, the light inside is
dimmed by the dense shade of a flourishing vine which climbs
over the whole building up to the roof. There you can lie and
imagine you are in a wood, but without the risk of rain. Here
too a fountain rises and disappears underground, while here and
there are marble chairs which anyone tired with walking
appreciates as much as the building itself. By every chair is a
tiny fountain, and throughout the riding-ground can be heard
the sound of the streams directed into it, the flow of which can
be controlled by hand to water one part of the garden or another
or sometimes the whole at once.

Pliny excuses the length of this letter by the fact that he has been indulging the affection he feels for all the places he has laid out himself or where he has improved on an earlier design ('praeterea indulsi amori meo; amo enim, quae maxima ex parte ipse incohavi aut incohata percolui'). There are also several letters which describe constructive works of man or natural phenomena: the building of Trajan's harbour at Centum Cellae, the source of the river Clitumnus, suddenly rising from level ground as it still does today, Lake Vadimon with its sulphurated waters, floating islands and vanishing stream, which he describes to a friend who shares his interests ('nam te quoque ut me nihil aeque ac naturae opera delectant').[47] Licinius Sura is sent an account 'fully worthy of your great learning' of the intermittent spring still to be seen in the grounds of the Villa Pliniana at Torno, on the eastern shores of the lake, and of the various explanations Pliny offers for this phenomenon one of them is near the truth: the spring works on the siphon principle, 'so that the stream diminishes and flows slowly while water accumulates after it has emptied, but flows faster and increases when the supply is sufficient'.[48]

This gift for direct observation and clear description is rare in the ancient world, but in many ways Pliny's detached curiosity is more scientific than his famous uncle's. He is not interested in marvels as such nor in antiquarian tales, and so he presents the well-known ghost stories as problems in psychology, and the behaviour of the dolphin at Hippo as an interesting example of unusual animal behaviour.[49] His letters describing the eruption of Vesuvius,[50] written twenty years after the event to provide information for Tacitus's *Histories*, are remarkable for their sober factual presentation. Martial wrote of the widespread flame and ashes as an act of the gods which they would regret having had in their power to bring about (IV.44.7–8.):

> . . . Cuncta iacent flammis et tristi mersa favilla:
> nec superi vellent hoc licuisse sibi.

And at Misenum, says Pliny, during that dreadful darkness 'many besought the aid of the gods, but still more imagined there were no gods left, and that the universe was plunged into eternal darkness for evermore'. He himself has no such sentiments, but nothing could convey the horror of the situation better than his plain words about the first sight of the cloud 'like an umbrella pine', then the shooting flames and rain of pumice, the wheeled carriages running in all directions; and, as he and his mother left Misenum, 'a dense black cloud was coming up behind us, spreading over the earth like a flood'. Then 'darkness fell, not the dark of a moonless or cloudy night, but as if the lamp had been put out in a closed room' ('. . . et nox non qualis inlunis aut nubila, sed qualis in locis clausis lumine extincto'). Few of us, surely, would resist the temptation to dramatize memories like these, but Pliny's sober facts are infinitely more telling.

He is also exceptional in that he romanticizes neither the past nor the rural scene, though the idea of a Golden Age was fashionable among his contemporaries, and city dwellers at all times have been apt to believe that the simple virtues of the past are to be found in an idealized country life. 'I am an admirer of the ancients,'[51] he writes, 'but not, like some people, so as to despise the talent of our own times. It is not true that the world is too tired and exhausted to be able to produce anything worth praising. . . .' ('sum ex eis qui mirer antiquos, non tamen (ut quidam) temporum nostrorum ingenia despicio. Neque enim quasi lassa et effeta natura nihil iam laudabile parit.') He gives a gentle dig at Suetonius who proposes to buy a country retreat near Rome:[52] 'Scholars turned landowners, like himself, need no more land than will suffice to clear their heads and refresh their eyes, as they stroll around their grounds and tread their single path, getting to know each one of their precious vines and counting every fruit tree. . . .', and can write wistfully in Rome that it is 'a long time since I have known what peace and quiet are, or even known that lovely lazy state of doing and being nothing'; but when he visits his Tuscan property his tenants seize the opportunity to voice their grievances, and 'claim their right after my long absence to vex my ears with their complaints. The necessity of letting my farms is also becoming urgent and giving a good deal of trouble, for suitable tenants can rarely be found.'[53] He wrote to Trajan for permission to absent himself from the *aerarium Saturni* for the month of September to attend to his affairs at Tifernum: 'The farms I own in the district bring in more than 400,000 sesterces, and I cannot postpone letting them especially as the new tenants should be there to see to the pruning of the vines, and this must be done soon. Moreover, the series of bad harvests we have had are forcing me to consider reducing rents, and I cannot calculate this unless I am on the spot.'[54] This was written in 99, and there were more troubles at Tifernum in the period covered by Books VIII and IX of the *Letters*, with poor grape harvests so that Pliny had to compensate the contractors, who stood to lose heavily, and also reduce his tenants' rents; he even considered changing his practice of five-year leases for the *mezzadria* system, or payment of rent by a share of produce to the landlord.[55] Letter VIII.17 vividly describes floods of the Anio and Tiber after prolonged stormy weather; and at Comum, when hail has done damage to the vines in Tuscany, a bumper harvest has resulted in a fall in price. Even at Laurentum, where Pliny owns only the house and garden, there are times when he has to apologize for not being able to send a friend some fresh fish 'as long as the weather is so bad'.[56] He can laugh at himself on occasion for 'playing the part of proprietor, but only to the extent of riding round part of the estate for exercise' ('et patrem familiae hactenus ago, quod aliquam partem praediorum, sed pro gestatione percurro'), or when he writes of himself as gathering in the grape harvest 'which is poor, but better than I expected; if you can call it "gathering" to pick an occasional grape, look at the press, taste the fermenting wine in the vat . . .' ('ipse cum maxime vindemias graciles quidem, uberiores tamen quam expectaveram colligo, si colligere est non numquam decerpere uvam, torculum invisere, gustare de lacu mustum...').[57] But the general picture he gives us is of a landlord who takes a practical interest in management, has no illusions about his peasant farmers, and is characteristically generous to them when they are seriously in trouble.

Pliny shows no great originality in his literary judgments, and his scattered remarks on art are conventional for his time: realism in representation is his ideal. He shows a knowledge of at least ten Greek and fifteen Roman authors, but apart from his detailed discussion of the Attic orators in Letter IX.26, nearly all his verbal quotations come from the *Aeneid* and the *Iliad*. He has only one reference to Horace, and none to Ovid; he quotes twice from Euripides but never from Sophocles or Aeschylus; he refers twice to Plato and never mentions Aristotle. He does not appear to be interested in philosophy nor in political theory – nowhere does he mention the principles motivating the Stoic opponents to the emperors, although he admires them personally. The *Panegyricus* and the two letters which discuss his reasons for expanding and publishing it are the exception, and in fairness to Pliny I think we should not separate the speech from the *Letters* – it was, after all, Pliny's creation, and enthusiastically received by his invited audience, and although it is undeniably far too long and often absurd in its sheer exuberance, its political message is clear. Through the conventional vote of thanks demanded of the new consul Pliny hoped that 'good rulers should recognize their own deeds and bad ones learn what theirs should be' ('boni principes quae facerent recognoscerent, mali quae facere deberent' (*Pan.*, 4.1)). This he confirms in Letter III.18: 'I hoped in the first place to encourage our emperor in his virtues by a sincere tribute, and, second, to show his successors what path to follow to win the same renown, not by offering instruction but by setting his example before them.' Throughout the speech he emphasizes that the *optimus princeps* should be less despotic than Domitian and more effective than Nerva, while continuing to act in the interests of his people, so that he builds up a picture of the ideal ruler that Trajan's grateful subjects hope he will be.

No other speech of Pliny's survives whereby we can judge him as an orator, though he discusses oratorical style in two long letters,[58] and makes it clear that he preferred something fuller and more colourful than the pure 'Attic' style with its rather arid standards of brevity and correctness. Elsewhere he criticizes 'Asian' flamboyance in Regulus or a Bithynian advocate. His master Quintilian divides oratory into three styles, and the middle or mixed one would best suit Pliny. Many of his letters discuss literary topics, and he seems to value most the versatility which can match style to theme – his own great gift as a prose writer. The specimens he quotes of his own verse are poor, and two sets of verses by Martial and Sentius Augurinus are almost as trivial,[59] so that one doubts his literary judgment – the much-praised poems of Calpurnius Piso and Vergilius Romanus may have been equally uninspired. The reading aloud of an author's works for discussion and advice from his friends seems to us an improbable way of achieving original creative work, though Pliny rarely failed any of his friends and often mentions his own readings. Juvenal, of course, found the whole practice an intolerable bore and waste of time.[60]

As a prose stylist Pliny is in the first rank. He has no obvious mannerisms (apart from a liking for diminutives and a rapid succession of verbs or epithets for dramatic effect) but no one can write with greater virtuosity and variety. Here, for example, is the dolphin playing with the boy in the sea at Hippo Diarrhytus; the sentence is as flexible and quick-moving as the dolphin itself, while any English equivalent is ponderous (IX.33.4).

> Delphinus occurrit, et nunc praecedere puerum nunc sequi nunc circumire, postremo subire deponere iterum subire, trepidantemque perferre primum in altum, mox flectit ad litus, redditque terrae et aequalibus.

> (A dolphin met him and swam now in front, now behind him, then played round him, and finally dived to take him on its back, then put him off, took him on again, and first carried him terrified out to sea, then turned to the shore and brought him back to land and his companions.)

To Valerius Maximus, going out to Greece on a commission like that of Pliny's in Bithynia, he sends advice in language which is almost Ciceronian (VIII.24.2):

> Cogita te missum in provinciam Achaiam, illam veram et meram Graeciam, in qua primum humanitas litterae, etiam fruges inventae creduntur; missum ad ordinandum statum liberarum civitatum, id est ad homines maxime homines, ad liberos maxime liberos, qui ius a natura datum virtute meritis amicitia, foedere denique et religione tenuerunt.

> (Remember that you have been sent to the province of Achaea, to the pure and genuine Greece, where civilization and literature, and agriculture, too, are believed to have originated; and you have been sent to set in order the constitution of free cities, and are going to free men who are both men and free in the fullest sense, for they have maintained their natural rights by their courage, merits, and friendly relationships, and finally by treaty and sanction of religion.)

Then there are the *ioca*, trifles written in light conversational style which often recalls Martial, such as the following (IV.29):

C. Plinius Romatio Firmo suo s.
Heia tu! cum proxime res agentur, quoquo modo ad
iudicandum veni: nihil est quod in dextram aurem fiducia mei
dormias. Non impune cessatur. Ecce Licinius Nepos praetor!
Acer et fortis et praetor, multam dixit etiam senatori. Egit
ille in senatu causam suam, egit autem sic ut deprecaretur.
Remissa est multa, sed timuit, sed rogavit, sed opus venia fuit.
Dices: 'Non omnes praetores tam severi.' Falleris; nam vel
instituere vel reducere eiusmodi exemplum non nisi severi,
institutum reductumve exercere etiam lenissimi possunt. Vale.

(Now then, you really must come along somehow to take your
place on the bench next time the court is sitting – you can't rely
on me to let you sleep soundly; if you default, you will suffer.
Along comes our stern praetor, Licinius Nepos; bold man, he
has just fined a senator! The culprit made his defence before
the Senate, but he had to plead for pardon. He was let off the
fine, but he had a fright; he had need of mercy and had to beg
for it. You may say that all praetors are not so strict, but you
are wrong there. It may take a strict one to establish or revive
such a precedent, but once that is done the mildest of men can
act on it.)

He writes in a style nearer that of oratory in his more impassioned outbursts (such as the one on the honours paid to Claudius's freedman Pallas)[61] and his vocabulary is more poetic in his descriptions of natural scenery; in the account of the harbour at Centum Cellae his debt to Virgil has been noted. When his subject is literary criticism his language is that of Quintilian, and his style is very much *pressus sermo purusque* – concise and simple it may be, but its studied elegance defies translation. For example (IV.20):

C. Plinius Novio Maximo suo s.
Quid senserim de singulis tuis libris, notum tibi ut quemque
perlegeram feci; accipe nunc quid de universis generaliter
iudicem. Est opus pulchrum validum acre sublime, varium

elegans purum figuratum, spatiosum etiam et cum magna tua
laude diffusum, in quo tu ingenii simul dolorisque velis
latissime vectus es; et horum utrumque invicem adiumento fuit.
Num dolori sublimitatem et magnificentiam ingenium, ingenio
vim et amaritudinem dolor addidit. Vale.

(I gave you my views on each section of your book as I finished
reading it; now you shall have my general opinion of the work
as a whole. It is a noble achievement, powerful and penetrating:
its language is dignified, varied and well chosen, the style pure
and rich in metaphor, the comprehensive scale has a breadth
which will win you recognition. You were swept on by the force
of genius as well as of indignation, and these have reinforced
each other; genius has added dignity and grandeur to your
indignation, and this in its turn has given your genius power
and fury.)

Pliny always recognizes Tacitus as his superior in judgment and
literary style, and hopes that posterity will remember them
together; 'for me,' he writes, 'the highest position is the one
nearest to you.' For though he is often unself-critical, he is
not self-satisfied; and the letters about his many benefactions and
acts of kindness which may jar on us should be read in the light
of the Roman system of patronage between friends, where
beneficia conferred can properly expect *officia* and gratitude in
return. His views on equity go beyond what was officially recognized, and several times he writes to justify his holding to the
spirit rather than to the letter of the law.[62] His professional
honesty is beyond question, and he is quite free from professional
jealousy. He is a loyal and reliable friend, indefatigable in his
assistance to promising young men, and suitably grateful to the
older generation, men like Corellius Rufus and Vestricius
Spurinna, from whom he had received support in furthering
his own career. He is a good and considerate master, both to
individual members of his household in whom he is specially
interested, and in his policy of allowing privileges to his house
slaves and in his readiness to grant them their freedom,[63] and
he is an appreciative son-in-law as well as an affectionate husband.
He always practises tolerance himself and preaches it to others,
defending on occasion an erring servant or a spendthrift son,

or even the sophisticated entertainments which he personally dislikes.[64] But he has no use for affectation in any form, whether it is that of a popular rhetorician or of people who make a show of superiority, and he condemns the crowds at the Races because they have no real interest in the horses or the drivers' skill.[65] His attack on snobbery at a dinner-party is as sharp as Juvenal's, and his contempt for M. Regulus is as much for his exhibitionism as for his lack of principle.[66] We come to know him well through the *Letters*, and that is perhaps why they can be read at many levels; for social historians and Latin stylists Pliny is important, while for everyone he is surely a most likeable man.

Notes

1 VI.16; 20; X.96–7; II.17; V.6; VII.27; IX.33.
2 II.1.8; II.15; IX.7.
3 VI.20.5.
4 II.1.
5 IV.13; VI.6.3.
6 *CIL*, V.5262.
7 I.18.3; V.8.8.
8 III.11.5; VII.31.2.
9 VII.16.2; I.23.2.
10 VII.16.2.
11 VI.29.8; VII.33.4.
12 III.11.3.
13 *CIL*, V.5262.
14 IX.13.
15 V.14.5.
16 III.13; 18.
17 X.3a; II.11–12.
18 III.4.
19 II.14.
20 VI.11; IV.22; VI.31.
21 IV.9; V.20.
22 IV.8; X.13.
23 V.14.
24 X.17a.
25 IX.13.4.
26 VI.30.1.
27 VII.5; VIII.10–11.
28 I.3; VII.11.5.
29 I.8; IV.13; VII.18; *CIL*, V.5262.

30

Caecina Paetus = elder Arria
|
Thrasea Paetus = younger Arria
|
(1) = Helvidius Priscus = (2)Fannia
|
Helvidius = Anteia
|

Helvidius   2 daughters

31 III.11.3.
32 IV.21.3.
33 VI.11.
34 IX.39; III.6.
35 III.15; VI.16; II.19.
36 IX.2.3.
37 IX.2.
38 X.96–7.
39 X.93.
40 X.81.
41 X.17a; 23; 37; 39; 90; 98.
42 X.41–2; 61–2.
43 V.1.5; IV.8.3.
44 X.37; 90.
45 IX.7.
46 II.17.
47 VI.31; VIII.8; VIII.20.
48 IV.30.
49 VII.27; IX.33.
50 VI.16; 20.
51 VI.21.
52 I.24.
53 VIII.9; IX.15.
54 X.8.5.
55 VIII.2; IX.37.
56 IV.6; V.2.
57 IX.15; 20.
58 I.20; IX.26.
59 VII.4.6; 9.11; III.21.5; IV.27.4
60 Juvenal, *Sat.*, I 1–13; VII. 39–59.
61 VIII.6.
62 II.16; IV.10; VII.11.
63 V.19; X.5; VIII.1; 16.
64 IX.21; 12; 17.
65 IV.11; VI.17; IX.6.
66 II.6; 20; IV.2.

VII

Latin Prose Panegyrics*

Sabine MacCormack

1   Definitions and rhetorical textbooks

The development of Latin eulogistic oratory was at first intermittent rather than continuous. So far as can be judged by the
extant evidence, a period of continuity began in the late third
century A.D.: late antiquity was the golden age of panegyrics.

Latin prose panegyrics were derived from Greek rhetorical
theory as regards their arrangement of topics and rhetorical
methods. But in their manner of implementing Greek theory,
Latin panegyrists were largely independent of their Greek pre-
cursors and contemporaries, and relied instead on Cicero,
especially his Caesarian speeches and his *De lege Manilia*, and on
Pliny's *Panegyric*. This characteristic of Latin panegyrics in prose
also differentiates them from panegyrics in verse, where different
language and imagery were employed. Latin prose panegyrics
can therefore be studied profitably in their own right, as required
by the present context.

Epideictic oratory, the *genus demonstrativum*, is one of the three
fields of oratory distinguished in Greek and Latin textbooks of
rhetoric,[1] the other two being the *genus iudicale* (δικανικόν) and
the *genus deliberativum* (δημηγορικόν). Epideictic oratory comprises
different types of speeches of display, in particular praise and
vituperation.[2] The praise of individuals, especially rulers, formed
only one branch, but the most important one, of the former
class. The literary prototype was the *Evagoras* of Isocrates. The
term *panegyrikos* was at first applied in Greek only to Isocrates'
oration in praise of Athens, designed to be recited at a festival,
πανήγυρις.[3] In Latin, the term *panegyricus* was initially used with
the same restricted meaning,[4] and speeches of praise in general
were called ἐγκώμια in Greek and *laudes* or *laudationes* in Latin.
The word *panegyricus* to describe a *laudatio* of an individual had
become the accepted term in Latin by the fourth century. It was

* See note on p. 192.

used in the corpus of the *XII Panegyrici Latini*,[5] which was compiled in Gaul by a Gallic rhetor, perhaps by Pacatus,[6] the author of the latest panegyric in the collection, the speech of 389 on Theodosius.

Most rhetorical treatises gave instructions for the composition of epideictic speeches. Among the methods generally suggested are comparisons, amplification of particular topics, an elevated style commensurate with the importance of the theme, and careful subdivisions to make clear the overall structure of the work, whether biographical or analytical, that is, praise or vituperation according to virtues or vices. The chief aim of an epideictic discourse, as repeated frequently in rhetorical literature, was to please the listeners by any means possible.[7] Aristotle's *Rhetoric*, which, apart from the so-called *Rhetorica ad Alexandrum* is the earliest surviving rhetorical treatise, gives instructions as to how to compose an epideictic speech, and also suggests the heroes of the mythological and historical past as fitting subjects for eulogies.[8] In other words, Aristotle bore in mind chiefly speeches for the delectation of the audience, although the example of Isocrates shows that such speeches could have a practical application; could serve to propound political views and ideals. Aristotle treated eulogies briefly as being only a minor aspect of rhetoric, and the same was done by the authors of Latin rhetorical works.[9]

In the later third and early fourth century A.D., however, two comprehensive treatises on eulogistic discourses were composed; one of these is by the *rhetor* Menander, the other probably not, although both have been attributed to him.[10] The τέχνη περὶ τῶν πανηγυρικῶν going under the name of Dionysius of Halicarnassus probably dates from the late second or the third century.[11] The date of these treatises suggests that eulogistic oratory was acquiring greater importance and regard in later antiquity than previously, a suggestion which is corroborated by the dates of the surviving Latin panegyrics, which, apart from Pliny's, are late Roman.

The principles of composition which were laid down in the treatises attributed to Dionysius and Menander were the same as those in earlier works, but, particularly in the latter, they were worked out in greater detail, with plenty of examples.[12] At times it is almost as though one hears the teacher of rhetoric addressing his class, first stating the principle in question in the abstract, then applying it in practice.[13] The authors of the treatises attributed to Menander were certainly very well aware of all the quandaries in which a panegyrist might find himself, and resourceful in suggesting solutions. The treatises are school books, which were designed to prepare the young orator for what was in late antiquity one of his chief functions as a public speaker, the praise of emperors, generals and government dignitaries.

The treatises outline speeches for different types of occasion, such as arrivals, departures, marriages and the presentation of wreaths – the last applicable to the *aurum coronarium* offered to Roman emperors.[14] There is also a basic scheme for the *basilikos logos* which could be adapted, depending on the occasion, although the scheme remained similar.[15] Apart from pointing out some general methods, such as comparisons to the heroes of myth and history,[16] and careful and clear subdivisions of the speech, so that the listeners may follow more easily,[17] the basic scheme outlined the order in which topics had to follow one another.[18] After an introduction, where alternatives were proposed, the home-country, family, birth and education of the subject were to be praised briefly; if any of these was likely to cause embarrassment, it was to be left out. In the main part of the speech, the deeds, divided according to deeds of war and of peace, were to be praised in detail, and the author was to point out how in his deeds the subject of the panegyric practised the different virtues.[19]

The methods suggested here and in earlier textbooks were observed, at least in outline, in almost all the panegyrics to be discussed here. They served to differentiate a panegyric, or, more broadly, an epideictic discourse, from judicial and deliberative speeches.

There is one aspect of panegyrics of which the existence and importance cannot easily be gathered from the rhetorical textbooks, and that is their role, at least potentially, in practical, political terms. In this sense the textbooks were a product of the world of the schools, which could be, but was not always, disengaged from the world of politics and the constantly shifting aims and priorities of imperial government into which some of the Latin panegyrics give a particularly clear insight. The two treatises attributed to Menander recount all the various possibilities of different types of speeches of praise without ever pointing to the contemporary significance that the time-honoured commonplaces and tricks of panegyric could be made to acquire and did acquire in a specific situation.

The political relevance of panegyrics is most apparent in late antiquity, when they were used to propagate imperial programmes and policies, and when most of the extant panegyrics, Latin as well as Greek, were composed. Panegyrics featured most prominently, as will be seen, when they could be utilized politically. The link existing between the rhetorical, cultural and artistic aspects of panegyrics and their political significance accordingly forms a guideline in the present enquiry. This guideline will emerge most clearly in the treatment of late antique panegyrics. Developments in Latin eulogistic oratory previous to late antiquity will be seen to lead up to the formation of panegyric into an instrument of political propaganda.

2 *Laudatio funebris*

The contemporary and political relevance of Latin panegyrics may be regarded as a Roman contribution to eulogistic oratory which had its roots in the republic. Greek textbooks, which, as regards rhetorical theory, served as models for the Latin ones, worked out the methods whereby a person could be praised. There existed, however, in republican Rome, a type of eulogistic speech with a political significance which initially developed independently of the Greek tradition and was regarded by contemporaries as specifically Roman: the *laudatio funebris*.[20] Roman tradition had it that Brutus, the first consul, was honoured with a state funeral and a *laudatio funebris* delivered by his colleague Poplicola.[21] An occasion of this kind was described by Polybius.[22] The deceased was carried in a reclining or seated position to the Rostra, amidst persons who wore the masks of his ancestors and had with them the insignia of the offices which those ancestors had held. Then a son or close relative delivered the oration. The ceremonial was peculiarly Roman, and the republican *laudatio* had features which distinguished it from Greek eulogies. The ancient Roman ceremonial for state funerals was still documented by Dio Cassius, Herodian and the *Historia Augusta*; the *laudatio funebris* of Pertinax was delivered from the Rostra by Septimius Severus.[23]

One of the Roman features of the *laudatio funebris* was pointed out by Polybius. Whereas Greek schemes invariably proceeded from the praise of ancestors to that of the subject proper of the speech, the *laudatio funebris*, according to Polybius, began with the deceased and then proceeded to his ancestors.[24] Surviving fragments of funerary *laudationes* of the republic confirm that ancestors were praised, but it is impossible to tell what part of the speech these ancestral *laudes* occupied. Another peculiarity of some funerary *laudationes*, which is to be gathered from the fragments and from historians' renderings of *laudationes*, is that they addressed the deceased in the second person. This is the case in Brutus' *laudatio* of Appius Claudius[25] and Augustus' *laudatio* of Agrippa, a fragment of which has survived in a recently discovered Greek translation on papyrus.[26]

Although the *laudatio funebris* of individuals at both public and private funerals was in origin a Roman custom, it, like other aspects of Roman culture, was subject to Greek influence;[27] Greek rhetorical theory regarding the disposition of eulogies probably influenced republican funerary *laudationes*, although from the fragments one cannot tell their disposition. Dio's version of Antony's *laudatio* of Caesar differs widely from Appian's, and unlike the latter follows the Greek rules.[28] Although neither version probably records Antony's words, they both provide examples of the possible content and arrangement of a *laudatio funebris*. The style of funerary *laudationes*, like their arrangement, was influenced by Greek theory, but not universally. The fragment of the *laudatio* of Scipio Aemilianus by Laelius, like to a lesser degree the fragment of Caesar's *laudatio* of his aunt Julia,[29] has a complex rhetorical structure, whereas other *laudationes* were composed in a simple, non-rhetorical manner. Among these, so far as one can judge by the Greek translation, was Augustus' *laudatio* of Agrippa, the surviving part of which enumerates Agrippa's deeds without any attempt to order the sentences in a rhetorical manner.[30]

Republican funerary *laudationes* at state funerals could be a vehicle of political propaganda, for they could be used as a means of bringing the deceased and his family to public notice. Delivering the *laudatio* of a famous – or even not so famous – ancestor, like speaking in the law courts and competing for the junior magistracies, was a way in which a young candidate for a political career could catch the public eye, as Caesar did when he delivered the *laudatio* of his aunt Julia. As might be expected, *laudationes* made false claims, and their value as historical evidence was doubtful, a fact which was noted by Cicero and Livy.[31] Indeed, the whole genre of speeches of praise was viewed with suspicion in Rome, and Cicero, although he gave instructions as to how a laudatory speech should be handled, regarded purely laudatory compositions as un-Roman.[32] The specifically Roman features that can be traced in funerary *laudationes* lend some support to his view, but none the less, by Cicero's time, laudatory speeches, composed according to all the rules of the art, that is, Greek rules, were firmly established in Roman public life and in Latin literature. Speeches in law courts, as witness Cicero himself, gave ample opportunity for praise and for its rhetorical counterpart, vituperation.[33] The methods for both were similar.

3 From Cicero to Pliny

These very methods appear in Cicero's *De lege Manilia* and the Caesarian speeches. These speeches were carefully studied and much alluded to by late antique panegyrists, and, as regards both method and content, were extremely influential.[34] Just how pervasive their influence was, is shown, as it seems to me, by one of the illustrations at the end of the *Notitia Dignitatum* for the East;[35] this shows a number of *codicilli* in a rectangular framework surmounted by a shallow triangle. On the four corners are the busts of *Virtus, Scientia Rei Militaris, Auctoritas* and *Felicitas*, set into medallions and identified by inscriptions; these are the very virtues which Cicero praised in *De lege Manilia*.[36] In the apex of the triangle in the illustration appears the bust of *Divina Providentia*, a concept which was also treated by Cicero in the second book of *De natura deorum*,[37] but which in Christian late antiquity could be interpreted independently of Cicero; by means of this concept the military virtues of Pompey, now impersonalized, acquired a contemporary relevance.

The collapse of the republic brought with it the disappearance of Roman political oratory. The *vir bonus dicendi peritus* had to turn to administering the empire, and did so with considerable success. Oratory in Rome, apart from oratory in law courts, became what it had already been for centuries in the Greek East, a means of popular entertainment. History, myth, the absurd, and contemporary affairs, the latter mostly of local relevance only, were the topics of the *declamationes* with which *rhetors* both Roman and Greek, but especially Greek, delighted their audiences.[38]

Panegyrics, as a branch of epideictic oratory, which with the disappearance of political oratory became increasingly important during the empire, formed part of the repertoire. In Rome itself, however, the earliest imperial panegyrics were composed in verse, not prose.[39] The idiom was non-political, even if political undertones were intended in the *Carmina Einsiedlensia* and the eulogistic poems of Calpurnius Siculus[40] and Statius,[41] which are the ones to survive from a genre that was much practised in the first century A.D.

In this situation, Pliny created what came to be regarded in late antiquity as something of a prototype for imperial prose panegyrics. Pliny's *Panegyric*, or *gratiarum actio* for the suffect consulship of A.D. 100, heads the collection of the *XII Panegyrici Latini*. In part it also survives in the same palimpsest as the panegyrics of Pliny's imitator Symmachus,[42] an indication of the conscious preservation of tradition in late antique Rome.

The custom whereby the consuls thanked the emperor for their office in a speech in the Senate became established under Augustus;[43] it originated in the republic, when the consuls, on entering office, thanked the people for their election.[44] Pliny's *gratiarum actio* therefore had many antecedents, of which, however, none survive. After pronouncing his speech in the Senate, Pliny expanded and improved it and recited it to a select group of literary friends.[45] It is this expanded and published version that survives.[46] It is impossible to tell how far Pliny's *Panegyric* differs from the many earlier consular *gratiarum actiones*. It owes much of its importance in the Latin eulogistic tradition to the fact that it was published and could serve as a model for later panegyrists. From this point of view, Pliny made an important contribution towards the creation of Latin prose panegyric as a genre.

Like Cicero's *De lege Manilia*, Pliny's *gratiarum actio* is political in content. His arrangement is basically biographical, though not in strict chronological order. The speech describes Trajan's conduct in and outside Rome and makes of him an emperor such as the Senate would approve of. How far this would actually be the case remained to be seen at Pliny's time of speaking. [47] In September A.D. 100 Trajan had only been in Rome for a few months, and Pliny was in no position to know what his policies would be. He could not, therefore, do what some of the late antique panegyrists did so well, that is, announce a programme and interpret imperial policies for a local audience.

Pliny's *Panegyric*, and prose panegyrics in general, differ from verse panegyrics in the idiom they use. Verse panegyrics were more or less fanciful in their setting and imagery – the pastoral panegyric was particularly popular in the early empire. [48] Prose panegyrics, on the other hand, discussed what the audience might have seen or would have liked to have seen in reality. Latin prose panegyrics treated politics directly, rather than in the imagery appropriate to poetry. After the eclipse of Roman republican oratory, the publication of Pliny's *gratiarum actio* initiated the re-establishment of rhetorical method in the field of eulogy in terms of the practice of oratory. Pliny's teacher Quintilian covered all fields of rhetoric from the theoretical angle.

Pliny was conscious and proud of his role as an orator, but the audience to which he addressed himself was not the *plebs* of Rome that Cicero had spoken to, or the courtiers and townspeople that the later panegyrists addressed. Rather, Pliny's audience consisted of a small literary circle of senators who were eager to appreciate and discuss each other's works. It was the literary occasion, the recitation of the expanded speech to his circle of erudite friends that Pliny valued and wrote of in his letters. [49] The panegyric was viewed first as a work of literature and only second as an instrument of politics. Pliny was thus particularly pleased with its style and rhetorical disposition: [50]

> nam invenire praeclare, enuntiare magnifice interdum etiam barbari solent, disponere apte, figurare varie nisi eruditis negatum est. nec vero adfectanda sunt semper elata et excelsa. nam ut in pictura lumen non alia res magis quam umbra commendat, ita orationem tam summittere quam attollere decet.

> (For even though the uneducated are capable of flights of the imagination and powerful delivery, only cultivated men can devise an appropriate disposition and manifold figures of

speech. Indeed, one must not always aspire to the elevated and the sublime. For just as in painting light is brought to the attention by shadow, so the style of an oration should be in part a subdued, and in part an elevated one.)

Fronto, like Pliny, regarded panegyrics as works of literature, rather than as instruments of politics.[51] He spent much trouble and time composing the *gratiarum actio* to Antoninus Pius, which he pronounced in the Senate for his suffect consulship of A.D. 143, in order to save it from the oblivion which normally befell panegyrics.[52] His panegyric on the British victories of Antoninus Pius was known in the late third century,[53] and, like his *gratiarum actio pro Carthaginiensibus*, perhaps still in the sixth.[54]

4 Developments after Pliny; panegyrics as distinct from historical writings

The panegyrics which Fronto mentioned in his letters[55] are only a few among the hundreds which were delivered, but of which no trace survives. There is no mention of Latin panegyrics in prose for the third century, but the occasions on which panegyrics were held in the second century are likely to have been observed also in the third. The first late antique panegyric dates from A.D. 289, and apart from Pliny's, it is the earliest oration in the Gallic corpus of the *XII Panegyrici Latini*. The surviving late Roman panegyrics are a very small sample of the discourses which were delivered throughout the empire on numerous imperial occasions.[56] Any conclusions one draws from these panegyrics, therefore, must not be regarded as automatically valid for the empire at large, or even the Latin-speaking part of it, but as relevant chiefly for the context from which particular panegyrics came.

The late third-century panegyrists saw themselves as the continuers of the Roman republican traditions and those of the second century A.D. The orator of 297 mentioned Fronto's panegyric on the victory of Antoninus in Britain,[57] and the orator of 312 compared five years of Constantine's reign to Cato's *lustrum* as censor and referred to Cato's speech *De lustri sui felicitate* as well-known;[58] Cicero and Pliny were extensively quoted, though not mentioned by name.[59] This consciousness of a continuity with the Roman republic and the period of the good emperors of the second century A.D. survived into the fifth century and later. Macrobius associated Pliny with Symmachus, for both were, as he said, representatives of the *genus pingue et floridum*; this association is reflected in the manuscript tradition.[60] Symmachus' letters, in imitation of those of Pliny, were published in ten books, the tenth book in both cases consisting of official correspondence.

Although there may have existed some continuity in the composition of panegyrics between the second and late third century, for which support can be adduced from what is known of a continuity of tradition in higher education, the very long gap in the panegyric tradition – at least so far as the survival of panegyrics is concerned – must not be set aside.[61] Developments took place in this period, the results of which can be ascertained from the late Roman panegyrics, but the actual course of which remains obscure. These developments concern the difference between panegyric and history, and the precise nature and aim of panegyric.

A letter sent by Lucius Verus to Fronto gives an idea of the content of eulogies in the second century.[62] Verus submitted to Fronto materials which Fronto was to use to compose a history of Verus' war against the Parthians. He seems to have written only the preface.[63] Fronto was instructed to magnify Verus' deeds as much as possible by means of a series of devices which are familiar from panegyric: for, Verus said, although the nature of his deeds would not thereby be changed, they will appear to be such as Fronto portrays them.[64] Fronto in his reply used the term *historia* for the work:[65] Verus wanted his deeds recorded in *historia* rather than *laudatio* for the very good reason that *laudatio* was in bad repute for disregard of truth – in short, Verus was hoping to have it both ways.

Lucian, in his *How to write History*, mocked and criticized precisely this kind of historical writing, with specific reference to devices of praise, examples of which are to be found in Fronto's preface.[66] Pliny also used some of these devices, but more discreetly.[67] There was here, as Lucian pointed out, a confusion between the genres of panegyric and contemporary history.

In late antiquity, however, a deliberate distinction was drawn between these two, both by panegyrists and historians, and a special term was applied to panegyric: it was the *stilus maior*. Pacatus stated that his *Panegyric* would provide material for historians and artists, and that the latter should leave off illustrating the deeds of Liber and Hercules.[68] Pacatus' *Panegyric* was indeed more suitable than others for supplying material for history: the war against Maximus, the theme of the central part of the work, was told in continuous narrative with the chronological and geographical framework that is needed for history but was often lacking in panegyrics. More important, however, and more decisive, was the distinction made by Eutropius and Ammianus, at the end of their works, between history and panegyric. Eutropius' *Breviarium*, dedicated to Valens, ends with the death of Jovian.

quia autem ad inclitos principes venerandosque perventum est, interim operi modum dabimus. nam reliqua stilo maiore dicenda sunt. quae nunc non tam praetermittimus quam ad maiorem scribendi diligentiam reservamus.

(But since now we have reached the period of our illustrious and revered emperors, we will for the time being end our work; for what remains should be pronounced in a higher style. This task we do not so much set aside as reserve for a more elevated manner of composition.)

Ammianus, who probably read Eutropius, ended his work in similar fashion, by exhorting any who might continue the narrative to use the *stilus maior*.[69] Eutropius betrayed a distinct reluctance to describe the reigns of Valentinian and Valens in anything but the *stilus maior*. Unlike Ammianus, he did not say that he would not attempt the task, but only that it was of a different nature. The position was that contemporary history, which began with the accession of the ruling emperor, was a subject for panegyric, past history for historical writing. Once a panegyric was out of date *qua* panegyric, it could be used as a source for history.[70]

The panegyrics of late antiquity were a development of, and in some senses an improvement on, the *Panegyric* by Pliny. They were, it is true, if one is to judge them by the standards of Classical Latin literature, inferior to Pliny and certainly to Cicero, from the literary and linguistic point of view. Where Pliny tried to create methods of expression and literature, the fourth-century panegyrists used the expressions made available to them by the authors of the past, especially Cicero. They did not aim to create literature for its own sake. Also, their panegyrics were less comprehensive as a record, much shorter and less factual. However, these characteristics were in many respects an advantage. By means of them panegyrics could be differentiated more clearly from history and were turned from pure eulogy – something pleasant for the subject of the panegyric and the general audience to listen to, duly embellished with linguistic finesses for those who could appreciate them – into an instrument of propaganda. Such panegyrics had to be concise, systematic and comprehensive, but simple. Detail of narrative, linguistic and structural complexity, yielded to clarity.

These principles do not exclude the rules of Menander, but in many ways they modified what had been said about amplification.[71] The late Roman panegyrists observed Menander's rules, but they did so very selectively.[72] Among the omissions are not only those parts of eulogistic speeches which had to be passed over because, as Menander himself said, they could not always apply, or would strain the credulity of the audience,[73] but also matters which could perfectly well have been said but were none the less left out. The late Roman panegyrists were deliberately not writing history, and most of them did not aim at completeness, even as regards the emperor's good qualities. Rather, they interpreted a particular situation for a particular purpose, place and time. In short, their panegyrics were written in what historians, without attaching either praise or blame, could call *stilus maior*. Panegyric was an acceptable genre of literature in late antiquity.

5 Occasions of panegyrics in late antiquity; setting and ceremonial

By the fourth century A.D., a pattern of occasions had emerged on which panegyrics were customarily held, but the better part of this pattern was already established by the second century. The earliest kind of imperial panegyric to be regularly delivered was probably the *gratiarum actio* by the consuls. In Pliny's *gratiarum actio* the actual thanksgiving at the end of the work is almost

totally submerged by the laudatory part of the speech. Mamertinus' *gratiarum actio* of A.D. 362, on the other hand, falls into two
almost even parts, which is perhaps the more usual form that such
a speech would have taken. Imperial consulships were another
occasion for praise, which was utilized by Statius, who wrote a
laudatory poem on Domitian as Consul; for the fourth century,
there are Symmachus' panegyric on Valentinian I,[74] and Claudian's three consular panegyrics on Honorius. Consulships of
private individuals could be similarly praised. The anniversary
of the emperor's accession was marked by special religious
observances, and Latin panegyrics survive from Constantine's
quinquennalia and *quindecennalia*.[75] The time to celebrate imperial
victories could be adjusted to coincide with such anniversaries,[76]
which were also used as occasions for the emperor to take up the
consulship,[77] and in themselves could provide the occasion for
a panegyric. Instances are Constantine's capture of Rome, and
Theodosius' defeat of the usurper Maximus.[78]

Panegyrics in late antiquity formed part of the ceremonial
on various imperial occasions. They were one of the accompaniments of legitimate rule, a form of consent. As will be seen, this
is one aspect of their revival in the Ostrogothic kingdom. As
part of imperial ceremonial, they needed a setting, an architectural framework: the extensive imperial building programme
of the later Roman empire, which was emulated by the Ostrogothic kings, can be viewed in the context of imperial ceremonies
that stood in need of a backcloth. At Trier, Aquileia, Milan, and
other capitals of the empire, the palace and its accompanying
buildings formed a nucleus of imperial activity and propaganda,
as well as of local pride. The panegyrist of 310 referred to the
buildings of Trier as rivalling those of Rome:

> video circum maximum, aemulum, credo, Romano, video
> basilicas et forum, opera regia, sedemque iustitiae in tantam
> altitudinem suscitari ut se sideribus et caelo digna et vicina
> promittant.

> (I see the great circus, resembling, I believe, the circus of Rome,
> I see the basilicas and the forum – kingly works – and the seat
> of justice being raised to such a height that they promise to be
> worthy of the stars and the sky to which they come so close.)

The '*sedes iustitiae*' is probably the extant basilica at Trier and is to be identified with the building where Ambrose was received by the tyrant Maximus and where, earlier, Ausonius delivered his *gratiarum actio*.[79] According to him, it was an awe-inspiring and holy place:[80]

> atque non in sacrario modo imperialis oraculi, qui locus horrore tranquillo et pavore venerabili raro eundem animum praestat et vultum, sed usquequaque gratias ago, tum tacens, tum loquens. . . .

> (And I will not only give thanks in the shrine of the imperial oracle, a place of quiet worship and reverend awe, where the face can only seldom express what is in the soul, but I will give thanks everywhere, now silently, and now with words. . . .)

In such a place the emperor could be seen enthroned under a *ciborium* in the apse, ready to receive the homage of those who were so privileged as to be admitted – as Mamertinus said of Diocletian and Maximian in 291:[81]

> quale pietas vestra spectaculum dedit, cum in Mediolanensi palatio admissis qui sacros vultus adoraturi erant conspecti estis ambo et consuetudinem simplicis venerationis geminato numine repente turbastis!

> (What a spectacle was vouchsafed by your Piety in the palace of Milan, when you were both seen by those who were admitted to adore your sacred countenances, men who, being accustomed to revering only one emperor, were troubled by a twofold majesty!)

Late antique people had a very highly developed sense for the appropriate architectural setting of various imperial activities. In art, the emperor was often represented in an architectural framework which was in keeping with the function he was represented as performing. Thus Theodosius on the missorium in Madrid is seated in his palace between Valentinian II and Arcadius, giving the *codicilli* of his office to a dignitary. This consciousness of the imperial architectural setting survived unbroken in the West until the Ostrogothic kingdom. It is probable that in the original version of the mosaic of the Palatium in

S. Apollinare Nuovo in Ravenna, Theoderic was to be seen in the gate of his palace, flanked on either side by dignitaries of his court. Iconographically, the mosaic and the missorium are related: both show a schematized symmetrical structure.[82] The ruler occupies the central part of a tripartite entrance, while those subordinate to him are shown in the parts of the building which are subsidiary to the main, central structure.

One of the ceremonies where the architectural setting emerges very clearly is that of imperial *adventus*. In art, the ceremony was often depicted against the background of a city gate from which citizens or a personification emerged to greet the emperor. The panegyrist of 312 expressed the relevance of the architectural setting particularly well when he said, *à propos* of Constantine's arrival at Autun in 310:[83]

di immortales, quisnam ille tum nobis illuxit dies . . . cum tu, quod primum nobis signum salutis fuit, portas istius urbis intrasti, quae te habitu illo in sinum reducto et procurrentibus utrimque turribus amplexu quodam videbantur accipere!

(Immortal gods, what a day shone upon us . . . when you, bringing us the first token of our salvation, entered the gates of this city, which, being shaped in a hollow curve, with projecting towers at either side, seemed to receive you in a kind of embrace!)

Such a gateway, with towers protruding at either side, appears on a Constantinian gold multiple from Trier.[84] *Adventus* was a frequent and important theme in panegyric, and could be adapted for different contexts: instances are the meeting of Diocletian and Maximian in Milan in 290, Constantius' entry into London in 296, Constantine's accession and his entry into Rome after the defeat of Maxentius, Julian's progress to Constantinople and Theodosius' entry into Haemona in 389 *en route* for Italy. The theme of *adventus* still appears in Cassiodorus' panegyric on the consulship of Eutharich, delivered in 518 or 519, where, as in numerous earlier panegyrics, the joy bestowed by the ruler's presence was described.[85] The typology of *adventus* was used in panegyric to cover any ordinary imperial arrival as well as special occasions like accession and victory. It is the context, different for each occasion, that determined the particular colours and shades of meaning that the orator would put into the tableau in which the scene was generally described in panegyric.

The ceremony of *adventus* was one of the occasions on which panegyrics were customarily delivered, and the treatise attributed to Menander as well as the τέχνη περὶ τῶν πανηγυρικῶν of Ps. Dionysius of Halicarnassus gave instructions regarding panegyrics for arrivals.[86] The treatise by Ps. Dionysius also suggests that the panegyric could be delivered by one of the dignitaries who were to meet the arriving ruler outside the city walls, before the welcoming crowd together with the ruler and his train entered the city.[87] The practice in the West, however, was that the panegyric was delivered after the formal arrival was accomplished, in the Curia if it was in Rome, or in the local curia or palatium if it was elsewhere.

The delivery of a panegyric necessitated a well-ordered formal setting, which was provided by the fixed ceremonial for the various imperial occasions. The panegyrics themselves, when describing imperial actions, described them as orderly and planned, and often as having splendour and beauty.[88] This also was a sign of legitimate rule. Chaos and disorder, on the other hand, were accompaniments to the rule of a usurper. This emerges very well in Ammianus' description of the usurpation of Procopius in 365.[89] Procopius was acclaimed by a disorderly group of soldiers – and not very many of them – he was hustled to the palace, and the whole scene bears the imprint of hasty, ill-prepared and surreptitious action. The acclamation of Julian as Augustus, on the other hand, in fact probably no less chaotic, was described by Ammianus in such a way as to convey the divine and human consent which were betokened by ceremonies carried out with dignity and in the prescribed order.[90]

It was generally thought that a large audience should be present to hear the panegyric: the orator of 312 actually stated that he did not speak on an earlier occasion because not enough people were present.[91] Most panegyrics addressed not only the emperor, but also the audience: the Senate of Rome was always specifically addressed, and a number of panegyrists made a point of selecting their topics so as to interest and involve the local audience. This could be done very specifically, with reference to contemporary political issues.[92] The delivery of a panegyric on an imperial occasion and in a formal ceremonial setting was not merely a method of making propaganda, but also a token of legitimate rule, and a form of popular consent which was demonstrated by the presence of the audience. A panegyric by Cassiodorus, probably delivered on the occasion of the marriage of Vitigis and Matasuntha, Theoderic's granddaughter, in A.D. 536, illustrates the element of consent particularly well. Having praised Vitigis' deeds in war, Cassiodorus paused for the army to acclaim the king, and to attest the truth of his statements.[93]

The order and beauty attributed by panegyrics to imperial actions, and implied by the very delivery of panegyrics, was also conveyed in the formalized and carefully structured iconographic schemes which were employed by late antique imperial art. On the *largitio* and *adlocutio* panels of the arch of Constantine, on the base of the obelisk in the hippodrome of Constantinople and on the column base of Arcadius, emperors were shown receiving, in various forms, the homage of subjects and barbarians, and appearing as the central figures in a structured and rigorously-ordered composition.

6 Late Roman panegyrics as expression of imperial politics

Above, the formal features which differentiate late Roman panegyrics from history have been discussed. These panegyrics were selective and composed for a particular purpose. According to Lucian, historical writings ought to be written so as to be appreciated by posterity.[94] Late antique panegyrics, on the other hand, had a certain in-built obsolescence, for they addressed themselves to contemporaries, and then mainly to a particular group of contemporaries, that is to those locals who were present to listen. It is thus important to realize the potential and the limitations of panegyrics. On the one hand, a panegyric could crystallize in considerable detail and depth one specific moment in a specific place, but on the other hand, in its particularity lay its limitations. Panegyrics are not a good basis upon which to generalize. It is a mistake to extract from them singly or collectively an amalgam of qualities attributable to the late antique 'ideal emperor'.[95] Particular imperial qualities found expression in relation to particular circumstances, places and groups of people. Thus Constantine in Trier in 310 was portrayed as the merciless conqueror of barbarians, but in 313 in Trier and in 321 in Rome his generosity towards the enemy was emphasized.[96] The Theodosius of Pacatus' *Panegyric* is barely recognizable as the subject of Ambrose's *Consolatio*.

The temporary and relative validity of panegyrics, the way in which they were circumscribed by a particular context, also becomes apparent when one examines them as sources for historical facts. The historian who disentangles facts from panegyrics has a frustrating task, not only because of the conventions of the genre, according to which, for instance, an enemy was often not referred to by name,[97] amd place-names and chronology could be avoided,[98] but also because the aim of most late Roman panegyrics was suggestion and allusion rather than demonstration and proof. In this, late Roman panegyrists differ greatly from Pliny, who was more thorough and therefore more neutral and impartial in his treatment of facts.

In late Roman panegyrics, events were not necessarily narrated in detail, but could be explicitly or implicitly passed over to make room for descriptions of states of affairs and of imperial actions in terms of pageants and ceremonies. Instead of hearing of historical facts, the audience heard of facts as symbols and as tokens of imperial majesty. These characteristics are especially pronounced in some panegyrics of the late third and early fourth century and in Mamertinus' *gratiarum actio* of 362. These panegyrics were all used as a medium to announce imperial programmes and policies in such a way as to embrace both political and religious matters, while avoiding any details that would detract from the central themes. This will be illustrated in some examples.

It was a panegyric commonplace to say that the emperor's achievements were too great and too numerous to be narrated in detail. The audience was more likely to be convinced by this if the orator did not actually go into the detail he had promised to avoid; if he could make his message clear, concise, and relevant to the local situation. Thus Mamertinus in 289 very appropriately merely reminded his hearers of imperial victories in the East,[99] and concentrated on the situation in Gaul which was of more immediate concern to the people of Trier whom he addressed. Similarly in 291, rather than going through the four cardinal virtues, he only praised the emperors' *pietas* and *felicitas*.[100] They had *pietas* towards the gods and towards each other. The latter was very skilfully illustrated by an account of the meeting of Diocletian and Maximian in Milan in 290, described as a victorious *adventus*,[101] where fact and symbol flow into each other, and are juxtaposed one to expound the other without the tedium of actual explanation and definition. The hardships of the journey, the rejoicing of the population at the approach of the emperors, their reception in Milan and residence in the palace there, were all described in some detail as illustrating the emperors' affection and devotion for each other, their endurance and their command even over the elements. But the subject of the deliberations in Milan was not mentioned with one single word. The historical event did not matter as much as the event which could be made into a symbol. In the second part of the panegyric, the empire's prosperity, the fertility of the fields and imperial victory were used to demonstrate the emperors' *felicitas*. This speech was very skilfully composed, for while imperial virtues were expressed by the well-being of the subjects, they were also expressed – in the description of the *adventus* scene – in the majesty, the exalted position of the emperors. In this way imperial virtues created a link between ruler and ruled, which, characteristically, was not stated directly, but emerged from the panegyric as a whole.

Even in a more factual panegyric, like that on the *quinquennalia* of Constantius, celebrating his victory over Allectus and re-conquest of Britain, in 296, the narration of imperial deeds was prefaced by an introduction on the world-wide victories of the Tetrarchs[102] and an exposition of Tetrarchic rule in terms of symbols. The fourfold division of the Tetrarchic empire was not explained so much with regard to frontiers needing defence and provinces requiring the presence of an emperor to provide a local focus of interest and to retain the loyalty of the provincials. Such an explanation would belong to the realm of historical writing. Rather, the panegyrist compared the four emperors to the four elements, the four seasons, the four cardinal points and the four luminaries of the sky, Sol and Luna, Vesper and Lucifer,[103] and thereby integrated imperial dominion into the eternal order of nature. The narration of Constantius' campaign against Allectus, although sufficiently factual for the events of the war to be reconstructed in outline, yet emphasized the world-wide and supernatural aspects of the victory as much as its practical importance. The victory was used to illustrate the *felicitas* and divine protection which the emperors enjoyed;[104] it was understood as a symbol for imperial *felicitas* as well as extolled in its own right.

Events which a panegyrist did not want to develop could be alluded to or passed over explicitly in a *praeteritio*,[105] or they could be ignored. Mamertinus in his *gratiarum actio* of 362 to Julian gave an example of both *praeteritio* and omission which is distinguished by the superb confidence of a real master in this art of saying the unsaid. After mentioning Julian's activities in Gaul, Mamertinus said:[106]

> mitto cunctam barbariam adversus vindicem Romanae
> libertatis in arma commotam gentesque recens victas et
> adversum iugum nuper impositum cervice dubia contumaces in
> redivivum furorem nefandis stimulis excitatas – quae omnia
> obstinatam et immobilem principis maximi tandem vicere
> patientiam. itaque cum in ipso molimine oppressisset
> Alamanniam rebellantem, qui paulo ante inaudita regionum,
> fluviorum, montium nomina exercitu victore peragraverat, per
> ultima ferarum gentium regna, calcata regium capita
> supervolans, in medio Illyrici sinu improvisus apparuit.
> vidimus, felicis istius viae comites, stupentes urbium populos
> dubitasse credere quae videbant.

> (I pass over the whole barbarian world rising up in arms against
> the defender of Roman liberty; I pass over the nations recently
> conquered but still rebellious under the yoke newly imposed
> on their insubmissive necks, nations which were aroused to
> renewed uproar by nefarious schemes: all these troubles at last
> conquered the steadfast and unmoved patience of our emperor.
> Thus it was that he who with his victorious army had traversed
> regions, rivers and mountains whose names were heretofore
> unknown, hastening through the remotest kingdoms of
> uncivilized peoples, and trampling over the heads of kings,
> appeared unexpectedly in the heart of Illyricum. We, the
> blessed companions of that journey, beheld the astonished
> populace of cities suspending belief in what they saw with their
> own eyes.)

The narrative of the occurrences here referred to occupied

lengthy sections in Ammianus; the events in question were the battle of Strassburg, and the rebellion of the Alamanni, which, according to Ammianus,[107] Constantius had incited against Julian. One is left to think whatever one likes of the sentence beginning 'itaque . . .'. It may refer to Julian's action against the barbarians, where Constantius is also implied, or to Julian's usurpation, or to both, for by the end of the next sentence, Julian has arrived in Illyricum and is on his way to Constantinople. He was heading for armed conflict with Constantius, although Mamertinus suggests, without actually saying it, that Julian's inroad into Illyricum was just part of his campaign against the barbarians. Mamertinus then leads his narrative into the terminology of a victorious *adventus*, and that is all he says about Julian's becoming sole emperor. Julian's proclamation as Augustus in Gaul, the reasons for it, the events leading up to it and the events following after are all ignored. Mamertinus never allows himself to betray the cause by giving any details or any explanation of any matter at all that is likely to lead him into difficulties or to require apologies. It was a superb performance which left potential objectors in Constantinople with little chance to reply. Mamertinus, while giving his listeners a good and thorough picture of Julian in general, really told them no facts; that is, he deprived them of the opportunity of any rejoinder, there being nothing in what he said that they could deny. There is little narrative of events in the historical manner in this panegyric. All is evaluation, allusion, argument. The listener was definitely not left to make up his own mind.

Late Roman panegyrists explained and propagated past imperial actions, as is illustrated by the above examples. But this was only one of their possible tasks. They could also elucidate for their listeners imperial policies for the future. Such panegyrics, for instance that of 362, could prepare the scene for action: a number of them were delivered on the occasion of an arrival, a time of potential uncertainty, when a definition of past events could be used to lay down attitudes for the future. In particular this was the case during the aftermath of a war against a rival emperor or usurper; the panegyric would make sure that the point of the war was properly understood,[108] and considerable liberty could be taken with the facts. Here again the approach was non-historical.[109]

This becomes especially clear where panegyrics are close to-gether in time and where changes of policy had to be explained. The type of problem that arose is illustrated in the panegyrics that document the ascendancy of Constantine. The panegyrics of 289, 291, 297 and 298 praised the institutions and emperors of the Tetrarchy with great skill and conviction, and gave the impression that the Tetrarchic system had been worked out to last for ever – as indeed it was intended to do. With the panegyrics that follow, however, the reader is in for a shock – but it cannot be anything like as big as the shock of those who witnessed the events after 305 and listened to the panegyrics. The panegyric of 307 praised what amounted to the collapse of the Tetrarchy. Constantine, having emerged from Britain in what looked like a usurpation, made a makeshift alliance with Maximian, who had returned to a sem-blance of power after his retirement, by means of a dynastic marriage between himself and Maximian's daughter Fausta. The panegyrist's task was to publicize these facts in a manner and a setting which would convince people that the arrangements in question were valid and final. He had to back up the emperors' military effort of preventing further usurpations. Facts were duly selected and tailored to suit that programme. But the orator did not choose themes that might suit the occasion at random by leafing through his copy of Menander or equivalent, as one might suppose if one studies only the way in which panegyrics repeat commonplaces and observe the textbook rules.[110] He introduced and pointed to themes which turned out to be of great importance in Constantine's later policy.

The themes which emerge in the panegyric of 307 are the dynastic aims of Constantine and the collapse of the Tetrarchic religious programme. These were two features which were to make an essential difference between the regime of Constantine and that of the Tetrarchs. The dynastic theme is of course an obvious ingredient in a panegyric for a marriage: this panegyric, however, is not the traditional *epithalamium*, for the bride is hardly mentioned at all, but a political speech. The omission of any religious programme, of a religious interpretation of empire, which distinguishes this panegyric from the Tetrarchic ones, was deliberate. The panegyric of 307 was an attempt at interpret-ing recent events. When compared with the earlier panegyrics, this one gives an impression of slight unease and uncertainty which is expressed in the indistinct divisions of the speech and its lack of unity and coherence.

The panegyric of 307 was only an introduction to the changes in the empire which were made by Constantine. Further rhetorical convolutions had to be gone through to take account of the situation three years later when Maximian was dead and Constantine sole ruler of the *tres Galliae*. In the panegyric of 310, Maximian figured as the tyrant who had abused Constantine's generosity, while Constantine was the legitimate emperor who ruled by virtue of his descent from Claudius Gothicus and Constantius, and by virtue of the consent of the gods and mankind.[111] The Tetrarchic religious programme had gone, but it was now replaced by something new and positive, the personal relationship between Constantine and his god, Apollo, or, according to the coinage, Sol. The panegyrist, using the late antique identification of Sol and Apollo, adapted the empire-wide numismatic slogan of *Sol invictus comes Augusti* to the personal interests of his Gallic listeners by recounting a vision Constantine had in a Gallic temple of Apollo:[112]

... ubi deflexisses ad templum toto orbe pulcherrimum, immo ad praesentum, ut vidisti, deum. vidisti enim, credo, Constantine, Apollinem tuum comitante Victoria coronas laureas tibi offerentem... et immo, quid dico 'credo'? vidisti, teque in illius specie recognovisti, cui totius mundi regna deberi vatum carmina cecinerunt. quod ego nunc demum arbitror contigisse, cum tu sis, ut ille, iuvenis et laetus et salutifer et pulcherrimus, imperator.

(... when you turned aside to visit the most beautiful temple on earth, and came into the very presence, as you saw, of the god. For I believe, Constantine, that you saw your own Apollo, attended by Victory, who offered you wreaths of laurel.... But indeed, why do I say 'I believe'? You did see him, and recognized yourself under the aspect of him to whom, as the songs of poets have told, belong all the kingdoms of the world. I now hold that his rule has at last come to pass, for you, our emperor, like he, are young and gay, a healer and most beautiful.)

The panegyrists who used the medium of praise most success-fully for propaganda and the announcement of imperial pro-grammes in clear imaginative language, were men who had some close connection with the emperor or the court. They were the Tetrarchic panegyrists, the panegyrist of 310, and Mamertinus, the consul of 362. They were all pagans who were able to use the familiar idiom of paganism and adapt it as required. The possibilities ranged from the Tetrarchic concept of Iuppiter and Hercules as the *parentes* and models of the emperors, to Con-stantine's Apollo – Sol, to Julian's more impersonal ideal of philosophy as expounded by himself and Mamertinus.[113]

7 The impact of Christianity

Some panegyrists did not give a clear and positive impression of imperial actions and programmes. One of the explanations of the change in the nature of panegyrics, I would suggest, is to be sought in the religious changes introduced by Constantine, which resulted in his conversion to Christianity. These changes obliged panegyrists to be less open and explicit in their statement of imperial policies. Among the panegyrists in question are the orator of 307, already referred to, Nazarius and Pacatus. The orator of 307 and Pacatus have one feature in common: they spoke very shortly after fundamental changes in government. All three were unknown men who came forward to comment – or rather, so far as possible, avoid comment – on a new situation. Having such a panegyrist enabled the emperor not to commit himself concerning the ultimate aims of his policies.

The content of the panegyric of 307 indicates the overthrow of the Tetrarchy, but much of the ideology of the panegyric is still drawn from the Tetrarchy. Constantine filled the role of a Tetrarchic Caesar, Maximian that of an Augustus. The passage describing this aspect of the arrangement[114] in terms of a pageant of empire, evoking a visual experience, is among the most con-vincing in the panegyric. The author here used the vocabulary of the past to adapt the Tetrarchic system without its religious foundations to hereditary monarchy. Like Mamertinus in his panegyric on Julian, he divulged as few facts as possible. One can detect in the panegyric a certain distance from the emperors as the orator works out the relationship between them.[115] He gives the impression of being an outsider to the court, chosen to make what he could of policies hanging in the air.

Nazarius, delivering the panegyric for the *quindecennalia* of Constantine in Rome in the emperor's absence, was in a similar position, for in 321 he had to resort to the events of 312 as his central theme. He treated it, however, without the use of imagery, in which consisted much of the appeal of the panegyric of 307. He was not in sufficiently close contact with the emperor to say anything about the – admittedly complex and obscure – events between 312 and 321. He was the first of the Gallic orators represented in the corpus of the *XII Panegyrici* to come, not from Autun, but from Bordeaux, like, later, Pacatus, as well as Ausonius. The school of Autun had been rebuilt and patronized under the Tetrarchs, and its teachers composed most of the panegyrics on the Tetrarchs and the young Constantine which survive in the corpus of the *XII Panegyrici Latini*.[116] The choice of Nazarius may indicate a dissociation on the part of Constantine from the school of Autun and thereby from Tetrarchic policies. Nazarius' daughter was a Christian,[117] and it is possible that he himself, figuring as he does in Jerome's *Chronicle*, was at least a Christian sympathizer.[118] Relations between Constantine and the Senate of Rome, whom Nazarius addressed, were strained at this period, and in 325 the first Christian *praefectus urbi* – a Spaniard, of equestrian origin into the bargain – was appointed to an office generally held by senators of Rome.[119] Nazarius' panegyric, entirely unrevealing about the contemporary situation in any direct sense, by its very silence illustrates the complexities of the time, for which no satisfactory official explanation could be made available.

Pacatus' oration is structurally the most complex of the surviving Latin panegyrics, and, apart from Pliny's, the longest. Both the virtues and the deeds of Theodosius are praised; among the latter was the victory over Maximus, which provided the occasion for the panegyric, and which is related with some historical detail.[120] No personal picture of the emperor and his policies emerges, however, and it is impossible to tell from the panegyric anything about either the emperor's or the author's religion.

On matters of religion and empire the panegyrics of the Tetrarchy had provided a clear guideline by presenting the religious foundations of the Tetrarchy as an integral part of imperial rule.[121] After the accession of Constantine, and particularly after his conversion to Christianity, this incorporation of religion into imperial policy ceased being possible in Latin panegyrics. Nazarius said nothing of it, and even Mamertinus was cautious, if definite, in referring to restorations at Eleusis and mentioning that philosophy was now again enthroned side by side with the emperor. Pacatus picked up this image and changed the person of philosophy into the more neutral figure of *amicitia*,[122] while saying nothing of Christianity.

Religion as treated in panegyrics was a public matter, involving the emperor, his representatives and subjects in an official capacity. The adoption of Trajan in the temple of Iuppiter,[123] the relationship between the Tetrarchs and Iuppiter and Hercules, even Constantine's vision of Apollo in 310, relate to the role of the gods as protectors of emperors in their capacity as emperors. This did not, however, exclude the possibility of a personal religion of the emperor coalescing with the official one, like the devotion to Mithras by the Tetrarchs.[124] In this context it is significant that Eusebius in his *Life of Constantine* tried to give to Christianity an official relevance, whereby the religion of the emperor affects the whole empire: Constantine's religion was not merely a personal matter, but the instrument of his victory.[125] The personal religion of emperors was not a subject for panegyrics, which had a certain official value. Thus Mamertinus very properly left the topic out, apart from his references to philosophy and to Eleusis, and a very discreet passage on divination:[126] both philosophy and divination could, and under Julian did, have a public role affecting the empire officially.[127] Julian's conversion to paganism, however, like conversion to Christianity before it became the religion of the empire, and often thereafter, was a personal matter, which was as such not suitable for panegyric.[128] But there were methods whereby to make conversion officially effective, and Constantine's building programme was one of them – duly utilized by Eusebius in the *Life of Constantine*. He also recorded that the bishops who came to Nicaea did so on the *cursus publicus*, like any imperial official.[129] The role of the council itself, timed to coincide with Constantine's *Vicennalia*, was official and imperial, and the unity of religion was to support the unity of the empire.[130]

Notwithstanding the religious developments of the fourth

century, the Senate of Rome still regarded paganism as the official religion of the empire, the gauge of victory and security.[131] Thus it is quite explicable that Pacatus, even if he himself was a Christian (which, however, is uncertain) speaking about a Christian emperor, omitted that aspect when addressing the Roman Senate in his panegyric. The pagan members of the Senate, probably still in the majority in 389,[132] would dispute the official role of Christianity, and in the circumstances it was undiplomatic to raise the point. Therewith, religion was excluded altogether, for Christianity, if it could only figure as the personal religion of the emperor, was irrelevant. The method of avoiding the whole question was to follow very carefully, as Pacatus did, the rules for composing panegyrics, which the Tetrarchic panegyrists, being freer in their choice of topic, were able to use much more selectively.

Pacatus' method, which was also used by Libanius in his panegyric on Constantius and Constans – easily the most boring panegyric extant – was one solution to the problem of composing the official address to a Christian emperor on an official occasion. Another was found by Ausonius in his *gratiarum actio* for his consulship to Gratian, held at the end of his term at Trier in the presence of the emperor, who had come specially to hear him.[133] Ausonius explicitly avoided producing the usual *gratiarum actio* in the form of a panegyric, and delivered instead a personal thanksgiving which did not follow the rules of panegyric. It is in some senses comparable to Pliny's personal *gratiarum actio* at the end of his *Panegyric*, and to Mamertinus' second section, where the personal position of the author of the panegyric and his relationship to the emperor were discussed. Ausonius spoke as a Christian to a Christian emperor, and in order to do so avoided the traditional literary form of panegyric.

Not only was Christianity both as official and as personal religion unsuited to panegyric, but also, Christians had qualms about the genre in itself. The reason is to be sought partly in the content of panegyrics, even leaving religion aside, and partly in the historical background.

One of the chief topics of panegyric was imperial success in war and the practice, by the emperor, of the warlike virtues. Christians, even in official orations, as will be seen, attempted to pass over and deny the importance of this aspect of imperial activity. In this they were in accord with the argument of Orosius' *Historia*, according to which war was an evil, which Christian emperors had laudably sought to minimize, so far as was possible. According to Orosius, as well as Augustine in the *City of God*, war in itself was not glorious, and not a subject for praise.

As for the historical background of panegyrics, the Tetrarchy had been militantly pagan, and the panegyrics emphasized this feature, particularly Mamertinus in his *Genethliacus* of 291, in which he expounded the adoption of the names Iovius and Herculius by the emperors. Seven years later the centurion Marcellus was provoked into martyrdom during the celebration of the anniversary of this occasion in Africa[134] – quite possibly a panegyric here also formed a part of the official proceedings. Imperial celebrations of the kind where panegyrics were customary could produce strong Christian reactions: they provided an opportunity for both sides to assert themselves, and may have produced in Christians an innate distaste for speeches of imperial propaganda.[135]

Nearly a hundred years later, in 385, Augustine in Milan experienced such a distaste. He was required, as the *rhetor* of Milan,[136] to deliver the official panegyric on the consulship of the Frankish *magister militum* Bauto, which was to include the praises of the emperor.[137] On his way to the palace, tormented by anxiety about the occasion, Augustine was struck by a poignant perception regarding the worth of temporal felicity: he saw a drunken beggar in a side-street who had achieved that *laetitia temporalis felicitatis*, questionable as it was, which, in spite and because of prolonged labour, Augustine himself had failed to attain. The memory of that experience, that brief venture into public life, led Augustine to reflect on the falsity of the panegyric he had delivered, and threw him back to recall his longing for God, his friends and his home.

Meanwhile, however, other Christians were hoping to create a Christian variety of panegyric. After Theodosius' defeat of Eugenius, the Christian poet Endelechius encouraged Paulinus of Nola to compose a panegyric on the emperor. Paulinus sent a copy of this – now lost – panegyric to Jerome, who praised the *subdivisiones*, *sententiae* and arrangement of the work – merits which the pagan authors discussed here also aspired to – in terms that vividly recall Pliny's views on what a good panegyric should be in literary terms.[138] In the panegyric, Paulinus praised Theodosius, as he wrote to Sulpicius Severus,[139]

> non tamen imperatorem quam Christi servum, non dominandi superbia sed humilitate famulandi potentem, nec regno sed fide principem.

> (not so much as an emperor than as the servant of Christ, powerful not by the pride of dominion but by the humility of service, an emperor not because of his imperial authority but because of his faith.)

According to Gennadius,[140] Paulinus

> composuit ad Theodosium imperatorem prosa panegyricum super victoria tyrannorum eo maxime quod fide et oratione plus quam armis vicerit,

> (composed a panegyric in prose, addressed to Theodosius, about the victory he gained over the tyrants, because he conquered by faith and prayer rather than by arms.)

and from Jerome's reply it emerges that Paulinus also praised Theodosius' legislation, meaning, possibly, the laws against Arians and pagans.[141] As may be seen from these reports, the content of the panegyric was such that it could only apply to a Christian emperor, for the emphasis on faith and humility amounted to a denial of the traditional imperial and pagan military virtues which were customarily praised in panegyrics.

Specimens of this Christian form of praise survive in Ambrose's *Consolationes* on Valentinian II and Theodosius, where similar disclaimers regarding the primary importance of the successful conduct of war were made. These orations follow the classical rules for the disposition of *consolationes*,[142] but the content is uncompromisingly Christian. In Valentinian's *Consolatio* the spectacle of victory and empire, which is so prominent in a number of pagan panegyrics, is almost entirely lacking. The *Consolatio* on Theodosius does, however, display a tableau of magnificent proportions, where the rule of Theodosius is set against the background of Old Testament kingship and the *principes Christiani* of the fourth century, and where the virtue with which Ambrose endowed Theodosius – *fides, misericordia, humilitas* and love of God – were integrated into the teaching of the church.

Indicative of the method employed by Ambrose is the complex and beautifully modelled passage where he appeals for the loyalty of the soldiers – some of whom were present in the cathedral of Milan where the oration was delivered – to Theodosius' young sons.[143] He starts with the idea of the *fides militum*, formerly a slogan of the coinage, and ascends from there to an exposition of Theodosius' *fides* which has brought him victory on the Frigidus, and faith as the substance of things hoped for, faith by which the righteous – Abraham, Isaac and Jacob – had lived. That is on one level: on another, faith as the substance of things hoped for means the coming of age of Honorius and the future of the empire. In this oration, every traditional topic of the imperial *laudes* is either denied or turned to a different purpose. The pre-Christian empire is not mentioned with one single word: history progresses directly from the Old and New Testaments to the fourth century. This amounted to a breach of tradition such as not even the Christian court was prepared for – as is shown by the career of Claudian, whose first panegyric on Honorius, phrased in traditional and comfortably pagan terms, was pronounced two years after Theodosius' death.

The content of these Christian imperial *laudes* was too radical to be found acceptable, and, also, Christians did not show any sustained interest in imperial panegyrics. Jerome in his letter to Paulinus[144] sketches the development of Christian eloquence, past and future. Although Paulinus' panegyric is the starting point of his considerations, Jerome rapidly turns to questions which are of more immediate concern to him, the exposition of the Scriptures and of Christian teaching. Late antique Christian programmes of education concentrated on the instruction of the faithful and of preachers, not of political orators, and the secular schools survived until after the barbarian conquest.[145] No tradition of Christian panegyric developed and in the panegyrics of the early sixth century, as will be seen, a few Christian comments were simply added to the existing pagan framework.[146]

On the other hand, as has already been seen, and as will be elaborated in the sequel, the Christianization of the empire was one of the factors which disrupted the equilibrium that had made the Gallic panegyrics of the late third and early fourth centuries possible. Panegyrists after that date never succeeded in recapturing the confidence and concision, and the grasp of imperial policies, which had distinguished their Gallic predecessors.

8 The relationship between court and schools in Gaul and its collapse; Symmachus

The Gallic panegyrics of the late third and early fourth century illustrate a situation of co-operation and contact between the court and the schools – a stable situation – which enabled the panegyrists, especially those of the Tetrarchy, to phrase imperial policies so as to make them comprehensible and relevant to the local townsfolk, especially the people of Trier, where most of the extant panegyrics were held. The panegyrist, the court orator, is a figure who emerges particularly clearly in fourth-century Gaul. Pronouncing the imperial *laudes* was a task which a *rhetor* at a Gallic university was expected to be able to perform himself and to teach to his pupils, for it was one of the chief functions of oratory. The orator's role as panegyrist was stated particularly emphatically during the Tetrarchy and the early reign of Constantine, and again during the Ostrogothic kingdom. These were periods when rulers, unlike for instance Constantine in his later years and Julian, were not very vocal themselves in propagating their policies and selected orators to perform this task for them.[147]

The *gratiarum actio* of Ausonius is one of the indications that the arrangement between schools and court which had worked so well during the Tetrarchy, was no longer functioning. Julian's edict prohibiting Christians from teaching in an official capacity may have contributed towards upsetting the balance between court and schools by creating and defining divisions and borderlines which could have remained fluid.[148] Julian himself seems to have been aware of that problem: the edict deprived of his post Julian's former teacher at Athens, the same Proairesios to whom Julian had written in the preceding year offering to send materials for a description of his expedition from Gaul to the East. Julian wanted to exempt Proairesios, but the latter did not accept.[149]

Maximian, Constantius, Constantine and Julian, who are the subjects of ten out of the eleven Gallic panegyrics, all had strong connections with Gaul and resided there during important periods of their reigns. But most of the panegyrics date from 289–313, precisely the period when an emperor was continuously resident in Gaul and when the atmosphere of co-operation and mutual confidence that is required for the production of convincing panegyrics could be maintained. After 313 a number of factors converged to destroy this atmosphere of confidence. Constantine was in Gaul only in 316 and 328,[150] and until Julian, Gaul had no legitimate, permanently resident emperor.[151] By the mid-fourth century, Christianity had effected changes in the intellectual climate of the court which Mamertinus in his *gratiarum actio* could ignore, but which were expressed in the *gratiarum actio* of Ausonius. In 389, after Theodosius' victory over the usurper Maximus, Pacatus, a friend of Ausonius, was sent from Bordeaux as the emissary to assure Theodosius of Gallic loyalty, and, perhaps, to contribute towards re-creating that atmosphere of co-operation and confidence which had been lost. An imperial acknowledgment of the approach that had been made followed in 390, when Pacatus became proconsul of Africa. However, Pacatus was, so far as the available information goes, the last Gallic university teacher to deliver an imperial panegyric, and he was unable to handle the medium with the freedom and confidence of his predecessors of the early fourth century.

The gradual disintegration of the Gallic rapport between court and schools after 313 left a vacuum in the communication of imperial programmes, which, especially in the East, was filled by ecclesiastical propagandists, chief of them Eusebius. They did not, however, employ the traditional medium of panegyric, apart from the ephemeral adaptation of it which had been practised by Paulinus and Ambrose. This left a gap in the production of imperial propaganda which had not existed in the late third and earlier fourth century. Among pagans, Symmachus was one of the few to realize that an opportunity had arisen and could be made use of, and he was equipped by his education to do so. Gaul, in the fourth century, was the home of Latin oratory and panegyric, and Symmachus, after careful consideration by his father, was taught by a Gallic *rhetor*.[152] But learning rhetoric was one thing; pronouncing panegyrics on the emperor was quite another. The fact that Symmachus, as one of the leading senators of Rome, should condescend to employ a genre of literature generally practised only by teachers, is significant.

He used the medium as a means of communication between Senate and court, cautiously in 369, when as the emissary of the Senate he delivered a panegyric on the occasion of Valentinian's *quinquennalia* and another on Gratian's accession, and more boldly in the following year in the panegyric on Valentinian's third consulship and particularly in 376, in his speech *Pro Patre*.[153] Of all these orations substantial fragments survive.

The panegyric of 369 on Valentinian is composed strictly according to the textbook rules, with comparisons and *sententiae*, and the topics are arranged in chronological order, beginning with Valentinian's home-country and birth. It seems that there was also a subdivision of deeds of war and of peace, but the main part of the latter section is lost. The speech was somewhat hampered by ignorance, and little was said that would not have been generally known. It is not so much the exposition of an imperial programme as a record of *res gestae* in the idiom of panegyric. The oration of 370 concentrates on recent events and is more circumstantial, but there are still no tableaux, no symbolism, and no pageantry of victory, although victory was Symmachus' main theme. Instead, he adhered closely to the rhetorical structure in the panegyric of 369, and to the facts in 370. The method he followed consisted of narration rather than of allusion, exposition and the painting of a picture. In this, the method resembles that of Pacatus and Nazarius. On the other hand, one can detect in the panegyrics of 369 and 370 undertones – clothed in rhetorical commonplaces – which may be regarded as senatorial suggestions: propaganda would be too strong a word. Symmachus balanced Valentinian's warlike achievements with civic activities, the practice of eloquence and the involvement of the *nobiles* in imperial affairs.[154] In the consular panegyric, he spoke as though the consulship were bestowed by the Senate on behalf of the *respublica*, and as though it were a senatorial reward for imperial victory.[155]

Symmachus treated these themes at greater length and more explicitly in the oration of 376, delivered before the Senate. This was in effect a *gratiarum actio* for his father's consulship,[156] which had been granted at the request of the Senate. The message of the oration, however, is that the senators acted as electors to the consulship together with the *principes*, thus constituting '*unum corpus reipublicae*', in which '*quisquis bonus est, iam designatus est*'.[157]

Elsewhere in the speech, Symmachus condemned in no uncertain terms the abuses of the past – referring by name to Maximinus, Valentinian's *praefectus annonae*, vicar of Rome and pretorian prefect – and used the topic to reassert the link existing between Senate and emperor. [158]

These panegyrics document the growing concreteness of senatorial aspirations, at least as understood by Symmachus. But these aspirations remained a matter of nuance: the issues were flexible and open to interpretation. This was not the case with the conflict between the court and the pagan senators regarding the restoration of the altar of Victoria in which Symmachus played so prominent a part. Here, as in Julian's edict against the Christian teachers, a hard line was drawn which forced people to take sides. It appears that in his *gratiarum actio* to Theodosius for his consulship of 391, Symmachus firmly placed himself on the pagan side by using the occasion to request, once more, the restoration of the altar. [159] The request merely served to emphasize divisions between the court and the pagan senators, which became explicit during the usurpation of Eugenius.

Rome, more than any other city, had the setting, the buildings, from which the emperor or his panegyrist might address the world. But since the Tetrarchy, Rome had ceased to be the effective capital of the empire, for, as the Gallic usurpations of the third century demonstrated, it was too far removed from the focal points of power in the empire, one of which was Gaul: panegyrics, like army units, were in evidence in those places where they were most needed. The panegyrics of Symmachus may be regarded as an attempt to put Rome on the map, to make it a place of importance. But success was of short duration. During the fourth century, Rome became a self-contained unit of government under the control of the senators, who in this way isolated themselves from the problems of the empire at large. [160] The isolation of Rome from Italy and the empire was also, as will be seen, a feature of the Ostrogothic kingdom.

Symmachus was one of the most prominent pagan literary figures of his day. Like Pliny, he was a member of a literary circle, and his speeches, among them panegyrics, carefully edited before publication, had not only political and practical aims, but also literary ones. The latter in particular were intended to be appreciated by those of Symmachus' friends and acquaintances who received copies of his works.[161] These literary aims of Symmachus' speeches are in accord with the senatorial programme which he expressed in his panegyrics. The practice of literature and of politics by senators was to constitute a return to the golden days of the republic and the second century A.D. That these hopes were not to be realized was shown by the usurpation of Eugenius and is illustrated by the subsequent history of panegyrics. The literary circle of which Symmachus was a member still stirred the imagination of Macrobius in the 430s, but as an author of prose panegyrics on emperors, Symmachus had no immediate successor either in senatorial circles or among the *rhetors* of Gaul.[162]

After 394 the regular basis of co-operation and mutual adjustment between court and Senate, which could produce senatorial panegyrics, disappeared. Claudian praised Honorius and Stilicho from the point of view of the court, whereas Symmachus and the Gallic *rhetors* had, in their various ways, spoken as representatives and on behalf of groups of people other than the court, whose interests and enthusiasms they conveyed.

9 Imagery in panegyrics

The language of late antiquity was rich in images, and this was particularly so in the case of panegyrics. Certain parts of panegyrics, as has been seen, describe an imperial tableau rather than events in historical narrative, and they describe facts as symbols rather than facts merely in themselves. Their words, as will be shown here, could be translated into images. In this, the panegyrics open up one aspect of the Classical perception of a harmony in the different arts. Earlier, Pliny, preceded by Cicero, among others, had explained the characteristics of literary styles in terms of light and shade as used by painters, and Quintilian matched the achievements and characteristics of particular orators with those of particular painters and sculptors.[163] Viewing the question from the angle of the visual arts, Philostratus said:[164]

Whosoever scorns painting is unjust to truth; and he is also unjust to all the wisdom that has been bestowed upon poets – for poets and painters make equal contribution to our knowledge of the deeds and the looks of heroes – and he withholds his praise from symmetry and proportion, whereby art partakes of reason.

The way in which some panegyrists made a contribution to such knowledge of 'the deeds of the heroes' consisted in their ability to expound imperial actions in terms that would evoke images, like the tableaux that have been referred to above. Panegyrists often described rather than narrated, and in their descriptions of actions used the methods of ekphrasis, as employed, for instance, by Philostratus and Procopius of Gaza in descriptions of works of art.[165] Such descriptions, initially perceived through the sense of hearing, in fact appealed to all the senses, but particularly to the eyes. This is also the case in those panegyrics which evoke images.

On the one hand, panegyrics bring to mind specific and simple images in imperial art and slogans on the coinage; on the other, they express themselves in such a way as to evoke mental pictures which can be matched with existing works of imperial art or an iconographic scheme which is familiar. This is the tableau, the scene in panegyric which is in fact a picture. Thus, Pliny's account of the deeds of Trajan, where division into 'scenes', so pronounced in later panegyrics, is incipient, can be paralleled in the iconographic schemes used on the coinage of the second century,[166] and in the attic of the arch of Beneventum, Iuppiter appears handing his *fulmen* to Trajan, thereby leaving to the emperor the dominion of the earth, just as stated by Pliny.[167]

In late antiquity, imperial iconography, like panegyrics, became simpler, the images it used became fewer, and they were used more frequently, but often with great effectiveness. The message of imperial art, like the message of panegyrics, became more concise and compact. This factor in itself contributed to the more frequent correspondence of ideas in art and panegyric. Phrases in panegyric bring to mind images.

This is the case particularly in those panegyrics which above all were found to announce imperial programmes and policies in terms of symbols and pageants or tableaux, and which, at the same time, used a pagan idiom. Constantius, according to the panegyrist of 297, restored the prosperity of Gaul and Britain by his beneficent presence and is to be seen on medallions greeted by a kneeling province – to be identified as Britain – whom he is about to raise.[168] The coinage showed the emperor crowned by Victoria; the panegyrist of 310, in a passage quoted above, visualized Constantine similarly crowned in a Gallic temple of Apollo. He also praised Constantine's beauty, resembling the beauty of Apollo, who in late antiquity was often identified with Sol. Thus the Ticinum medallion of 313 shows jugate busts of Sol and Constantine, and on the reverse is depicted a FELIX ADVENTUS AUGG NN, where the mounted emperor is preceded by Victoria holding high a wreath.[169] The emperor depicted on the coinage in the act of victory, crushing a barbarian with his foot, has a verbal parallel in Mamertinus' *gratiarum actio*,[170] and another phrase of Mamertinus[171] is matched by a set of fourth-century coins showing the emperor standing in the prow of a ship. The origin of this type had been the third-century, ADVENTUS AUGUSTOR and TRAIECTUS AUG, but in the fourth century, legends were more general and the ship of state should not be excluded from the range of interpretation.[172]

Whether the coinage was deliberately used as an instrument of imperial propaganda is disputed.[173] What the parallels between coinage and panegyrics do make clear is that the former was used with a measure of planning to express ideas which were current at the time and to which, because of their appearance in both media, one can attribute some validity as expressions of imperial policy. Eusebius, characteristically, was aware of the possibilities of the coinage as a means of imperial advertising.[174] In the earlier fourth century, coinage and panegyric presented a uniform and coherent imperial programme. But the coherence of the two media began to disintegrate in the latter part of the reign of Constantine; this corroborates what has been said about the panegyric of Nazarius, and the decreasing effectiveness of panegyric as a medium of imperial propaganda and communication in the later fourth century.[175]

So far, only simple images in art and panegyric have been mentioned. The tableau of the panegyric, like some works of imperial art, is, however, a complex image with many strands. The method of narrative in the relevant panegyric passages resembles the literary genre of ekphrasis: these passages are descriptive of a scene, a prospect, in the same way that Philostratus, John of Gaza and Paulus Silentiarius were descriptive.

They appeal to sight as much as to hearing, and the appeal to the sense of vision is often explicit in the wording of the panegyric, as it is for instance in the speech of Mamertinus in 289, where he describes Maximian's entry on his consulship of 287:[176]

Vidimus te, Caesar, eodem die pro re publica et vota suscipere et coniunctim debere. quod enim optaveras in futurum, fecisti continuo transactum, ut mihi ipsa deorum auxilia quae precatus eras praevenisse *videaris* et quidquid illi promiserant ante fecisse. *vidimus* te, Caesar, eodem die et in clarissimo pacis habitu et in pulcherrimo virtutis ornatu.

(We have *seen* you, Caesar, taking up and fulfilling the vows for the state on the same day. For what you had desired for the future, that you performed yourself in the present, so that you were *seen* to anticipate the very aid of the gods for which you had prayed, and you achieved in advance what the gods had promised. We have *seen* you, Caesar, on the same day both in the most honoured attire of peace and in the most noble apparel of virtue.)

The link between imperial art and panegyric could be an explicit one, although perhaps a commonplace: Pacatus exhorted artists to illustrate in their works the deeds of Theodosius, which he had described, rather than those of Liber and Hercules; Symmachus appealed to Zeuxis and followers of Apelles, and the panegyric of 307 contains, as part of the *laudes*, the ekphrasis of a wall-painting in the palace of Aquileia, which represented Fausta presenting a ceremonial helmet to Constantine as a betrothal gift.[177]

More effective, however, are those passages which, unlike the above, evoke themes such as *adventus*, which are commonly illustrated in imperial art and which were appropriate for various contexts. Here the orator could begin with a particular event or fact which, on the one hand, he could use to support a generalization, and on the other, could make into an image, a tableau, or several images. Generalization and image frequently coincided, for in late antiquity imperial art came to represent, like some panegyrics, less the historical identifiable event than general aspects of the emperor's rule and character.[178]

The panegyric of 297, as has been seen above, generalized

and universalized Tetrarchic dominion by drawing parallels between it and the order of nature. The rule of the four Tetrarchs was described as being matched symbolically in the order of nature by the four lights of the sky and other quaternities. The symbol of the four lights, like other Tetrarchic ideas, was still used in the early reign of Constantine. On the arch of Constantine, the representations of imperial deeds are framed by two medallions, showing, the one, Luna with Vesper, and the other, Sol with Lucifer. [179] Thus the imperial deeds were set into a cosmic context, as was still done in imperial and then in Christian art after the fourth century, for instance on the column base of Arcadius, which will be discussed below. The particular value of the panegyric of 297 consisted in making the very widely used and very general formulae of cosmic imperial dominion specifically relevant to the Tetrarchy by emphasizing the number four. In Constantinian and later imperial propaganda, on the other hand, the application of this symbol to reality had to be more general.

The panegyric of 289 discussed the rise to power of Diocletian and Maximian. Characteristically, here also, historical and dateable events were only referred to by implication, but were used as the starting point for imagery and generalization. [180]

trabeae vestrae triumphales et fasces consulares et sellae curules et haec obsequiorum stipatio et fulgor et illa lux divinum verticem claro orbe complectens vestrorum sunt ornamenta meritorum...; sed longe illa maiora sunt quae tu impartito tibi imperio vice gratiae rettulisti: admittere in animum tantae reipublicae curam et totius orbis fata suscipere et... gentibus vivere et in tam arduo humanarum rerum stare fastigio, ex quo veluti terras omnes et maria despicias... accipere innumerabiles undique nuntios, totidem mandata dimittere, de tot urbibus et nationibus et provinciis cogitare... haec omnia cum a fratre optimo oblata susceperis, tu fecisti fortiter, ille sapienter.

(Your triumphal robes of state, your consular fasces, and your curule chairs, the glorious display of your subjects' allegiance, and that light which surrounds your divine head with a shining halo: these are the ornaments of your merits...; but much greater are the benefits which you in turn have imparted on the empire which has been bestowed on you: your concern is the care of so great a commonwealth, and the destinies of the whole

world are your responsibility. . . . You live for the nations and
stand in that most exalted pinnacle of human affairs whence, as
it were, you look down on all lands and seas. . . . You receive
messengers without number from all parts of the earth and
send out as many orders, and countless cities, nations and
provinces are the subjects of your consideration. . . . All these
tasks, which have been laid on you by your brother, you
perform them with fortitude and he with wisdom.)

The image here painted conveys the emperors enthroned high
above all, surveying the world. Their role is not identical, however, for Diocletian, whose *parens* is Iuppiter, acts *sapentier*, and
Maximian, whose *parens* is Hercules, acts *fortiter*. This contrast
was worked out throughout the Tetrarchic panegyrics.[181] The
image of the emperor enthroned above all recurs in the panegyric
of 307, where an attempt was made to preserve the ideology of
the Tetrarchy for new circumstances. It is now, to use the vocabulary of 289, Maximian who acts *sapienter*, and Constantine, in the
role of a Tetrarchic Caesar, who acts *fortiter*.[182]

te pater [Maximian] ex ipso imperii vertice decet orbem
prospicere communem caelestique nutu rebus humanis fata
decernere, auspicia bellis gerendis dare, componendis pacibus
leges imponere; te iuvenis [Constantine] indefessum ire per
limites qua Romanum barbaris gentibus instat imperium,
frequentes ad socerum victoriarum laureas mittere, praecepta
petere, effecta rescribere. ita eveniet ut et ambo consilium
pectoris unius habeatis et uterque vires duorum.

(Your role it is, Father [Maximian], to look out into the world
which you both rule from the very summit of empire, and to
decree the outcome of human undertakings by your celestial
volition, to grant the auspices for wars which have to be
undertaken, and to impose the terms when peace is to be
concluded. And your role, young [Constantine] it is to traverse
continuously the boundaries whereby the Roman empire is
defended against barbarian nations, to send many laurels of
victories to your father-in-law, to seek his instructions and to
report to him when they have been performed. So it will come
about that you both will work according to the counsels of
one mind, yet you will each have the strength of two.)

182

In visual art the emperors enthroned '*in vertice imperii*', '*in tam arduo humanarum rerum fastigio*', appear on the arch of Galerius, where Diocletian and Maximian are enthroned over the figures of earth and sky,[183] presiding over the other parts of the tableau, acting *sapienter*. On either side of them, the Caesars Galerius and Constantius, acting *fortiter*, introduce conquered provinces to the enthroned emperors. The scene is framed by the Dioscuri, Oceanus and Tellus and other divinities, represented to convey the worldwide and eternal nature of Tetrarchic rule, which was also propagated in the panegyrics.[184]

An explicit interpretation of a historical event as a symbol, suitably introduced by a *praeteritio* – '*transeo innumerabiles tuas tota Gallia pugnas et victorias*' – occurs in the panegyric of 289. The matter under discussion was Maximian's consulship of 287, referred to above,[185] which he entered upon in Trier. On the day of the celebrations occurred a comparatively minor barbarian attack on Trier not recorded elsewhere, which Maximian repulsed. In itself the event was of little significance, but it made an impression on the townspeople and it matched a common theme in imperial art and panegyric, the inter-relationship between imperial consulships and victory.[186] Thus, Mamertinus made of it a symbol, an ekphrasis, something to be seen with the eyes, as he repeated himself. The themes of the episode are a correlation of Maximian's roles in peace and war, expressed by his wearing the consular *toga praetexta* and armour on the same day. His role in peace was fulfilled by his sacrifice to Iuppiter with the vows appropriate for imperial consulships, and his role in war by the engagement with the enemy.

Similar themes, victory and a religious observance, are joined together on the *Decennalia* base in the Roman Forum, which is part of a monument that was erected in 303 on the occasion of the *Vicennalia* of Diocletian and Maximian and the *Decennalia* of Galerius and Constantius.[187] One side of the base, showing two Victories holding a shield inscribed CAESARUM DECEN-NALIA FELICITER over two crouching captives, the whole composition framed by two trophies, is devoted to imperial victoriousness, while the other three sides show the sacrifice of the *suovetaurilia* in the presence of Mars, Roma and Sol, a civil ceremony, performed by a togate emperor. The performance of this sacrifice, one of the most ancient Roman religious rites, by the emperor, has an antiquarian touch which also found expression in the panegyric of 289, where the legendary origins of Rome were recalled.[188]

A more integrated representation of the emperor's role in peace and war, of imperial consulship and victory, which in some senses is a better match to the panegyric, appears on the column base of Arcadius, to which I will return below.

Another tableau, where *adventus* and victory are intermingled, occurs in Mamertinus' *gratiarum actio* of 362. Some aspects of it have already been discussed in connection with the avoidance of issues not suitable for panegyrics, and in connection with parallels between individual phrases in panegyrics and iconographical schemes on the coinage. After stating, as has been seen, Julian's proclamation as Augustus by implication rather than expressly, Mamertinus went on to describe his welcome by the rejoicing populace of the Danubian provinces in the current idiom of imperial advents. He then contrasted the rejoicing of the Romans on one side of the river and the abject submission of the barbarians on the other:[189]

> quae navigationis illius fuit pompa, cum dexteriorem incliti fluminis ripam utriusque sexus, omnium ordinum, armatorum inermium perpetuus ordo praetexerat, despiceretur ad laevam in miserabiles preces genu nixa barbaria! omnes urbes quae Danuvium incolunt aditae, omnium auditae decreta, levati status instaurataeque fortunae, innumerabilibus barbaris data venia et munus pacis indultum.

> (How glorious was our progress during that voyage, when the right bank of the river was lined with an endless array of citizens of all ranks of society, men and women, soldiers and civilians, while on the left bank barbarians were to be seen sunken to their knees and uttering abject entreaties! The emperor visited every city on the Danube, heard the requests of all, raised their condition and restored their prosperity, and granted pardon and the gift of peace to countless barbarians.)

The '*genu nixa barbaria*' is a commonplace of imperial art.[190] It is more important that the image presented by the passage as a whole appeared on the column base of Arcadius. On the south side, Arcadius and Honorius were represented with a following of court dignitaries, while, in the register below, provinces wearing mural crowns made their offerings. On the west side, the emperors, attended by soldiers, received the submission of barbarians, shown in the register below with Victories and a trophy.

The occasion of the erection of the column base was the expulsion of Gainas and the consulship of Arcadius and Honorius in 402.[191] Accordingly, on the east side, the emperors were shown togate as consuls, attended by lictors, and, in the register below, by the senators of Rome and Constantinople. In the bottom register were mourning barbarians and piles of captured armour. This was an interpretation in art of the themes of consulship and victory as described in the panegyric of 289. However, on the column base these themes were placed into a Christian, not a pagan or neutral context: the figurations of all three sides of the column base were dominated by the cross or Chi Rho, supported by angels or Victories, and framed by the old symbol of Sol and Luna.

By the later fourth century, imperial art achieved the fusion of Roman imperial traditions and Christian concepts of empire which panegyric failed to achieve. Imperial art became Christian, and continued to express itself in stylizations and universalizations, tableaux in other words, rather than in the conventions of narrative art, whereas panegyrics remained pagan or neutral and ceased employing tableaux as a means of expression. The panegyrics of Nazarius, Symmachus and Pacatus contain few images, and none that can be matched in imperial art, and they have no tableaux. This lessened their effectiveness as propaganda and as announcements of imperial programmes, quite apart from their content.

As has been shown above, the most successful panegyrics of late antiquity arose out of an interchange between court and schools in Gaul and out of imperial patronage. As a result, in the fourth century, Gaul was one of the centres of oratory in the West. The Gallic orators of the late third century developed techniques which made their panegyrics particularly effective: they spoke by allusion, implication, symbol, and they presented facts and events as images and tableaux. It is here that one can trace connections between imperial panegyrics and imperial art.

From the point of view of imperial politics and propaganda, these connections and parallels show that the emperors were able to present a consistent, stable and continuous programme, which, because of its continuity, could be stylized and universalized and could be made to acquire symbolic meanings in art and rhetoric. The changes that occurred in the fourth century, especially after Julian, made it more difficult for panegyrists to use symbols and universalizations, partly because they – or at least those whose works survive – were too distant from the court, both physically and in outlook, and partly because imperial policies were too changeable for any fusion of art and panegyric to take place. From the point of view of the cultural history of the later empire, on the other hand, the parallels between art and panegyric illustrate a special sensitivity and skill on the part of the orators, for they succeeded in applying to the exposition of *res gestae* methods of description which had formerly been applied mainly to objects, in particular works of art. To achieve this, the orators utilized the genre of ekphrasis, description. Description, rather than narrative in the historical manner, was particularly suitable for panegyrics, the more so if it could evoke not only a visual experience in the imagination, but could also bring to mind actual works of imperial art and serve as a kind of commentary on them. However, the orators of the later fourth century returned to narrative in the historical manner: they spoke about facts and events rather than states of affairs and tableaux.

In verse panegyrics, on the other hand, images, personifications and divinities who also figured in late Roman and Byzantine art continued living a vigorous and picturesque existence: but verse panegyric was a different genre from prose panegyric, with different rules and conventions. Prose panegyrists under the Tetrarchy had created a specifically political and imperial imagery, which differed from the imagery of verse panegyric. Their expertise, the involvement of sight and hearing concurrently, was largely lost in the later fourth century. There occurred a change of awareness and ways of perception on the part of panegyrists, and perhaps their audiences. In the later fourth century, orators were not able or, perhaps, willing to convey emperor and empire as the theme that would absorb eyes and ears.

10 Ostrogothic panegyrics

The genre of prose panegyric was briefly revived during the Ostrogothic kingdom, together with some of the occasions which had formerly been marked by panegyrics. The revival was an aspect of the renewed awareness, in Ostrogothic Ravenna, of the need for a suitable ceremonial and architectural setting for royal activities, of which the formal delivery of panegyrics formed a part. This awareness has already been discussed above; it is reflected, as will be seen, in one of the panegyrics themselves.[192] A panegyric on Theoderic marked the beginning of Cassiodorus' public career. The date was in or after A.D. 500. It is possible that this was the oration which the king later asked to be published.[193] Among Cassiodorus' numerous subsequent panegyrics,[194] which are no longer extant, were a speech on Eutharic's consulship of 519, addressed to the Senate in Rome, and another on an Ostrogothic king and queen, probably Vitigis and Matasuntha, on the occasion of their marriage in 536, of both of which fragments survive.[195] The oration of 536 is the last recorded late antique Latin prose panegyric. Boethius was consul in 510, but no panegyric for the occasion is recorded; for the consulship of his sons in 522, however, he praised Theoderic in the Senate.[196] Only one Ostrogothic panegyric survives complete, that by Ennodius, then deacon of Milan, addressed to the king in Ravenna in spring A.D. 507.[197]

Politically, the revival illustrates an attempt at achieving something similar to the social and political cohesion of which the panegyrics of the early fourth century had been an expression. In Cassiodorus' view, as expressed in the *Variae*, panegyrics served to commend the ruler to his subjects, and were a token of lawful, rather than tyrannical dominion, a voluntary offering to rulers who were also patrons of letters.[198] Like the *Variae*, the panegyrics of Cassiodorus were a genuine attempt to mediate between the Gothic king and his Italian subjects, as well as the Senate of Rome, with which Cassiodorus had peripheral connections.[199] Cassiodorus, like Ennodius, presented Gothic kingship in the idiom of the Roman panegyrics of the past, with the traditional comparisons to the heroes of myth and history, especially those of the Roman republic.[200]

Christianity was only peripherally incorporated into this

structure of propaganda. Characteristically, the method of incorporation was that of the comparison, a much used device of panegyric. In Cassiodorus, Theoderic is found superior to the great men of the republic because he does not worship mindless images,[201] and Ennodius' Theoderic excels Alexander, among other reasons, because he is a Christian.[202] There is one passage which goes beyond the sterility of this somewhat laboured comparison, because it conjures up a fertile theme of Byzantine imperial theology and an aspect of Frankish kingship which was to emerge in the eighth century:[203]

> agis ut prospera merearis adipisci, sed potius universa adscribis auctori. exhibes robore, vigilantia, prosperitate *principem*, mansuetudine *sacerdotem*.

> (Your administration of affairs is such that our prosperity is to be ascribed to your virtues, yet you prefer to attribute everything to your creator. Your power, vigilance and success give you the aspect of an emperor, your mildness that of a priest.)

Ennodius did not explain his meaning any further, however, but rather by criticizing the *divi* and *pontifices* of antiquity, made one of the traditional sallies against the *maiores*, whose achievements, according to panegyrics, were always being excelled in the present.

Whether, however, the senators of Rome were as eager to welcome Gothic kingship in these terms, is open to question. The maintenance of the pagan religion in Rome in defiance of the court was in the fourth century a vehicle for the expression of local Roman patriotism and of a revival of the literary and artistic tastes of the earlier empire, of which Symmachus' panegyrics were one aspect. These panegyrics, as has been seen, were only a very partial and conditional exposition of imperial programmes. During the fifth century, contacts between Senate and court continued but became more sporadic, although, especially in the mid-fifth century, very intense. The pagan families of the fourth century became Christian, and urban feeling, which separated Rome from the imperial court, continued unimpaired.[204] In the absence of an emperor in Rome, the senatorial families satisfied the Roman taste for ceremonial and magnificence in the emperor's stead. Thus Boethius visualized the consulship of his sons in almost imperial terms:[205]

... cum duos pariter consules liberos tuos domo provehi sub
frequentia patrum, sub plebis alacritate vidisti, cum eisdem in
curia curules insidentibus tu regiae laudis orator ingenii gloriam
facundiaeque meruisti, cum in circo duorum medius consulum
circumfusae multitudinis expectationem triumphali largitione
satiasti.

(... when you watched both your sons, consuls at the same
time, proceeding from your house accompanied by a crowd of
senators and the rejoicing populace; when you yourself,
delivering the panegyric of the king in the Curia, in the
presence of your sons seated on their curule chairs, reaped the
glory of wit and eloquence; and when, seated between the two
consuls in the circus, you stilled the expectant multitude with
your triumphal largesse.)

All the *gloria* was concentrated on the actors of this scene, and
the glory of the absent Theoderic vanished behind that of his
orator. This outlook contradicted the role – resembling that of an
emperor – which Ennodius and Cassiodorus were attempting to
attribute to Theoderic, and could have affected the tenor of
Beothius' lost panegyric of 522. It probably did affect Theoderic's
reaction to the allegedly treasonable letter of Albinus, the discovery of which led to Boethius' death. [206]

Culturally, the revival of the literary genre of prose panegyric in the early sixth century was a manifestation of the Senate's
concern for the preservation of learning, of the Classical texts
and of Roman traditions, which were visualized chiefly as
republican and urban ones. [207] Ennodius used republican *exempla*,
and quoted, apart from Virgil, the panegyrics of Symmachus,
thereby reflecting the literary tastes of the senators. The surviving
Ostrogothic panegyrics display considerable erudition, but this
was not, as in many earlier panegyrics, subordinated to the
political function that panegyrics could have. The Ostrogothic
panegyrics were a homage to contemporary notions of eloquence
as much as to the king. Much of what the panegyrists said could
not have been appreciated except by a very small group of men
of letters, a literary circle reminiscent of the circle of Symmachus.
This confirms the conclusions reached above about the decline
of panegyrics during the later fourth century. Panegyrics became

less important when their primary aim was no longer the propagation of imperial programmes and policies.

Apart from this, the declining skill of the orators as public speakers – not so much as men of letters – played a role. This can be documented from late Latin rhetorical treatises and the panegyrics themselves. The threefold division of rhetoric – a matter of controversy in the earlier empire – had become a commonplace in late antiquity and was mechanically repeated in late Latin rhetorical treatises. These treatises indeed have little to recommend them. In the field of epideictic oratory nothing of the enterprise and skill of some of the panegyrists here discussed was utilized for rhetorical theory. Even a somewhat unusual passage, like Emporius' explanation of how the same information could be used for either praise or blame, where Julius Caesar's life was used as an object lesson, is static, theoretical and dry, a far cry from the lively adaptability displayed in the two treatises attributed to Menander and in several late Roman panegyrics. The authors were still aware of the type of topic that was to be discussed in panegyric, but instructions for the order in which topics were to be arranged were at best cursory. [208] Correspondingly, the arrangement of the surviving Ostrogothic panegyrics is imprecise. In Ennodius' *Panegyric*, the disposition, considered so important earlier, was omitted, and topics follow one another loosely and without proper introductions. Ennodius' arrangement of topics is chronological up to the death of Odovacar. There follow three further sections, two on deeds of peace and one on war, relating to the capture of Sirmium in 505. [209] There is no chronological reason why the deeds of peace in the first section should be thus divided from those in the last, and the arrangement is best explained by reference to the rhetorical scheme according to which deeds could be divided into deeds of peace and of war regardless of chronology. Ennodius' manner of combining these different patterns of panegyric, however, defeated the purpose for which the rhetorical rules were devised, because it led to obscurity rather than clarity. The obscurity is the more pronounced because Ennodius also uses an abstruse vocabulary, complex sentences and erudite comparisons; the latter generally serve to complicate, rather than elucidate, the issues in question. [210]

Ennodius displayed more emphatically the narrative methods

that have been noted above for Nazarius, Symmachus and Pacatus, and which differentiate these orators from the earlier panegyrists. That is, Ennodius used narrative of events rather than description, and he wrote partisan history rather than panegyric technically defined. There are no tableaux; it has been seen above that the tableau in panegyric, the passage which evokes a mental image, was produced by alluding to particular events in terms of generalizations, descriptions of states of affairs, and by interpreting events as symbolic of imperial majesty at large. The oration of Ennodius, however, adheres too closely to the course of events and to facts for tableaux, the type of generalization which they imply, and the treatment of events as symbolic, to become possible.

Cassiodorus, on the other hand, did produce a tableau, an ekphrasis, not of actions, however, as is the case with the pageants and tableaux of the Tetrarchy, but of objects and persons. In his panegyric on Vitigis and Matasuntha, the Virtues appear attending the queen as personifications, endowed with poetic epithets, and Matasuntha herself is greeted as more beautiful and radiant than any of her jewels. Cassiodorus' description of the jewelled royal throne and the palace adorned with marbles, painting and mosaic, evokes a picture of majesty clothed in all the ornaments of imagery and art that the age could provide.[211] This same picture is also conveyed by the art and architecture of Ostrogothic Ravenna. The throne of Christ in the Arian Bapistry is encrusted with jewels, and Theoderic's palace in S. Apollinare Nuovo shines with gold, mosaic work and precious marbles. Cassiodorus, a better panegyrist than Ennodius, if one may judge by the fragments, was at his best when portraying a still-life, a motionless picture of bejewelled kingship.

What captured the imagination of the orator in Ostrogothic Ravenna was what he himself saw. It had been the same during the Tetrarchy and in the fourth century. Throughout, panegyrists appealed to the spectacle before their eyes: '*haec magis diligo quae probavi*', said Symmachus,[212] a sentiment many times expressed by other panegyrists.

However, from the later part of the fourth century, imperial doings on the frontiers and in the provinces ceased being of sufficient interest and concern to stimulate an orator's imagination as much as they had done earlier, even if, like Symmachus, he had been a witness of them. One might relate this failure of the imagination regarding the secular *res gestae* of emperors and kings to the character of Christian eulogies in the West, in which such topics were absent or transformed into something new and different. The conduct of war, which had formed one of the chief topics of panegyrics, came to be, as it had not been earlier, spiritually as well as geographically remote from the capital, be it Symmachus' Rome or Cassiodorus' Ravenna. Hence Cassiodorus' interest in the still-life, the tableau of the metropolis,[213] which he had seen with his own eyes.

Concurrently, the corruption of the formal elements necessary for the composition of panegyrics contributed to the failure of the Ostrogothic orators to portray convincingly and imaginatively the royal *res gestae*. The disappearance of panegyrics in prose, as well as in verse,[214] preceded by a decline in the rhetorical skill of formulating imperial actions by means of imagery in the framework of the literary form of panegyric, constitutes an aspect of the decline of Latin secular letters after the end of the fourth century and of the disintegration of the political framework of the Roman empire in the West.

Notes

* I owe much to Dr Oswyn Murray, Gervase Mathew, Dr Hadwig Hörner and Dr Robert Markus, who have read drafts of this paper and made valuable suggestions, and to Dr J. F. Matthews, who discussed some problems with me. I would also like to thank the Craven Committee for a most generous study grant, which enabled me to spend more time on this paper than would otherwise have been possible.

1 Ps. Arist. (Anaximenes), *Rhet. ad Alex.*, 1. 1421b; Arist., *Rhet.*, I.3.1ff; *Ad Herenn.*, I.2; Quintilian, *I.O.*, 3.4; see also Hinks, 'Tria Genera Causarum', *CQ* 30 (1936), pp. 170–6. Later Latin treatises, below, n.262. Cf. Edna Jenkinson, 'Nepos – an Introduction to Latin Biography', in *Latin Biography* (Routledge 1967).

2 *Rhet. ad Alex.*, 3. 1425b f; 35. 1440b f; Arist., *Rhet.*, 1.9. 1f; 38–41 on amplification and comparisons, which are two devices characteristic of eulogy; cf. 3.14.1–7; Ps. Dionysius of Halicarnassus, *Ars Rhetorica* (ed. Usener and Radermacher) I, τέχνη περὶ τῶν πανηγυρικῶν, with details on different types of speeches of praise; *Ad Herenn.*, 3.10f, 13f; Cic., *Orator*, 37f; 42; 62f; 65f; 207f; Quintilian *I.O.*, 2.4.20; 3.7ff; surveys of the rules for the composition of epideictic discourses, R. Volkmann, *Die Rhetorik der Griechen und Römer*, 1885, 314–61; Kroll, *PW Suppl.*7 (1940), 1128–35.

3 Ps. Dionysius of Halicarnassus applied the term *panegyrikos* to speeches of praise as a whole, emphasizing their festive nature.

4 E.g. Cic., *Orator,* 37; Quint., *I.O.*, 10.4.4.

5 The most recent editions of the *XII Panegyrici Latini* are by E. Galletier, with French translation (Budé, 1949–55); R. A. B. Mynors (Oxford, 1964). The latter follows the order in which the panegyrics appear in the MSS., which is not chronological, whereas Galletier adopted a chronological order. The *Panegyrici Latini* are here cited according to Galletier's numeration, which appears in brackets in Mynors. The collection, in the MSS., is headed by Pliny's *gratiarum actio* for his consulship of A.D. 100, entitled *Panegyricus*; there follows the speech by Pacatus, also entitled *Panegyricus*. The speech by Mamertinus of 1 January 362 is called *gratiarum actio Mamertini de consulatu suo Iuliano imperatori*; *gratiarum actio* is the usual term for such a speech, but it was not applied to Pliny's in the collection. After Mamertinus there follow in the MSS. the '*panegyricus*' by Nazarius of 321, and next an overall heading, *incipiunt panegyrici diversorum VII*, to cover, in this order, the panegyrics of 312, 310, 307, 297, 298, 289, 291; of these the speech by Eumenius of 298 is not, strictly, a panegyric at all but a *suasio*; the speech of 291 has a sub-title, '*genethliacus*', cf. below p. 170 and n.134. The last oration is the panegyric on Constantine of 313, entitled *Panegyricus* in some MSS. only, which appears to have been added as an afterthought to make up the number twelve. Cf. Galletier's introduction to his edition and, for the use of the term '*panegyricus*', Ziegler, *PW*, 18.3 (1949), *s.v.* panegyrikos, where also the genre as a whole is surveyed.

6 Thus Pichon in *Les derniers écrivains profanes*, 1906, 285f. This work is still one of the best treatments of the *XII Panegyrici* and Ausonius; cf. Galletier, op. cit., I, p. ix.

7 Cic., *Orator*, 37–8; 65f; cf. Arist., *Rhet.*, 1.3.2, where the audience at epideictic speeches is described as θεωροί, spectators; i.e. they were present for enjoyment rather than as judges. Quint., *I.O.*, 3.4.6. Cf. Hinks, op. cit., pp. 172f.

8 Arist., *Rhet.*, 1.3.6 and 3.16.3, praise of Achilles; cf. 1.9.2; 3.14.3, praise of Aristides.

9 Cf. *Ad Herenn.*, 3.15; Hinks, op. cit., p. 176.

10 Menander, περὶ ἐπιδεικτικῶν, ed. Spengel in *Rhetores Graeci* III (1865), 329–446 and Bursian in *Abhandlungen d. kgl. bayerischen Akad. d. Wiss. philos. philol. Cl. München* 16 (1882), part 3. In his introduction Bursian demonstrates that the π.ἐ. is in fact two treatises by different authors, dating, one from the later third, the other from the fourth century.

11 See Radermacher's introduction to the Teubner edn of Dionysius (Opuscula, 1904–29), vol. II, 2, pp. xxiiff, esp. xxiv.

12 E.g. on birth, upbringing, etc., Spengel, p. 368; 369; 370, etc.; on deeds and virtues, Sp., 373, where also, for scenes of battle, Herodotus, Thucydides and others are suggested as models (cf. Lucian, *How to Write History*, 15; 18–19; 25, and below, n.66; 67); Homer also is a possible source, Sp., 374; on deeds of peace, 375; 376; etc.

13 E.g. Sp., pp. 375, 5f.

14 Sp., 377; 395; 399; 422 respectively. On the στεφανωτικὸς λόγος cf. Menander, Sp., 422, 29f . . . ἐπάξεις ὅτι τοιγάρτοι διὰ τοῦτο στεφανοῖ σὲ ἡ πόλις . . . with Synesius, De regno (speech accompanying the presentation of the aurum coronarium from Cyrene), 3, ed. Terzaghi, 'Εμέ σοι πέμπει Κυρήνη, στεφανώσοντα χρυσῷ μὲν τὴν κεφαλήν, φιλοσοφίᾳ δὲ τὴν ψυχήν . . .

15 Sp., 379: à propos of speeches of welcome the importance of logical division, a frequent theme, is pointed out; then praise of home-country, deeds, etc. is suggested; similarly for the στεφανωτικός, p. 422.

16 Sp., 376, comparison to predecessor.

17 E.g. Sp., 369; 372; 375; division of deeds of war and peace, 376, 13f.

18 Sp., 368f.

19 E.g. Sp., 373; 373, 7f, the four cardinal virtues; 374.

20 Dion. Hal., A.R., 5.17.3f; on the political relevance of praise in the republic cf. D. Earl, The Moral and Political Tradition of Rome (1967), pp. 16ff; cf. Cic., Brutus, 112; 162.

21 Dion. Hal., A.R., 5.17.2; Plut., Popl., 9.6f. Like many other traditions of early Rome, this one was remembered in late antiquity: Liber de Vir. ill., 10.7. The fragments of funerary laudationes were collected by Vollmer, Laudationum funebrium Romanorum historia et reliquiarum editio, Jhbb. f. class. Phil. Suppl. 18 (1891), 445–528; cf. Vollmer in PW 12, 992f. On state funerals, Vollmer, 'De funere publico Romanorum', Jhbb. f. class. Phil. Suppl. 19 (1892), 319–64; also Crawford, Classical Journal 37 (1941), 17–27.

22 Polybius, 6.53.1f, with F. W. Walbank, A Historical Commentary on Polybius I (1957), 737f.

23 Dio, 74.5.1; Herodian, 4.2.4; H.A. Pert., 15. The laudatio for Pertinax is the last recorded funerary laudatio to be delivered from the Rostra. Herodian, who described the obsequies of Septimius Severus, mentioned no laudatio. Cf. laudationes by Verus and Marcus Aurelius on Antoninus Pius (H.A., Marcus, 7, 11).

24 Polybius, 6.54.1f.

25 Vollmer (1891), p. 482 no. 6=Malcovati, Oratorum Romanorum Fragmenta liberae reipublicae, 2nd edn, p. 465.

26 Koenen, Zeitschrift für Papyrologie und Epigraphik 5 (1970), 217–83, where the earlier literature on funerary laudationes and sources is also cited.

27 There was a general awareness of Greek influence in oratory, noted for instance by Cicero in the Brutus, e.g. 77f; 114f; 151f; 325f and throughout the treatise; cf. A. D. Leeman, Orationis Ratio (1963), chs 1–2.

28 Dio, 44.36ff; Appian, B.C., 2.144f; cf. Suet., Caes. Divus Iulius, 84.2. On Caesar's funeral cf. Borzac, Acta Antiqua 10 (1962), 23–31.

29 Ed. Vollmer (1891)=Malcovati, op. cit., pp. 121; 389f.

30 The same was the case in the laudationes of Murdia, CIL 6. 10230= Vollmer (1891), no. 12, pp. 484f; Matidia, CIL 14, 3579=Vollmer (1891), no. 18 p. 516; and Turia, CIL 6, 1527=Vollmer (1891), no. 13, p. 491; this last has been edited with commentary by M. Durry, Éloge funèbre d'une matrone Romaine (Budé, 1950). For the non-rhetorical prose of funerary laudationes see Durry, Laudatio funebris et rhétorique, Revue de Philologie (1942), 105–14, where, however, the case is over-

stated, because the fragments of *laudationes* by Laelius and Caesar, where rhetorical devices are in evidence, are passed over.

31 Cic., *Brut.*, 62; Livy 8.40.4., cf. 27.27.13.

32 Cic., *Orator*, 42: epideictic oratory is *genus . . . proprium sophistarum, pompae quam pugnae aptius, gymnasiis et palaestra dicatum, spretum et pulsum foro*. From this type of praise Cicero clearly distinguished laudatory autobiography by statesmen, which he regarded as worthwhile and instructive (*Brut.*, 112; 162).

33 A *vituperatio*, see, e.g. *Act. in Verr.*, 2. lib. 1, 32f, preceded by a detailed *praeteritio*, a device much used in panegyric, cf. below, pp. 160; 162.

34 See Klotz, 'Studien zu den Panegyrici Latini', *RM*, 66 (1911), 531ff. (For Cicero's own judgment of the speech, see *Orator*, 102.)

35 Otto Seeck, ed., *Notitia Dignitatum* (1876), p. 101, line-drawing. For the date of the *Notitia* see A. H. M. Jones, *The Later Roman Empire* III (1964), pp. 347ff; p. 351 for date of the Eastern part: *c.* 395/413.

36 *De lege Manilia*, 10.28; 11.29; 15.43; 16.47.

37 The expression *divina providentia* is used in *De natura deorum* 2.87; 2.98; elsewhere *providentia deorum*. For the use of the work by the Latin fathers of the church see A. S. Pease, *M. Tulli Ciceronis de natura deorum* (1955), pp. 53f, cf. p. 83.

38 E.g. Dio Chrysostom, *Or.*, 11; 16; 61. Synesius still found Dio's encomium on hair pleasing and quoted from it extensively in his *In Praise of Baldness* (ed. Terzaghi, 1944), pp. 190f. Fronto's *laudes fumi et pulveris* (ed. Haines (Loeb), vol. I, p. 38), his *laudes negligentiae* (ibid., pp. 44f) and Lucian's *muscae laudatio*, among many other examples belong here.

39 On *Aeneid*, 6.778f see Norden *RM*, 54 (1899), 466–82; on a *laudatio* in verse by Varius Rufus on Augustus see H. Bardon, *La Littérature Latine inconnue* II (1956), 32–3. Cf. Suet., *Aug.*, 89.3. Augustus did not wish to be made the object of inferior laudatory versifications.

40 Cf. Momigliano, 'The literary Chronology of the Neronian Age', *Secondo Contributo alla Storia degli Studi Classici* (1960), 454–61.

41 Statius, *Silvae*, 4.1 on Domitian as consul; *Silvae*, 4.2; 3.

42 E. A. Lowe, *Codices Latini Antiquiores* I, (1934), no. 29.

43 M. Durry, *Pline le Jeune* (Budé, vol. IV) (1964), p. 86.

44 Cic., *De lege agraria* II, *ad populum*, 1–4.

45 Pliny, *Epp.*, 3.13.

46 M. Durry, *Pline le Jeune, Panégyrique de Trajan* (1938), 5–14.

47 Pliny did not and could not give a complete picture of Trajan, but what he wrote was sufficiently convincing, to an audience ready to be convinced, to create a legend that became accepted in historiography (see Durry, op. cit., 15–21).

48 Cf. above, n. 40; also Virgil, *Eclogues*, I.

49 H. P. Bütler, *Die geistige Welt des jüngeren Plinius* (1970), pp. 30ff; 129ff; 147; the conflict of *otium/negotium*, so vividly felt by Cicero, was still alive, and literary activity had to be justified (ibid., pp. 41f). For the recitation of the panegyric see Pliny, *Epp.*, 3.13.

50 Pliny, loc. cit.

51 Fronto, letter to Marcus Aurelius, ed. Haines (Loeb), vol. I, pp. 108f where he also refers to several panegyrics he had composed on Hadrian.

52 Fronto (Loeb), I, p. 110; cf. pp. 126; 128; 302; he praised Antoninus Pius both as *consul designatus* and as consul.

53 *Pan. Lat.*, 4.14. 2f.

54 E. A. Lowe, *Codices Latini* . . ., I, no. 27, Fronto's letters, written in the late fifth century. A fragment of his *grat. act. pro Carthaginiensibus* survives from a palimpsest of the fourth or fifth century, rewritten in the seventh or eight century (ibid., no. 72).

55 Above, n. 51, and Fronto (Loeb) I, p. 142, where panegyrists addressing Marcus Aurelius in Southern Italy are mentioned. For another panegyric by Fronto on an uncertain occasion, see Loeb I, p. 134. His *grat. act. pro Carthaginiensibus* (Loeb II, 280–2) was eulogistic. *Pan. Lat.*, 8, A.D. 312, is a surviving specimen of this type of speech.

56 The delivery of a panegyric on a feast day was taken for granted, e.g. *Pan. Lat.*, 2.1.1; 3.1.1; 9.1.1. The corpus contains only a fraction even of the panegyrics held in Gaul.

57 *Pan. Lat.*, 4.14.2.

58 *Pan. Lat.*, 8.13.3. For the republican tradition in the panegyrics, which survived until the Ostrogothic kingdom (below pp. 187f), see also Sir Ronald Syme, *Emperors and Biography* (1971), 89ff.

59 Klotz, *RM* 66 (1911), 531f.

60 Macr., *Sat.*, 5.1.7; E. A. Lowe, *Cod. Lat. Ant.* I, no. 29.

61 On the cessation of literary activity in the third century see Fuhrmann, 'Die lateinische Literatur in der Spätantike', *Antike und Abendland* 13 (1967), 56–79, esp. 68f; Bardon, *La littérature latine inconnue* II, 245ff; p. 260 on oratory.

62 Fronto, ed. Haines, II, pp. 194–6.

63 Fronto, ed. Haines, II, pp. 198–218.

64 Ibid., p. 196.

65 Ibid., p. 198; the genres of history and panegyric were not clearly distinguished. On the second-century debate see Leeman, *Orationis Ratio*, 332–7; 366–79, and H. Homeyer, *Lukian, Wie man Geschichte schreiben soll* (1965).

66 Leeman, op. cit., 375f. Lucian, *How to Write History*, 7 (neglect of events in favour of praise of rulers and generals)=Fronto, preface 8ff; esp. 13f; Lucian 8 (adornment with myth)=Fronto 1f; Lucian 8; 13; 20 (exaggerations)=Fronto, e.g. 10–14. Lucian 14, (comparison to Achilles)=Fronto 1; comparison to Trajan 8ff; Lucian 15 (imitation of Thucydides)=Letter of Verus to Fronto (Loeb II, 196). Lucian's tract, like Fronto's preface, was occasioned by Verus' Parthian war (Lucian 2).

67 Pliny, *Panegyric*, neglect of events in favour of praise: e.g. considerations on adoption of Trajan, 5–9; on war, 12ff, and similarly throughout. N.B. 56, 1: *propositum est . . . principem laudare, non principis facta*. Exaggeration, e.g. 35.4f; Comparison, mainly to Domitian, 26; 49–50; 54f; also 2; 11; 30. Lucian 31 (mocking prophecies of future triumphs)= Pliny 17; *Pan. Lat.*, 2, 12; these also figure in Claudian and Sidonius.

68 *Pan. Lat.*, 12.44.5.

69 Straub, *Vom Herrscherideal in der Spätantike* (1939), 153.

70 As was done by Ammianus, who appears to have used Mamertinus' panegyric on Julian; on Trioptolemus, *Pan. Lat.*, 11.8.4=Amm., 22.2.3; on the Palladium, *Pan. Lat.*, 11.6.3–4=Amm., 22.2.4; but similarly Cic., *De lege Manilia*, 41; Julian as *sidus salutare*, *Pan. Lat.*, 11.2.3=Amm., 21.10.2; 22.9.15 cf. 15.8.21 and 24.2.21. See Galletier, *Panégyriques Latins* III, p. 9; Gärtner, 'Einige Überlegungen zur kaiserzeitlichen Panegyrik und zu Ammians Charakteristik des Kaisers Julianus', *Abhandlungen Mainz* (1968), no. 10; also above, n. 47; below, n.137. Ammianus, 16.1, introductory to Julian's deeds in Gaul is constructed as panegyric, with the customary comment on the insufficiency of words to describe the subject in hand, profession of veracity and comparisons. Note also Julian, *Epp.*, 31 (ed. Bidez) to Preairesies, offering materials for the composition of contemporary history.

71 E.g. Spengel III, 368.8ff; 372.19f.

72 This aspect of the panegyrics is studied in detail for the consul Mamertinus by H. Gutzwiller, *Die Neujahrsrede des Konsuls Claudius Mamertinus vor dem Kaiser Julian* (1942), 92-9.

73 Menander, Spengel III, 369.27f; 370.30 f; but note (371.11) that it is permissible to expand on matters incapable of proof or disproof, such as divine descent.

74 *Silvae* 4.1; Symmachus, *Or.* 2, ed. O. Seeck (1883), pp. 324f.

75 *Quinquennalia*: *Pan. Lat.*, 8, cf. Galletier II, 77f; *quindecennalia*: *Pan. Lat.*, 10. See Fink, Hoey, Snyder, 'The feriale Duranum', *Yale Classical Studies* 7 (1940), 85f, the proclamation of Alexander Severus by the troops; 89f, his recognition by the Senate. The accession of some past emperors continued being celebrated after their death. In the *fer. Dur.* such celebrations, mostly for the Antonines, express the dynastic claims of the Severi. See also Snyder, 'Public anniversaries in the Roman Empire', *Yale Classical Studies* 7 (1940), 230ff *passim*.

76 Fink, Hoey, Snyder, op. cit., 77ff, celebration of Severus' capture of Ctesiphon timed to coincide with Trajan's *dies imperii*. *Pan. Lat.*, 4, A.D. 297, was occasioned by Constantius' *quinquennalia* and praised his reconquest of Britain.

77 E.g. Honorius' sixth consulship, celebrated by Claudian after the defeat of the Goths in 403.

78 *Pan. Lat.*, 4, A.D. 297; 9, A.D. 313; 12, by Pacatus, A.D. 389; cf. *Pan. Lat.*, 3.5.1.

79 *Pan. Lat.*, 7.22.5; E. M. Wightman, *Roman Trier and the Treveri* (1970), p. 108; on the basilica as a whole and its date, pp. 103–9.

80 Ausonius, *Grat. act.*, 1.

81 *Pan. Lat.*, 3.11.1, with Galletier's note ad loc., cf. *Pan. Lat.*, 10.5.1.

82 E. Dyggve, *Ravennatum Sacrum Palatium, La Basilica Ipetrale per Ceremonie* (Copenhagen, 1941), 34f.

83 *Pan. Lat.*, 8.7.6; E. Baldwin-Smith, *Architectural Symbolism of Imperial Rome and the Middle Ages* (1956), 19ff reviews the buildings that figured in ceremonies of arrival and triumph.

84 *Roman Imperial Coinage*, ed. C. H. V. Sutherland (hereafter *RIC*) VII, p. 162, no.1=pl. 3.1, Ry. AUGG GLORIA, city gate of Trier; outside it, two seated captives, above it statue of emperor.

85 *Pan. Lat.*, 3.8ff; 4.19.1f; 7.9.4–5; 8.7.6–8.5; 9.7.3f; 19.1f; 10.30.4f; 31.1f; 12.37.1f; Cassiodorus *Or.*, 1, ed. Traube (in *MGH Auct. Ant.* 12 (reprint, 1961)), p. 470.

86 In both cases the technical term for a formal welcome was used; Ps. Dionysius, *Ars Rhetorica*, ed. Usener and Radermacher, (Teubner, 1904–29), p. 272, l. 7; Menander (Spengel), III, p. 378, l. 30, see Peterson, 'Die Einholung des Kyrios', *Zeitschr. f. systematische Theologie* 7 (1930), 682–702; cf. my article, 'Change and continuity in late antiquity: the ceremony of Adventus', *Historia*, 1972, 721–52.

87 Ps. Dionysius, op. cit., pp. 272–3.

88 E.g. *Pan. Lat.*, 3.8ff.

89 Ammianus, 26.6.11–19.

90 Ammianus, 20.4–5: the acclamation, 20.4.14 (the soldiers 'Augustum appellavere [Iulianum] *consensione firmissima*' (cf. 17)); the refusal of power, 20.4.16; the donative, 20.4.18; and the imperial *adlocutio*, 20.5.1 – these were the prescribed ingredients of the imperial accession ceremony.

91 *Pan. Lat.*, 8.1.5.

92 Instances are Ambrose's appeal for the loyalty of the soldiers in his *Consolatio* on the death of Theodosius, below, p. 172, and the description of Maximian's assumption of the consulship, *Pan. Lat.*, 2.6, below, p. 180.

93 *Or.*, 2, ed. Traube, p. 475.

94 *How to Write History*, 38–42; 61–3.

95 E.g. Born, 'The perfect prince according to the Latin Panegyrists', *AJPhil* 55 (1934), 20–35; also Lippold, 'Herrscherideal und Traditions-overbundenheit im Panegyricus des Pacatus', *Historia* 17 (1968), 228ff. Charlesworth, 'The virtues of a Roman Emperor', *PBA* 23 (1937), 105–35 emphasized the continuities of imperial virtues but also pointed to the changes. A good study of the ideological content of the *Panegyrici Latini* is F. Burdeau, 'L'Empereur d'après les Panégyriques Latins', in *Aspects de l'Empire romain* (1964), see esp. 6–9; the attempt to define the religious aspects of empire (10ff) is less successful, for the reasons here stated.

96 *Pan. Lat.*, 7.10–11; 9.6.1; 9.11–12; 10.8 and 21; for the connections between events and what Claudian in his role as propagandist said about them see A. Cameron, *Claudian: Poetry and Propaganda at the Court of Honorius* (1970).

97 Particularly if he was a rival emperor. Thus Allectus is not named in *Pan. Lat.*, 4, nor Maximian in *Pan. Lat.*, 7, nor Maxentius in *Pan. Lat.*, 9 and 10; Procopius in Symmachus, *Or.*, 1.17 is 'rebellis exsul'. Pacatus, however, mentioned Maximus by name (*Pan. Lat.*, 12–24.4; 38.1; 40.3; 41.2, etc.); this fits with the historical nature of the narrative dealing with the war against Maximus. For Mamertinus the consul of 362, see below, pp. 162f. For the historical material to be found in the *XII Panegyrici Latini*, see Galletier's introductions to the several panegyrics.

98 This is the case particularly when praise is arranged according to virtues, as in *Pan. Lat.*, 3; see also *Pan. Lat.*, 11; in Symmachus' panegyrics most place-names occur in *exempla*, and are therefore of no use historically.

99 *Pan. Lat.*, 2.9.2; 10.6–7. Arist., *Rhet.*, I.9.30 pointed out that a panegyrist should praise what would interest his audience; cf. Menander (Spengel), III, 368.21f.

100 *Pan. Lat.*, 3.5.1–6.1, *divisio*; 6.2ff, *pietas*; 13.1ff, *felicitas*.

101 *Pan. Lat.*, 3.8ff.

102 *Pan. Lat.*, 4.3.2f; 5.1–3.

103 *Pan. Lat.*, 4.4.

104 *Pan. Lat.*, 4.15 and 17.

105 E.g. *Pan. Lat.*, 3.5.1; 4.2.1. Cf. 4.21.3; 7.1.4–5; 7.7.1; Symmachus, *Or.*, 2.3.

106 *Pan. Lat.*, 11.6.1f. See the commentary by H. Gutzwiller, *Die Neujahrsrede*..., pp. 125ff, for the events alluded to.

107 Ammianus, 18.3.4ff. See also K. F. Stroheker, 'Alamannen im Reichsdienst', in *Germanentum und Spätantike* (1965), 48ff.

108 The relevant panegyrics are cited in n. 95, above.

109 The 'tyrant' endowed with numerous vices was, in some panegyrics, contrasted to the emperor, his opposite: *Pan. Lat.*, 7.14f on Maximian is cautious in comparison to *Pan. Lat.*, 9.3.4f; 16.1f and *Pan. Lat.*, 10.12 on Maxentius, where there is much distortion (for a reconstruction of Maximian's policies, see H.v. Schoenebeck, 'Beitr. zur Religionspolitik d. Maxentius und Konstantin', *Klio Beih.* 43 (1939)); see also *Pan. Lat.*, 12.23f on Maximus.

110 Mesk, 'Zur Technik der lateinischen Panegyriker', *RM* 67 (1912), 569–90, analysed, most informatively, the rhetorical structure of panegyrics and literary influences on them; from this, however, results a picture of uniformity which the panegyrics do not have. Similarly in Maguiness, 'Some methods of the Latin Panegyrists', *Hermathena* 47 (1932), 42–61; 'Locutions and formulae of the Latin Panegyrists', *Hermathena* 48 (1933), 117–38.

111 *Pan. Lat.*, 7.2.1f; 7.7.4; 7.8.2.

112 *Pan. Lat.*, 7.21.3f.

113 *Pan. Lat.*, 11.23.4.

114 *Pan. Lat.*, 6.14.1f. See also below, pp. 182f.

115 *Pan. Lat.*, 6.3.1f; 8.1f; 13.1f.

116 For the rebuilding see the oration of Eumenius, *Pan. Lat.*, 5; T. Haarhoff, *Schools of Gaul* (1920), 136–50 on imperial patronage (with adverse judgment on panegyrics); cf. Galletier (ed.), *XII Pan. Lat.*, I. xi–xiv.

117 *Anthologia Latina* I², ed. Riese (1870), nos 767; 768. Jerome, *Chron.*, ad ann. 339.

118 Jerome, *Chron.*, ad ann. 329.

119 A. Chastagnol, *La Préfecture urbaine à Rome* (1960), 400; 401ff; Stroheker, 'Spanische Senatoren ...' in *Germanentum und Spätantike*, p. 58.

120 Cf. above, n. 95.

121 W. Seston, *Historia* I (1950), 257–66; *Diocletien et la Tétrarchie*, Bibl. des Écoles Fr. d'Athènes et de Rome 162 (1946), 196f; 209f; 211ff.

122 *Pan. Lat.*, 11.9.4; 11.23.4 with *Pan. Lat.*, 12.16.2.

123 Pliny, *Panegyric*, 8.1.

124 Inscription of Carnutum, CIL III.4413=M. J. Vermaseren *Corpus Inscr. et Mon. Rel. Mithraicae* II (1960), no. 1698, 'DISM fautori imperii sui Iovii et Herculii . . . sacrarium restituerunt'. Seston, *Dioclétien* . . . , p. 225 interprets this inscription as an official expression of imperial religion; the light imagery of *Pan. Lat.*, 3.9–10; 15 is taken as an expression of this imperial Mithraism. But Mithras is not mentioned in any panegyric, and the Tetrarchic panegyrics, like the coinage, show a deliberate return to ancient Roman religious institutions (*Pan. Lat.*,2.1f), cf. below, p. 183, on the Decennalia Base.

125 Euseb., V.C., 1.1–6; 37–8; 2.3–14; 16–17.

126 Above, n. 118 and *Pan. Lat.*, 11.23.5f.

127 Note the emphasis on philosophy in Julian's panegyric on Constantius, *Or.*, 2 (Bidez); reception of Maximus, Ammianus, 22.7.3; divination, Ammianus, 22.1.1; 12.6–8; 23.3.3; 24.6.17; 25.4.17.

128 Festugière, 'Julien à Macellum', *JRS* 47 (1957), 53–8.

129 Churches: Jerusalem, V.C., 3.25–39; 4.40; 43–7; church of the Apostles, V.C., 3.41ff, *passim*; 4.39; 58–60; bishops on *cursus publicus*, V.C., 3.6; 4.48.

130 *Vicennalia* at Nicaea, V.C., 3.15; also 4.40; 47 on the dedication of the church of the Sepulchre on Constantine's *tricennalia*; on the unity of faith and empire, see Constantine's letter to Arius, V.C., 2.64ff, esp. 65. Note also Eusebius' emphasis on the presence of bishops from all parts of the empire at councils, to signify universal consent, V.C., 3.7; 8; 4.43. In view of the prestige accruing to emperors from Persian embassies (*Pan. Lat.*, 2.10.5f; 4.10.4; 10.38.3; 12.22.4f; V.C., 4.57), the presence of Persian bishops noted by Eusebius is perhaps significant.

131 On Symmachus' *Relatio III*, see most recently, R. Klein, *Symmachus* (1971), 76ff.

132 Chastagnol, *La Préfecture urbaine*, 454f.

133 Ausonius, *Grat. act.*, 18.

134 Seston, 'Jovius et Herculius ou l'épiphanie des Tétrarches', *Historia* 1 (1950), 257–66.

135 The Christian mentality that was provoked into martyrdom by the institutions and ceremonies of the empire was particularly pronounced in Africa, cf. W. Frend, *Martyrdom and Persecution in the Early Church* (1965), 361f; note the incident narrated by Tertullian, *De corona*, 1f.

136 He obtained the appointment through a recommendation by Symmachus, then *praefectus urbi* (*Conf.*, 5.13.23).

137 Augustine, *Conf.*, 6.6.9f; *C. lit. Petil.*, 3.25.30.

138 Jerome, *Epp.*, 58 cf. above, n. 50. The rules of traditional imperial panegyric were also followed in eulogies of saints, H. Delehaye, *Les Passions des martyres et les genres littéraires* (1966), 133ff.

139 Paulinus of Nola, *Epp.*, 28.6.

140 *De vir. ill.*, 49.

141 See Augustine *C.D.*, 5.26; the picture drawn here of Theodosius is very similar to what may be gathered of the content of Paulinus' panegyric and to the *Consolatio* of Ambrose; see also Orosius, *Hist. adv. pag.*, 7.34–5. The similarity suggests that Augustine and Orosius may have been influenced by the panegyric and the *Consolatio*, and that Christian panegyric could act on Christian history as pagan panegyric did on pagan history, cf. above, n. 70.

142 F. Rozynski, *Die Leichenreden d. hl. Ambrosius*, Diss. Breslau (1910), 71ff.

143 *De ob. Theod.*, 6f.

144 *Epp.*, 58.

145 See Augustine, *De doctrina Christiana* and John Chrysostom, *On Vainglory* (translated in M. L. W. Laistner, *Christianity and Pagan Culture in the later Roman Empire* (1951)). On the survival of the secular schools, see P. Riché, *Éducation et culture dans l'occident barbare* (1962), pp. 45ff; 62f; 68f; 75f, etc. (I was not able to consult the revised edn, 1967). See also the analysis of the relationship between pagan and Christian education by H. I. Marrou, *Histoire de l'éducation dans l'antiquité* (1948), 451ff.

146 Below, pp. 187f.

147 *Pan. Lat.*, 3.3.1f, esp. 2; 4.1.2–3; 5.8.1–9, 4; 5.21.1–3; 7.23.1; 9.1.1; Ennodius, panegyric of Theoderic, 74, quoting Symmachus, *Or.*, 2.30; cf. Cassiodorus, *Or.*, 1 (ed. Traube), pp. 466; 470; 472.

148 Cf Marrou, op. cit., 463–5.

149. Above, n. 70; *PW* 18² (1957), 30–2 (Ensslin).

150 O. Seeck, *Regesten der Kaiser und Päpste* (1919), 164; 178.

151 Cf. Amminaus, 15.8.21; on the role of Trier as an imperial capital until *c.* 395, when it was replaced by Milan, E. Ewig, *Trier im Merowingerreich* (1954), 21ff, esp. 25–7, and Wightman, *Trier and the Treveri*, 52–70.

152 The older Symmachus had originally thought of sending his son to Libanius (Libanius, *Epp.*, 1004.8), but then chose a Gallic *rhetor* (Symmachus, *Epp.*, 9.88); Symmachus in his turn sent his own son Memmius to a Gallic *rhetor* (*Epp.*, 6.34, cf. D. Romano, *Simmaco* (1955), 14f).

153 *Or.*, 1, 3, 2 and 4, respectively, ed. O. Seeck, MGA AA 6¹ (1883), pp. 318ff; for the dates, ibid., pp. ccx f. Symmachus also delivered a panegyric on the usurper Maximus, for which he later had to apologize (Seeck, p. lvii and n. 228). The reason for this indiscretion is hard to see and the question needs explanation.

154 *Or.*, 2.30 and particularly *Or.*, 1.23.

155 *Or.*, 2.2; 27.

156 See Symmachus, ed. Seeck, p. xli f. A *gratiarum actio* before the consulship was taken up was not entirely unusual: for Fronto, see above, n. 52.

157 *Or.*, 4.2; 6; 7.

158 Especially *Or.*, 4.12. Romano, *Simmaco*, pp. 19ff also points out Symmachus' emphasis, in the panegyrics, on senatorial hopes and ideals. On the rhetorical methods of Symmachus, ibid., pp. 113ff.

159 Ps. Prosper, *De promiss. Dei*, 3.38.2; Symmachus, ed. Seeck, p. lviii.

160 As is illustrated by Symmachus' letters. For the Senate's disinterest in issues affecting the empire see J. A. McGeachy, *Q. Aurelius Symmachus and the Senatorial Aristocracy of the West*, Diss. (Chicago, 1942), pp. 44ff

(but somewhat biased). The urban prefecture of Rome was administered almost exclusively by Roman senators in the fourth century (Chastagnol, *La Préfecture urbaine*, pp. 391f), a trend which continued thereafter (Chastagnol, 'Le sénat Romain sous le règne d'Odoacre, recherches sur l'épigraphie du Colisée au Vᵉ siècle', *Antiquitas* 3 (1966), pp. 46f). The prosopography (pp. 79f) shows that a senatorial career which comprised non-Roman offices was an exception. This illustrates the isolation of the Senate from the rest of the empire. Cf. Fuhrmann, *Antike und Abendland* 13, (1967), pp. 72f, on the dissociation of court and the schools of Gaul after the Tetrarchy.

161 For the literary circle, Romano, *Simmaco*, pp. 74ff; edition of speeches Symmachus, ed. Seeck, pp. x–xv; sending works to friends, e.g. Symmachus, *Epp.*, 1.44 and 52; 1.78; 1.96 and 105; 3.7; 5.43; cf. 1.95.

162 Cameron, 'The date and identity of Macrobius', *JRS* 1966, 25–38. Merobaudes, who wrote a prose panegyric on the second (?) consulship of Aetius (fragments, ed. Vollmer, MGH AA 14, pp. 7–10) belonged to the senatorial order. See on the panegyric, Lenz, PW 15 (1932), 1043–4. The work shows knowledge of the rhetorical rules for panegyric, but as in Ennodius (below, p. 190), the division of deeds of war and peace, although hinted at, is not properly carried out.

163 Cic., *Brut.*, 63ff; cf. 141; 274 and *Or.*, 149; *Or.*, 3f; 7f; 36f; 65f; 73–4; *De Or.*, 3, 101; Quint., *I.O.*, 12.10. 1–12 (cf. Austin, 'Quintilian on painting and statuary', *CQ* 38 (1944), 17). A variety of points are made in these passages, showing a certain preoccupation with parallels in rhetoric and visual art, although no strict theory is worked out. Cf. the authors quoted by Lee, 'Ut pictura poiesis', *Art Bull.*, 22 (1940), 197f.

164 *Imagines*, I, preface (tr. Fairbanks; Loeb).

165 See P. Friedländer, *Johannes von Gaza und Paulus Silentiarius* (1912), esp. pp. 83f. I hope to discuss elsewhere the complex and important question of the links between late antique literature and the visual arts, which has been touched upon here.

166 E.g. *congiarium*, Pliny, 25f=RIC II, pl. 10, 177; buildings, Pliny, 51f= ibid., pl. 9, 150 BASILICA ULPIA; pl. 9, 153 FORUM TRAIAN; pl. 8, 146 and 11, 203 VIA TRAIANA. . . . Cf. J. M. C. Toynbee, *Roman Medallions* (1944), 110–11; G. Hamberg, *Studies in Roman Imperial Art* (1945), 32ff.

167 Pliny, *Panegyric*, 80, 4–5; but see Hamberg, op. cit., 64–7.

168 Toynbee, op. cit., pl. 8, 5; 6 (cf. pl. 6, 2) and pp. 174; 183; 195; the reverse legend of these medallions is PIETAS AUGG, cf. *Pan. Lat.*, 3.6ff, above pp. 160f. On the Arras medallion (Toynbee, pl. 8, 4) and panegyric, cf. MacCormack, *Historia*, 1972, p. 729.

169 *Pan. Lat.*, 7.21.4–6. On the coinage, e.g. RIC VII, p. 368, Ticinum A.D. 316 ℞ RECTOR TOTIUS ORBIS, Constantine seated, holding zodiac, crowned by Victoria; RIC VII, p. 474, Sirmium, AD., 324 VICTORIA CONSTANTINI AUG, Victoria standing, crowning standing emperor. The Ticinum medallion, Toynbee, op. cit., pl. 17, 11, pp. 108–9.

170 *Pan. Lat.*, 11.6.2, quoted above, p. 162. cf. Symmachus *Or.*, 2.1. H.
Cohen, *Description historique des Monnaies* 8 (1892), p. 51, no.
67 (Julian), Ry VIRTUS AUG N, Julian in military dress, holding standard and
laurel branch, placing foot on seated captive (cf. nos 68–70); also no.
75, Ry VIRTUS EXERC GALL, Julian in military dress holding captive
by hair (cf. nos 76–82); for Valentinian I, e.g. RIC IX, pl. 12, 2=p. 218,
32; pl. 3, 6=p. 14, 5.

171 *Pan. Lat.*, 11.9.4.

172 K. Kraft, 'Die Taten der Kaiser Constans und Constantius II', *Jhb. f.
Numismatik und Geldgeschichte* 9 (1958), 141f; 170f; 179–81, issues for
Constans and Constantius II, FEL TEMP REPARATIO; pl. 12, 3; 9.
The ship of state, e.g. *Pan. Lat.* 2.4.2.

173 A. H. M. Jones in *Essays in Roman Coinage presented to H. Mattingly*
(1956), pp. 14–16; C. H. V. Sutherland, *JRS* 49 (1959), 46–53.

174 V.C., 3.47; 4.15; 73. See also H. v. Schoenbeck, 'Religions-politik d.
Maxentius und Constantin', *Klio Beih.* 43, (1939) p. 46.

175 Above, p. 167; cf. below, p. 187.

176 *Pan. Lat.*, 2.6.3; the emphasis on sight also in, e.g. *Pan. Lat.*, 4.9.1 'quis
. . . deus . . . persuadere potuisset quod nunc vidimus et videmus, totis
porticibus civitatum sedere captiva agmina . . .' (cf. above, n. 84);
Pan. Lat., 11.6.3.

177 *Pan. Lat.*, 12.44.5; Symmachus, *Or.*, 3.5; *Pan. Lat.*, 6.6.2f.

178 J. Kollwitz, *Oströmische Plastik der theodosianischen Zeit* (1941), 58–62.

179 *Pan. Lat.*, 4.4 above, p. 161.

180 *Pan. Lat.*, 2.3.2ff.

181 *Pan. Lat.*, 2.4.2f; cf. 9.2f; 13.3f; *Pan. Lat.*, 3.3; 7.6; *Pan. Lat.*, 5.10.2.

182 *Pan. Lat.*, 6.14.1f.

183 According to Seston, *Dioclétien et la Tétrarchie*, p. 251, the emperors are
enthroned over Pluto and Hecate, on the ground of their Mithraic
devotion. I am doubtful of this interpretation, as it has no parallels
in imperial art, whereas the emperor enthroned over the sky does, e.g.
Euseb. v.c., 4. 69. The motif was adopted in Christian art, e.g. on the
sarcophagus of Junius Bassus, where the figure under the billowing
veil can only be Coelus. I hope to discuss the whole question of this
iconographic scheme elsewhere.

184 Cf. Seston, op. cit., 252–3; *Pan. Lat.*, 3.5–6; 14; 16; *Pan. Lat.*, 4.4;
20; 5.20.2ff.

185 P. 180; *Pan. Lat.*, 2.6.1f.

186 Cf. Alföldi, 'Insignien und Tracht der römischen Kaiser', *Röm. Mitt.* 50
(1935), 32f; the themes of victory and imperial consulship are particularly
clearly related to each other in Claudian's panegyrics on Honorius.

187 H. Kähler, *Das Fünfsäulendenkmal für die Tetrarchen auf dem Forum Romanum*
(1964), 5f; L'Orange, *Röm. Mitt.* 53 (1938), 1–38.

188 *Pan. Lat.*, 2.1.1ff.

189 *Pan. Lat.*, 11.7.2f.

190 E.g. the column of Trajan, scene lxxv, left end, Hamberg, *Studies in
Roman Imperial Art*, pp. 111f, pl. 20; H. Kähler, *Zwei Sockel eines Triumph-
bogens im Boboligarten zu Florenz*, 96. Winckelmannsprogramm (1936), pl.

3, imitated on the bases of the arch of Constantine, L'Orange and Gerkan, *Der Spätantike Bildschmuck* . . . (1939), p. 122, pl. 23; pp. 125–6, pl. 29; pp. 128–30, pl. 30.

191 Kollwitz, *Oströmische Plastik*, 27ff; 50ff; on the reliefs of the base, 33–58.

192 H. Usener, Anecdoton Holderi, *Ein Beitrag zur Geschichte Roms in ostgothischer Zeit* (1877), p. 4; 68 (Anecdoton also edited by Mommsen in Cassiodorus, *Variae*, MGH AA 12, pp. v–vi). Date of panegyric accepted by Courcelle, *Histoire littéraire des grandes invasions germaniques* (1964), p. 207, but cf. *Variae*, ed. Mommsen, p. x.

193 Usener, op. cit., p. 68, and n. 11; Cassiodorus, *Or.* 1, ed. Traube, MGH AA 12, p. 470.

194 *Var.*, *pref.*, p. 4, 27 (Mommsen); *Var.* 9.25.

195 Ibid., ed. Traube, pp. 465–84, cf. pp. 462–3.

196 Anecdoton Holderi; Boethius, *De cons. phil.*, 2, 3. The panegyric on the occasion of Theoderic's visit to Rome in A.D. 500, mentioned by J. Sundwall, *Abhandlungen zur Geschichte des ausgehenden Römertums* (1919), p. 102; 204 seems to be spurious.

197 Sundwall, op. cit., p. 41f; Courcelle, op. cit., p. 206 attributes the panegyric to the year A.D. 506.

198 See above, n. 194.

199 See Momigliano, 'Cassiodorus and Italian culture of his Time', *PBA* 41 (1955), 207–45 = *Secondo Contributo* (1960), 191–229.

200 Ennodius, *Panegyric*, 17f; 29f; 85; cf. 78f (Alexander); Cassiodorus, *Or.*, 1, pp. 467; 468; cf. *Or.* 2, p. 473 (Achilles); p. 483 (Semiramis; Cyprus).

201 *Or.*, 1, p. 468.

202 *Panegyric*, 80.

203 Ibid.; cf. E. Kantorowicz, *Laudes Regiae* (1946), 47; 56f; 57 n. 148; 112f; 124; O. Treitinger, *Oströmische Kaiser und Reichsidee* (1938), 124ff.

204 See A. Chastagnol, *Le sénat romain sous le règne d'Odoacre*, demonstrating sustained interest on the part of Christian senators in the traditional *laetitae* until the late fifth century; P. R. L. Brown, 'Aspects of the Christianisation of the Roman aristocracy', *JRS* 51 (1961), 1–11.

205 *De cons. phil.*, 2.3.

206 Cf. *De cons. phil.*, 1.4 where Theoderic is indirectly referred to as a tyrant, with M. A. Wes, *Das Ende des Kaisertums im Westen des römischen Reiches* (1967), 176f. Under both Odovacar and Theoderic, senatorial co-operation was at best conditional, Wes, 162–7; Sundwall *Abhandlungen*, 187ff, *passim*; p. 202, etc., on senatorial involvement with the papacy, which was another factor separating Rome and the Senate from the court. E. Stein, *Histoire du Bas-Empire*, II (1949), 130f; 254f.

207 O. Jahn, 'Über die Subskriptionen in den HSS römischer Classiker', *Ber. über die Verhandl. d. kgl. Sächs. Ges. d. Wiss. Leipzig, phil.-hist. Cl.* 3 (1851), 327–72; Lommatzsch, 'Litterarische Bewegungen in Rom. . . .', *Zeitschr. f. vergleichende Literaturgesch.* NF, 15 (1904), 177–92.

208 Praise and vituperation of Caesar, Emporius, ed. C. Halm in *Rhetores Latini Minores* (1863), 567f, with details on order of topics. The three *genera*, Chirius Fortunatianus, *Ars Rhetorica*, Halm, 81, 15f; Marius Victorinus on Cicero, *De Inventione*, Halm, 174, 39ff; cf. 182; 300; 304;

Martianus Capella, Halm, 456, 15f (463, 7f on *laus* and *vituperatio*); Cassiodorus, *Inst.*, Halm, p. 495=ed. R. A. B. Mynors (1937), p. 98; Priscian, *Praeexercitamenta ex Hermogene versa*, Halm, pp. 556–7, on *laus* and *vituperatio*, with indications on order of topics. This was one of the works which Priscian dedicated to Symmachus.

209 Ennodius, *Panegyric*, 1–55; 56–9; 60–70; 71–93.
210 Cf. above, n. 200.
211 *Or.*, 2, pp. 480f.
212 *Or.*, 2.3.
213 For the intensity of the propaganda conducted in Ostrogothic Ravenna by means of works of art, see O. G. von Simson, *Sacred Fortress: Byzantine Art and Statecraft in Ravenna* (1948).
214 See here the forthcoming article on panegyrics and advice to rulers by Oswyn Murray in the *Journal of the Courtauld and Warburg Institutes*.

Index